LIBERATED THREADS

Guided by feminist and antiracist perspectives, this series examines the construction and influence of gender and sexuality within the full range of America's cultures. Investigating in deep context the ways in which gender works with and against such markers as race, class, and region, the series presents outstanding interdisciplinary scholarship, including works in history, literary studies, religion, folklore, and the visual arts. In so doing, Gender and American Culture seeks to reveal how identity and community are shaped by gender and sexuality.

A complete list of books published in Gender and American Culture is available at www.uncpress.unc.edu.

LIBERATED THREADS

BLACK WOMEN, STYLE,

AND THE GLOBAL POLITICS

OF SOUL

Tanisha C. Ford

The University of North Carolina Press
CHAPEL HILL

This volume was published with the assistance of the Greensboro Women's Fund of the University of North Carolina Press. Founding contributors: Linda Arnold Carlisle, Sally Schindel Cone, Anne Faircloth, Bonnie McElveen Hunter, Linda Bullard Jennings, Janice J. Kerley (in honor of Margaret Supplee Smith), Nancy Rouzer May, and Betty Hughes Nichols.

Designed by Kimberly Bryant and set in Utopia
by Tseng Information Systems, Inc.
Manufactured in the United States of America

The paper in this book meets the guidelines for permanence and durability of the Committee on Production Guidelines for Book Longevity of the Council on Library Resources. The University of North Carolina Press has been a member of the Green Press Initiative since 2003.

Cover illustration: Olive Morris leading a rally in front of the Central Library in Brixton in 1978. Courtesy of the Lambeth Archives Department, London, England.

Library of Congress Cataloging-in-Publication Data
Ford, Tanisha C.
Liberated threads : Black women, style, and the global politics of soul /
Tanisha C. Ford. — 1 Edition.
pages cm. — Gender and American culture)
Includes bibliographical references and index.
ISBN 978-1-4696-2515-7 (cloth : alk. paper)
ISBN 978-1-4696-3613-9 (pbk. : alk. paper)
ISBN 978-1-4696-2516-4 (ebook)
1. Minority women—United States. 2. Women, Black—United States. 3. Feminine beauty (Aesthetics)—United States. 4. Beauty, Personal—United States. 5. Stereotypes (Social psychology) in fashion—United States. 6. Globalization—United States. I. Title.
HV1421.F67 2015
391.0082′0973—dc23
2015006177

Portions of Chapter 3 were previously published as "SNCC Women, Denim, and the Politics of Dress," *Journal of Southern History* 79 (August 2013): 625–58, and are reprinted here with permission.

MIX
Paper from
responsible sources
FSC
www.fsc.org   FSC® C013483

For Malik

Contents

Figures

Acknowledgments

Many people helped me take this project from an idea in my head to a completed book. First and foremost, I have to thank my parents, Amye Glover-Ford and Herman Ford, for giving me such a fine cultural and political education. Our house was filled with the soul sounds of such artists as Nina Simone, Gil Scott-Heron, Curtis Mayfield, and Aretha Franklin, and our walls were decorated with elaborate African-inspired artwork and masks. My mom dressed me in T-shirts that read "Black is Beautiful" and "The Revolution Will NOT be Televised." Though I did not realize it at the time, these things left an indelible mark on me. I also thank my son, Malik Ford, the best kid in the world. You have been so tolerant of me, even when I was stressed out, in tears, and on the verge of insanity while writing this book! Just like Nana and Papa enveloped me in love and gave me an invaluable cultural and political education, I have tried to do the same with you. Our family's tradition of passing on personal stories and cultural-political knowledge from generation to generation captures the spirit of community that is at the core of this book.

I want to thank my mentors and colleagues at Indiana University and the University of Wisconsin who have been there from the beginning and have watched this project develop. Claude Clegg, Amrita Chakrabarti Myers, Purnima Bose, Khalil Muhammad, and John Bodnar provided great insight, guidance, and wisdom. The women of my first writing group (led by Purnima Bose)—Laila Amine, Roxana Cazan, Anne Delgado, and Karen Dillon—kept me sharp and on top of my game. I owe sincere thanks to Audrey McCluskey, William Van Deburg, Christina Greene, Craig Werner, the late Nellie McKay, Stanlie James, Matthew Guterl, Debbie Cohn, Micol Seigel, Jason McGraw, Ellen Wu, Michelle Moyd, Ben Eklof, Carl Weinberg, Ebony Utley, and Ed Watts for reading drafts of my early work, suggesting readings, and offering mentorship.

My community at the University of Michigan helped me develop the project and expand the transnational components of the work. Special thank yous go to Tiya Miles, Brandi Hughes, Jessica Welburn, Martha Jones, Sherie Randolph, Stephen Ward, Stephen Berrey, Xiomara Santamarina, Meg Sweeney, Sandra Gunning, Kevin Gaines (now at Cornell University), Nesha Haniff, and Elisha P. Renne.

My friends and colleagues in the Five Colleges have been excellent conversation partners, readers, and editors. My deepest thanks go to Britt Rusert (we go way back to the Dublin days!), Whitney Battle-Baptiste, Tameka Gillum, Barbara Krauthamer, Joye Boyman, Julio Capó Jr., Priyanka Srivastava, Mecca Jamilah Sullivan, Emily Lordi, Bettina Judd, Carlos "Rec" McBride, K.C. Nat Turner, Chris Tinson, Karen "Kym" Morrison, Jim Smethurst, Yemisi Jimoh, Laura Doyle, Manisha Sinha, Rachel Mordecai, John Higginson, Marí Casteñeda, Keisha Green, Christina Knight, Khary Polk, Liz Pryor, Laura Lovett, Micaela Díaz Sanchez, Amilcar Shabazz, Dee Shabazz, Marla Miller, Daphne Lamothe, Banu Subramaniam, Laura Briggs, Miliann Kang, Alex Deschamps, Svati Shah, Angie Willey, Armanthia Duncan, and Rosa Clemente. A special thank you is due my research assistant, Kingsley Bradley, for organizing my archive and deciphering my "academic speak." To the students who have come through my Feminisms and Fashion and Black Women in Popular Culture courses: our conversations have influenced this book in meaningful ways. Thanks for teaching me how to write for your generation.

Many colleagues and friends have contributed to my intellectual growth and emotional well-being. To my besties from the Wisconsin Afro-American studies days, Phyllis Hill, Sherry Johnson, and Naaborko Sackeyfio-Lenoch (my mother calls us "The Posse"): I love you ladies dearly, and I'm happy that our friendship continues to blossom. Eric Darnell Pritchard, Robin Brooks, Michelle Gordon, Shannen Dee Williams, Charles Hughes, and Crystal Moten, I benefited greatly from our conversations both in and out of the classroom. To my IU grad school family, Siobhan Carter-David, April Faye Smith, Kimberly Stanley, Regina Bradley, Byron Craig, Fredara Hadley, Alyssa and David Amponsah, Cory Broadnax, Carl Suddler, and Bergis Jules: our gatherings and conversations helped me survive grad school! Thank you for keeping me positive and spiritually nourished. Jasmin Young and Janine Mobley: thank you for being such wonderful thinking partners and friends during my fellowship year in London. To my homegirls Treva B. Lindsey, Jessica Johnson, Brittney Cooper, and Joan Morgan: love y'all. It's been a pleasure to travel the world with you. Tiffany Gill and Noliwe Rooks, thank you for providing me with the blueprint for how to do this type of cultural history. You are awesome colleagues and mentors. Mark Anthony Neal, Davarian Baldwin, Dayo Gore, Imani Perry, Jennifer L. Morgan, and Iwan Morgan: thank you for always offering me sound guidance and mentorship. Special thank yous go to colleagues whom I have presented with on panels, who met with me to write, or who read and offered feedback on parts of my manuscript: Robin D. G. Kelley, Salamishah Tillet, Joshua Guild, Natanya Duncan, Krystal Frazier, Marlo David, Nadia Brown, Anne-Marie Angelo, Dan Magaziner, Marissa Moorman, Christina Greer, Randal Jelks, Heather Ann Thompson, Rhonda Williams, Ruth Feldstein, Nichelle Gainer, William Sturkey, Laurence Ralph, Emily Skidmore, and Tianna Paschel. To the global fashion and beauty scholars I have connected with while writing this book, Sharon Heijin Lee, Denise Cruz, Christina Moon, Thuy Linh Tu, Minh-Ha T. Pham, Mimi Thi Nguyen, Kimberly Hoang, and Monica L. Miller: collaborating with you has changed the way I think about my work. Special love goes to my *Feminist Wire* family, especially Heidi R. Lewis, Aishah Shahidah Simmons, Hakima Abbas, Aimee Merideth Cox, Darnell Moore, David J. Leonard (aka "D2"), Tamura Lomax, and Monica Casper.

My friends and family outside of the academy provided me with places to stay and warm meals during my travels. Cheers to my very special chosen family, Khai and Herana-daze Jones, Shamika Lee, Rose Yazdani, and Dahni-El Giles. No matter what was going on, I always knew I could count on you all to give me a place to crash. Thank you to Laura Smishkiss for letting me live in your home while I was on research leave. Many of the final elements of this book were completed in my room in your beautiful Brooklyn brownstone. My cousins (who are more like sisters) Aziza Bailey and Brandy Ford Knight are my everything. Thank you for always being a tremendous source of support. A special thank you goes to my loving godmothers, Elaine Pruitt and Janice Tharp, for their unconditional love and support. "Big up" everyone I grew up with in my hometown of Fort Wayne, Indiana! I carry the spirit of home with me everywhere I go. To the writers, intellectuals, activists, actors, and media folks who make up my New York City community: thanks for helping me get my LIFE . . . on a regular, lol! Our "Black and Brilliant" brunches were the highlight of my weekends. Thanks for making my life look as cool as those of the folks in the black cultural-political collectives I study.

I have workshopped parts of this book in various seminars over the years. I would like to thank Donald Pease and the participants at the University College Dublin's Clinton Institute for American Studies Summer School, Stephen Clingman and my peers in the UMass Institute for Interdisciplinary Studies seminar, Sue Dickman and my junior faculty comrades who participated in the Five College Crossroads in the Study of the Americas seminar, and Kwame Nimako and Stephen Smalls and the participants in the Black Europe Summer School. You all asked important questions that helped me develop the conceptual and analytical framework of the book. Thank you also goes to the participants in the Rutgers

University Black Atlantic Seminar, especially to Deborah Gray White and Jesse Bayker for helping me think through some of my arguments in chapter 5 over dinner at Sahara.

This project has been supported by several foundations, institutes, and universities. Without their contributions, I would not have been able to do such broad research around the world. Thank you to the Ford Foundation, the Andrew W. Mellon Foundation, the Schomburg Center for Research in Black Culture, the Organization of American Historians, the Center for Black Music Research, the University of London's Institute for the Study of the Americas, and the University of Michigan's Department of Afroamerican and African Studies. I am also appreciative of the Publication Subvention Grant from the University of Massachusetts Amherst's Office of Research Development. Special thank yous go to the faculty and staff of Princeton University's Center for African American Studies and the University College London's Institute of the Americas for hosting me as a visiting researcher.

I would like to thank the archivists and librarians of the Schomburg Center for Research in Black Culture; the Center for Black Music Research at Columbia College, especially Monica Hairston O'Connell and Suzanne Flandreau; the Archive of African American Music and Culture and the Herman B. Wells Library at Indiana University Bloomington, especially Celestina Savonius-Wroth and Bradley Cook; the Wisconsin Historical Society; the George Padmore Institute (London); the Black Cultural Archives (London); the Lambeth Archives (London); the National Jazz Archive (Loughton, England), especially David Nathan; Princeton University Firestone Library; and the University of California-Berkeley Library.

Several others contributed rare documents and other source material to the project. Doug Yeager, Odetta's manager, sent me some of Odetta's personal property, including a cartoon of Odetta and Joan Baez. I gained valuable insight on Afro-British history and culture during my months in London from the diverse group of radical feminists who made up the Remembering Olive Collective, including Kimberly Springer and Ana Laura Lopez De La Torre. These women worked tirelessly on the Do You Remember Olive Morris Oral History Project, and because of their efforts I had access to several oral interviews with people affiliated with the Black Power movement in Britain. I would also like to thank Portia Maultsby for giving me a copy of the Harvard Business School report on the soul music market (Columbia Records denies that the document exists!). And I thank my mother for letting me use many of her old photographs of the clothes she designed when she was in college.

My sincerest thanks go to the editorial professionals I worked with throughout this process. Mark Simpson-Vos and the team at the University of North Carolina Press: you are incredible. Mark, you made a promise to me at the very beginning of this project, and you kept every word of it. And let me tell you, that meant so much to this first-time author. Grey Osterud, thank you for being my thinking partner, coach, and cheerleader all rolled into one. You helped me pull the ideas from my head and put them on the page. You are brilliant.

Last, but certainly not least, I would like to extend my biggest thanks to the women who allowed me to interview them for this book. Thank you for entrusting me with your narratives. Your stories have helped me capture the global soul era in ways that I would not have been able to do otherwise. *Liberated Threads* is truly a labor of love written for you.

I traveled across four continents, eighteen countries, and countless cities while writing this book. I truly believe that the project benefited from my interaction with the peoples of various races, cultures, and national origins whom I encountered along the way. Each location taught me new things about the practice of getting dressed, about the importance of the social body, and about how black culture transcends national boundaries.

INTRODUCTION

Black Women and
the Making of a Modern
Soul Style

In 1970, the FBI placed scholar-activist Angela Davis on its "Ten Most Wanted Fugitives" list after guns registered in her name were used in the kidnapping and murder of a Marin County, California, judge. As Davis zigzagged across the country eluding the FBI, which was notorious for assassinating Black Power activists, the agency blasted images of Davis across TV screens and print media that instantaneously become iconic. Davis's "halo" Afro, which loomed large in the photographs, has attracted the attention of many scholars who read it as a symbol of her resistance to the cultural and political status quo. A close look at her clothing as well as her hair reveals that both were significant in the construction of her radical image. In the first picture on the FBI poster, Davis sports her Afro above a dark-colored, conservative blouse. In the second picture, taken just a few months later, her Afro is complemented by a dashiki—a popular version of an African men's shirt—and fashionable round "granny glasses." Examined together, the two pictures the FBI selected to represent Angela Davis's turn from black middle-class respectability to radical activism reveal the deep significance of the visual markers of a mode of dress that was known in the 1970s as "soul style" and point to a vital yet virtually unknown story of the body politics of the civil rights–Black Power era. During these years, black women struggled to redefine themselves over and against layers upon layers of stereotypes about the black female body that circulated in both mainstream and activist culture. In the everyday choices that black women made as they dressed themselves and styled their hair lay a revolutionary politics of style.[1]

Davis, her Afro, and her radical mode of dress

quickly became visual shorthand for revolutionary glamour as journalists clamored to shape Davis's public image. While some mainstream news outlets deemed Davis unattractive and awkward, others labeled her a fashion-forward beauty who embodied the transformative idea that "black is beautiful." They constructed Davis—who was a striking five feet eight inches tall, 140 pounds, with high, chiseled cheekbones—as if she were a model rather than a professor and revolutionary.[2] In the June 1972 issue of *Essence* magazine, writer Maurice Peterson claimed that Davis was "one of the most controversial" political figures in America, and "certainly the most glamorous."[3] In an interview with Davis at UCLA in 1969, after Ronald Reagan and the California Board of Regents fired her for being a member of the Communist Party USA, a reporter switched the focus of the conversation from her political views to her attire. "Can I ask you a very simple question? How can I describe your skirt? Is it leather? Is it a brown miniskirt?" After a few back-and-forth comments, Davis replied, "It's a skirt. Just say a skirt, that's all." Reporters frequently asked her if "her sexuality disrupted class."[4] In sum, the media interpreted Davis as a femme fatale with more sex appeal than intellect.

For many black youth across the diaspora, Davis was a role model, and her controversial image was a powerful symbol of black resistance and rebellion. Her soul style image proliferated throughout the African diaspora on posters, buttons, and other ephemera. Sociologist Maxine Leeds Craig argues that the circulation of Angela Davis posters helped to launch her celebrity status and created a new cultural iconography that illustrated the liberatory potential of soul style for black women coming of age in the 1960s and 1970s.[5] Davis reflected the changing aesthetic tastes and political ideologies of college women of color in particular. For example, when my mother, Amye Glover, was a freshman at Indiana University Bloomington in 1972, she hung an Angela Davis poster in the dorm room she shared with a young white woman. Displaying the image of the assertive activist in a space where she got dressed each day allowed my mother to feel a sense of black pride as she armed herself sartorially to deal with the hostility she faced on her predominantly white campus in a region commonly referred to as "Klan country."[6] In England, Afro-Britons decorated black community spaces with Davis posters and books to proclaim their transnational political and cultural solidarity with African Americans. Members of the London-based Black Panther Movement displayed copies of Davis's book *If They Come in the Morning* (with her image on the cover) in the Panther house. The owner of Desmond's Hip City record store in London's Brixton neighborhood hung an Angela Davis poster on the wall.[7] In Dar es Salaam, Tanzania, Afro-sporting and miniskirt-clad young women heralded Davis as a symbol of a hip, chic urban soul culture. In state-sanctioned newspapers, however, reporters used images of Davis to position her as an emblem of Western imperialism and capitalism, which they believed encroached upon traditional African ways of life and modes of adornment.[8] These three examples of the varied spaces and disparate ways in which Davis's image was displayed and interpreted speak both to the power of her image and to the global circulation of and contention over a women-centered soul style in the African diaspora during the 1970s.

Davis influenced and was influenced by other stylish black women, yet scholars of the Black Freedom movement have not treated dress and style as a critical aspect of the movement. Davis acknowledged that she was "emulating a whole host of women—both public figures and women I encountered in my daily life—when I began to wear my hair natural in the late sixties."[9] Davis did not ignore the fact that natural hairstyles and African-inspired clothing were fashionable in the Black Power era. She contextualized her style within a longer international history in which Africana women incorporated the concept of "styling out," or dressing fashionably, into the quest for black freedom and gender equality.[10] Using Davis's own admission as a launching point, I set out to bridge the seem-ingly disparate fields of fashion studies and civil rights movement history to think critically about dress as a political strategy and to offer an alter-native perspective on the civil rights and Black Power movements.[11] The eclectic archive I have assembled to excavate this understudied history—including album covers, posters, fashion magazines, yearbooks, personal correspondence, rare photographs, organizational papers, FBI files, and oral interviews—helps to remedy the disconnect between scholarship on fashion and scholarship on the social movements of the 1960s and 1970s. In turn, I have facilitated an interdisciplinary conversation between histo-rians and scholars of cultural studies, black studies, and women's studies and have extended the conversation to include activists as well. My in-terpretation of the history of soul style highlights the importance of em-bodied activism, illustrating that, in substance and symbolically, soul and style politics writ large are more critical to the black liberation and women's liberation struggles than we have previously recognized.

My research reveals that throughout the global Black Freedom struggle, black women have incorporated beauty and fashion into their activism. In the early 1960s black women led protests against white-owned wig shops in Harlem, in the late 1960s they engaged in violent confrontations with the police in front of black-owned record stores in London, and in the 1970s they armed themselves with stiletto heels during protests in apartheid-era South Africa to defend themselves from the police. Black women also purchased and made their own African-inspired clothing to imagine and perform their own vision of freedom. South African women made miniskirts and hot pants out of Zulu, Xhosa, and Sotho printed fabrics as a form of resistance to Afrikaner culture. Women activists in the United States reclaimed and repurposed fabrics such as denim that their enslaved ancestors had been forced to wear. Afro-Caribbean women in Britain wore colorful head scarves to draw attention to their natural hairstyles and their adornment traditions from home. Yet we hardly ever hear about these transformative choices when we learn about the Black Freedom movement. These seemingly disparate forms of dress became the core elements of soul style. Soul style comprises African American and African-inspired hairstyles and modes of dress such as Afros, cornrows, denim overalls, platform shoes, beaded jewelry, and dashikis and other garments with African prints that became massively popular in the 1970s when "Black is Beautiful" was a rallying cry across the African diaspora. Yet this narrative of cultural self-fashioning is not as harmonious as previous scholarship suggests. Black women who wore the style were targets of state-sanctioned policing to a greater degree than were Afro-sporting black men. Women in southern Africa had to pay exorbitant fines for violating gendered dress codes. In Great Britain and the United States, Afro-coiffed women members of the Black Panther Party were beaten and sexually assaulted by police officers. I argue that by studying the quotidian practice of getting dressed, we can learn more about the innovative ways that black women responded to state-sanctioned violence and about intraracial notions of feminine propriety.

Liberated Threads takes up these issues of black women's radical activism, the politics of style, and the global circulation of soul culture. On its most fundamental level, this book examines how well-known women like Angela Davis and lesser-known Africana women such as Amye Glover and a host of others turned getting dressed into a political "strategy of visibility."[12] Black women in the mid-twentieth century explicitly aimed to reconnect themselves to both real and imagined precolonial cultures in order to redefine notions of beauty, black womanhood, and style on their own terms. In wearing African-inspired clothing and large hoop earrings and sporting Afros and cornrow braids, Americans and Britons of African descent envisioned soul style as a symbolic baptism in freedom's waters through which they could be reborn, liberated from the cultural and social bondage of their slave or colonial pasts.

In this book, I weave together threads of political solidarity and cultural contestation. Beginning in South Africa, moving to the United States and England, and concluding in South Africa, I uncover how and why black women incorporated dress into their activist strategies. Body politics assumed many forms as black women across the diaspora fought to define their dressed bodies on their own terms. In uncovering this history, I explain the massive popularity of soul style in the years between 1954 and 1994 as African Americans drew inspiration from the influx of Africans, such as South African singer Miriam Makeba, to the United States in the late 1950s and early 1960s. From then on, soul style flourished as a black American creation. I chronicle the gender, racial, and cultural dynamics that ensued as magazines, album covers, films, and youth travel helped the now well-defined soul style circulate outside of the United States to other parts of the African diaspora—including continental Africa, where many of its core features had originated. I demonstrate how beauty salons, black-owned fashion boutiques, record stores, and nightclubs functioned as nodal points that connected grassroots community activists, celebrities, and ordinary people in an international dialogue about race, gender, and liberation. These sites of resistance were just as critical in the fight for black liberation as buses and lunch counters were because, while most blacks were not involved in formal political organizing, many were invested in beauty culture and fashion. The battle for liberation was waged through black people's everyday encounters with one another and with their white counterparts and through cultural practices, making beauty and fashion a vital arena for struggle alongside formal politics.[13]

But what was "soul style"? Why was it a symbol of black liberation, race pride, and gender nonconformity? How did it become a global fashion trend? These three questions are at the heart of *Liberated Threads*. Soul style is not simply a hermeneutic device that I am using to name this brand of fashion. Soul has a language derived from the black American lexicon that was commonly used to describe cultural traditions believed to be unique to the black experience in the United States and in other parts of the Americas and that reflected African cultural retentions and traditions.[14] In many Western and indigenous African-derived religions, the soul is regarded as the mind, will, and emotions of a woman or a man. Many people of African descent on both sides of the Atlantic believed that the deep well of one's innermost thoughts and feelings could be imparted to food, clothing, and music, which would then evoke an emotional response from those who ate the food, dressed in the clothes, and listened to the music. Although people struggled to capture the meanings of soul in words, they claimed to be able to identify soul when they saw, tasted, or heard it. Over time, the word "soul" came to symbolize the cultural manifestations of the feelings, thoughts, and emotions of a black person's inner being, a spirit that had survived the Middle Passage, slavery, and Jim Crow, as well as apartheid. Soul provided a cultural language through which people of African descent could speak about the horrors of slavery and colonialism while also serving as a source of cultural pride and political solidarity.[15]

Once blues and jazz music gained international popularity in the first half of the twentieth century, elements of black soul culture began to reach a broader audience. As blues women and men poured their souls out in songs that addressed issues ranging from love lost and found to the savory tastes, sounds, and smells of the Deep South and crime on city streets, they developed a language of soul that permeated popular culture.[16] Terms including "soul" itself, as well as "funk," "gutter bucket," and "black," were part of this language used to describe an indigenous African American culture. Jazz artists such as Abbey Lincoln, Max Roach, Nina Simone, Miriam Makeba, and Lou Donaldson not only offered their own interpretation of this language and culture in their music but also created a visual aesthetic, including natural hairstyles and African-inspired clothing that were often reflected on their album covers and promotional materials in the early 1960s. Record companies such as RCA and Blue Note recognized that they could package this soul culture with its radical new visual aesthetic and sell it to hip, socially conscious consumers who were becoming politically mobilized.[17] During its peak in popularity in the early 1970s, soul was synonymous with black, and the two words were often used interchangeably. Black youth were grooving to high-energy songs such as James Brown's anthem "Say It Loud—I'm Black and I'm Proud," and news stories about the Black Power movement were ubiquitous in the black press. Black people across the diaspora were clamoring to embrace blackness and redefine it by erasing negative stereotypes linked to black bodies. Companies that sought to appeal to the black-conscious consumer evoked the language of soul to sell everything from Afro Sheen to alcohol.[18] Unearthing soul's early roots in corporate marketing as well as in complex negotiations over questions of identity politics that were enacted in the black press in the United States and abroad helps to explain how soul style developed its popularity.

In this moment when soul was ubiquitous in the United States, there was a heavy emphasis on the importance of style both as a response to social and physical violence and as a source of pleasure. As fashion theorist Carol Tulloch argues, the word "style" implies a significant degree of agency because it reflects "the construction of self through the assemblage of garments, accessories, and beauty regimes that may, or may not, be 'in fashion' at the time of use."[19] The politics of style has a long history. Under systems of slavery and colonialism, white plantation owners throughout the Americas dictated how people of African descent dressed and wore their hair. Bondwomen subverted plantation dress codes by sewing their own clothes to wear to church—garments of more brilliant colors made from materials they purchased with their own earnings.[20] In the early twentieth century, juke joints and dance halls became places where black women domestics could shed their work uniforms and dress in their own clothing.[21] During World War II, African Americans used non-traditional fabrics and unusual cuts to popularize dramatic fashions like the zoot suit, with its long, baggy jacket and tightly tapered pants.[22] In the 1970s, soul sisters and soul brothers expressed their black consciousness and cool through dress. Exhibiting "soul style" became a way to convey that a person was hip, in the know, and worldly in their style sensibilities.

Like their foremothers and forefathers, youth of the Black Power era pieced together raw materials such as cowrie shells and animal-print fabrics to make innovative new looks. But style was about more than simply clothing; for black women in particular, it expressed an entire approach to body politics. Cultural theorist Carolyn Cooper argues that the black body bore the literal and figurative scars of generations of corporal punishment. The international struggle for black liberation provided a space for black people to use clothing to not only adorn but also re-aestheticize the black body. In doing so, Africana people believed they were rebuilding their psyches and healing emotional and physical wounds. This led to a re-aestheticization of blackness, which created new value and political power for the black body.[23] In the twentieth century, black women were using clothing to write new "body narratives," new renderings of their personal narratives that reflected their more expansive view of freedom; through their clothing, they projected a sense of sexual freedom, gender nonconformity, and upward social mobility.[24] Drawing on my numerous interviews with Africana women from three different continents, I show how soul style was born out of their interconnected experiences of violence and pleasure.

Black women's creative styling practices sparked international fashion trends in the mid-1970s. Black college women were the leaders of soul style innovation. Women like my mother, who could design and sew their own soul style garments, became campus fashionistas who set the trends for others to follow. These women soon became the subjects of *Essence* magazine's "College Issue." Beginning in 1973, *Essence* highlighted fashions on black college campuses, using student models to showcase the latest hairstyles and clothing, giving tips on how to incorporate thrift store finds into their wardrobe, and advising women on how to apply makeup properly.[25] It was not long before the mainstream fashion industry picked up on these trends and began mass-producing them.[26] This move coincided with a moment at which African designers living on the continent, such as Swaziland's Zora Kumalo and Nigeria's Shade Thomas-Fahm, were gaining visibility in African magazines such as *Drum* for their original designs that blended local techniques and adornment sensibilities with popular silhouettes such as miniskirts and midi-skirts, hot pants, maxi dresses, and caftans. Africana women across the diaspora were turning themselves into modern black subjects. What is interesting is that black American women were looking to African women as a model of womanhood and pride that seemed freer and less restricted by cultural norms than in the United States. Meanwhile, African women were borrowing from the culture of the West as a way to see themselves as progressive and not bound by the remnants of colonialism that often prompted elders in the community to cleave to traditional modes of womanhood, which many modern, educated African women found restrictive. Black British women, who were located between these two major cultural hubs, were drawing inspiration from both while trying to establish black cultural institutions in places like London that had previously lacked a thriving black cultural presence. The convergence of African American and African fashion scenes and the intermixing as the style aesthetic circulated through the Americas, Britain, and Africa helped to make soul style ubiquitous and to place black women in the forefront.[27]

The export and import of soul culture ephemera and stories about soul culture in the black press, together with black women's and men's travels through the well-worn routes of the black Atlantic world, established circuits of cultural and political exchange that were instrumental in creating a cultural sense of diaspora. In order to weave together the threads that black women established in the diaspora as well as to identify the limits of those linkages, it is imperative to explore a transnational geographical terrain. In my interrogation of soul style in Johannesburg, South Africa; New York City; Jackson, Mississippi; Bloomington, Indiana; Los Angeles; and London, England, I illustrate how soul was shaped by often-tenuous cross-racial and cross-ethnic political alliances among people of African descent, white ethnics, and South Asians, as well as by cultural chafing with normative white American, Afrikaner, and English traditions.[28]

Carol Tulloch argues that we must study the circulation of black fashion through a diasporic "network" that posits London, New York City, and Johannesburg as critical sites in the development of black style.[29] At first glance, these three locations in Western and/or highly Europeanized, largely English-speaking locales reinforce the problematic notion that fashion is a Western endeavor. But, I argue, these locations were important sites of radical activism. Moreover, these large urban areas were also centers of regional, national, and transnational migration, creating a vibrant mix of peoples who contributed to the development of soul style. This mapping allows us to examine translocal and transnational circulations of soul style and the ways in which black youth participated in the underground black fashion network, which relied upon black-owned boutiques, thrift stores, and do-it-yourself fashion. I do not mean to suggest that soul style had no cultural relevance outside of these three major nodal points.[30] Rather, I situate Johannesburg, London, and New York City as major points on a larger terrain that includes such places as Atlanta; the Bahamas; Kingston, Jamaica; Dar es Salaam, Tanzania; and Bamako, Mali, where the vocabulary of soul was used to construct innovative responses to local conditions. This framework disrupts narratives of harmony between and among people of African descent and the white Left. This book is as much concerned with the fraying of political and sartorial threads as it is with the interweaving of layered threads that connect black people in diaspora. The diaspora is a process of doing and undoing, of cultural remixing on the local level. Expanding the geographic framework of soul reveals that the meaning of soul was constantly being reinterpreted in different contexts.[31]

Soul is a useful language to unpack because it becomes clear that the people of the day were using it to do various, often competing, forms of cultural and political work. Sometimes soul was synonymous with black, and the two words were used interchangeably. For example, the popular phrase "Black Power" was often alternated with "Soul Power" to communicate the conviction that power was as much a community-wide cultural pursuit as it was a political matter. Other times, soul was used on a more individual level to prove or legitimize a person's blackness and commitment to the cause. In that sense, soul was considered something that could be performed by using the proper accoutrements. Black people believed they were sharing a common language, but when we dig deeper it becomes clear that its meanings were pervaded by contradictions and that soul was similar in form but different in practice in specific regional and national contexts. In thinking about how soul functioned as a language for style, I aim not to flatten out these differences but instead to show that these complexities made soul culture vibrant and powerful.

Telling the stories of women activists whose experiences have often been erased helps to show that soul style was actually used to express tensions within the global Black Freedom movement. In this way, we can explore competing ideas about soul sisters' identity and activism. In each chapter I trace the varied and often contradictory ways that black women defined and employed soul style based on their own notions of fashion-ability, feminine propriety, and political efficacy. Chapters 1 and 2 examine how women soul singers Miriam Makeba, Nina Simone, and Odetta; the Harlem-based Grandassa models; and the U.S. black press developed a language of soul in the late 1950s and early 1960s that was then marketed and exported to various parts of the African diaspora. Drawing from archival material such as personal correspondence, organizational documents, and photographs, along with magazine and newspaper articles, films, song lyrics, and album covers, I demonstrate that cultural producers created this language of soul to construct an aesthetic, political, and sonic representation of modern blackness.

Chapters 3 and 4 examine two major historical moments in the U.S. black student movement to trace how soul style developed in historically black and mainstream institutions in the 1960s. Chapter 3 asks how and why women activists in the Student Nonviolent Coordinating Committee (SNCC) abandoned their "Sunday best" attire for denim overalls and jeans. Interviews with SNCC field secretaries reveal that in the early 1960s, they stopped wearing dresses in large part because such attire was not practical on the front lines. But by 1964, they were also doing it to forge political ties with the sharecroppers they were helping to organize and as a way to reject middle-class notions of feminine propriety. Chapter 4 uses magazines, yearbooks, interviews, and archival materials to explore what happened as soul style became more widely visible and commodified in the 1970s. I argue that the college campus is an important site for examining how soul vocabulary was adopted and adapted by a generation of black women students to contest the status quo.

Chapters 5 and 6 move beyond the United States to examine how women activists in London and Johannesburg used soul style to envision a new identity and political reality for themselves despite de facto segregation in London and de jure segregation in South Africa. Afro-Caribbean activists in London adapted the raw material of U.S. soul to combat racial discrimination and sexism in England. Members of the Black Panther Movement Youth League in Brixton appropriated the language and imagery of U.S. soul to frame their own version of Soul Power that drew upon their Afro-Caribbean musical, culinary, aesthetic, and political traditions and responded to the discrimination and violence they encountered in their daily lives. Delving into the landscape of South Africa's black and coloured townships, chapter 6 examines the growing popularity of soul style, called the "Afro look" in the region. It circles back to the starting place for chapter 1 to examine South Africans' beauty and fashion culture during the era in which antiapartheid activism intensified among student activists. The first generation of recognized fashion and jewelry designers, inspired by the history of social activism in their country, redefined beauty politics and adornment in underground social spaces. This chapter offers a close reading of *Drum* magazine and draws on interviews I conducted with South African fashion designers, models, jewelry makers, and ordinary women who came of age in the 1970s.

Over the course of forty years, Miriam Makeba, Judy Richardson, Angela Davis, Olive Morris, Amye Glover, and a host of other women positioned themselves as political leaders, cultural revolutionaries, feminists, and socially conscious fashionistas. This is not always a happy story, given the ways in which soul style emerged, in large part, out of violence. The years between 1954 and 1994 saw the countless murders of black women and men as well as brutal sexual assaults against black women activists from Jackson to Johannesburg. While notions of soul were often uneven and problematic, the ways in which Africana women around the globe took space within the Black Freedom movement to redefine themselves on their own terms not only are a powerful testimony to the past but are vital to our understanding of the history and culture of modern social movements. In that sense, this book presents a humanistic story of the possibilities and difficulties of social, political, and cultural transformation.

In the early years of Miriam Makeba's U.S. career, RCA Records aimed to efface the singer's South African roots by marketing her as a sultry lounge singer in the bourgeois styling of African American singer-actress Diahann Carroll. After the commercial failure of Makeba's self-titled first album in 1960, RCA dropped the Xhosa songstress from its record label. But by 1964, label executives recognized that there was a growing audience with an interest in the African independence movements and African culture more broadly, prompting RCA to re-sign the singer. This time around, the label decided to make Makeba's Africanness a hypervisible element of her branding. The cover of Makeba's 1964 album, *The Voice of Africa*, is evidence of this shift, with the title touting Makeba as a spokeswoman for the continent. The cover art features a drawing of an ornate African-style mask in the colors of the Universal Negro Improvement Association's pan-African unity flag, red, black, and green, with a small picture of Makeba imposed on its center (figure 1.1). The image was a symbol of African nationalism, though none of the album's track titles explicitly address the political movements in Africa. As Makeba remembered, her outspoken opposition to apartheid transformed her public image from "just an African singer" to "a symbol of my repressed people."[1] Her "people" included not only Africans but black people around the globe, as Makeba became an icon of diasporic black militancy and African-inspired fashion that could be packaged and distributed to the masses.[2]

Between 1958 and 1964, Miriam Makeba, a host of African diplomats and students, and a group of African American soul singers reshaped the style of New

1
REIMAGINING AFRICA

How Black Women
Invented the Language
of Soul in the 1950s

Figure 1.1.
Miriam Makeba,
The Voice of Africa,
RCA Records, 1964.

York City. Makeba, Nina Simone, Odetta, and Abbey Lincoln helped create a politically charged language of soul that established soul style as a fashionable expression of blackness. Not only did they lend their voices to local, national, and international civil rights movements through the simple act of appearing in public in styles that subverted expectations of what a respectable black woman's body should look like, they also gave a generation a new set of terms and tools for asserting themselves. In a world where black women's bodies were often objectified and used as placeholders in a variety of competing ideologies—whether as symbols of "primitive" black sexuality or as keepers of black respectability—women's choices to adorn themselves differently became political. These singers were fashion icons and arbiters of black aesthetics whose international platform helped soul style reach a broad, diverse audience.

International black publications such as *Ebony* and South Africa's *Drum* magazine used their pages to discuss African independence and the role of African culture in the creation of a modern African diaspora. For African Americans and Afro-Europeans, establishing a tie to Africa that was not solely about slavery allowed for a reimagining of blackness built upon new aesthetic interpretations of style and beauty. What emerged was a soul style that was considered more African in form, origin, and inspiration than previous incarnations of black style. Performing this type of African-inflected soul—through music as well as clothing—made a person a modern citizen of the world. As members of this soul generation adopted, adapted, and innovated with the vocabulary that soul gave them, their everyday choices created a rich cultural-political discourse. Exploring the connection between activist-entertainers of the 1950s and the broader struggle for black human and civil rights offers a new way of analyzing the often-overlooked history of soul style.

Miriam Makeba and Style Politics in Africa

Miriam Makeba began building her reputation as a style icon in the mid-1950s, during her years singing in the nightclubs of Johannesburg's Sophiatown and Alexandra Townships. Townships were suburbs of the predominantly white urban centers of South Africa's major cities, including Cape Town and Durban as well as Johannesburg. Sophiatown and Alexandra were among the only townships in which blacks could own property. After the "white flight" of the 1920s, these spaces were largely inhabited by people of color: blacks, coloureds (the label the government assigned to people of mixed race), and South Asians. Sophiatown in particular was known for being a multiracial cultural hub. It was a nexus of black writers, jazz musicians, and other entertainers, as well as political figures.[3] Sophiatown's and Alexandra's nightclubs continued to flourish even in the early years of apartheid, a system that barred nonwhites from leaving the township at night, working outside of the township without an employment pass, drinking alcohol, or having intimate relationships with people of a different race. Under these conditions, nightlife was an important social outlet for people of color. Miriam Makeba and the men in her jazz group, the Manhattan Brothers, performed in these nightspots before audiences that ranged from gangsters to journalists and socialites. Dressing stylishly was a critical aspect of moving through the nightclub scene. The gangsters who frequented Makeba's shows had nicknames that spoke to their sartorial flair. Makeba remembered a man called "Styles" attending several shows in Alexandra dressed in "a hat, a belted jacket, and those Florsheim shoes."[4] The Manhattan Brothers' fashion was just as important as their sound, which blended U.S. jazz styles with traditional Xhosa and Zulu music. Their "debonair" style projected the air of sophistication that they associated with the U.S. borough of Manhattan in New York City. They wore tailored suits with matching ties and kerchiefs and expensive imported Florsheim dress shoes.[5] As the sole woman in the group, Makeba had to look the part in order to win over the opinionated crowd. Makeba's stylist (and cousin), actress-singer Peggy Phango, helped her develop her signature stage look that consisted of "Western style outfits: the stiff petti-coats that flare out" or "tight, strapless evening dresses."[6] Makeba's style could be described as sexy urban street wear meets youthful feminine ele-gance. Her blend of edgy and respectable destabilized notions of feminine propriety that black South African women were expected to adhere to, making Makeba a model of the modern girl. Her look was also significant because it did not fit what African Americans imagined as African.[7]

Style was critical for township residents outside the nightclubs as well. Even among the nation's poorest women and men, fashion was crucial to defining liberation on one's own terms, and black South Africans strove to express themselves with innovative new styles. The authors of *Life Soweto Style* suggest that, "far from restricting fashion choices, poverty has pro-pelled [South African style] towards careful quality selection, and a sure, often ingenious touch."[8] South African women, like most African women across the continent in the 1950s and early 1960s, ordered their clothing from Western mail order companies.[9] While early modes of soul style in South Africa were heavily influenced by European and North American fashions that were grouped together under the label "Western fashion," township residents brought individual flair to the textiles to create a style that reflected their urbanity. It was the sense of style that they applied to the raw material of the garments that gave their outfits a distinctly South African feel. In this fashion context, wearing Western attire was not akin to a desire to be white; it was more about the quest to be modern, global citizens. Modernity was important because township inhabitants could imagine and perform as liberated citizens of the world who were not bound by the spatial and material strictures of apartheid. By being mod-erns, they could distinguish themselves as city dwellers who were more progressive and upwardly mobile than blacks who lived in rural commu-nities and wore the traditional garments of their ethnic group. To be sure, there was tension even within the townships between those who equated Western clothing with imperialism and cultural encroachment and those who did not. It was from this cultural chafing that soul style was birthed.[10]

An example of the complexities of style politics and modernity lies in the short, natural hairstyle that Makeba helped to make internationally popular. As Makeba became a megastar in the United States, her hair-style began to represent a liberated African beauty aesthetic for Afri-can Americans. But it had a different historical meaning in South Africa. Under the Bantu education system, which mandated that the races re-ceive completely separate educations, young black girls were forced to shave off their plaits and ornate "cornrow" braids (rows of thin braids close to the scalp). Such ethnic hairstyles held special meaning for young women. The apartheid government aimed to erase intraracial ethnic differences in order to establish a heterogeneous "black" race. Cutting girls' hair became a form of forced uniformity, denying any sense of individuality, cultural pride, or community. A photograph taken at a Bantu schoolgirls' hostel in the southeastern part of South Africa around 1950 depicts a large group of black girls dressed in matching uniforms, all with their hair closely cropped.[11] Girls found ways to subvert the rules regarding hair cutting by hiding their plaits. But they were usually caught by the women who enforced the grooming rules at the school.[12] South African jewelry designer Nonhlanhla Ngozi recalled, "I had to cut my hair when I went to school. The plaiting of the hair was a privilege. I remember I was wearing a [bell cap] to cover my hair. Accidentally, I went up, and the teachers said, 'Take off your bell, and let us see your hair.' And they saw it, and said it was unacceptable."[13] The teachers proceeded to cut Ngozi's hair. Like the young women in the picture, Ngozi, who grew up in the Johannesburg townships, had to find a way to feel whole again after being violated and stripped of her hair. For some, the short hairstyle was emblematic of the ways that apartheid controlled every aspect of black life. For others, choosing to keep wearing short hair after one completed school challenged respectable notions of femininity. Women who continued to wear the style long after they had been forced to do so were cultural revolutionaries who gave the hairstyle new political meaning.[14]

For the thousands of black girls who had to cut their hair in order to attend school, Makeba was a beauty icon. Lette Matthebe, who came of age during the height of the antiapartheid movement, remembered the anguish she felt when she had to cut her long plaits before entering first grade in a school just outside of Pretoria. Seeing herself with short hair for the first time in her young life, Matthebe found inspiration in Makeba: "Mma. Miriam Makeba was the role model growing up. . . . She and her background singers were always so beautiful. Her makeup, her hairstyle, the dresses she used to wear were cool."[15] By referencing Makeba as "Mma.," a title of respect, Matthebe was expressing her high regard for the singer. Matthebe's invocation of the word "cool" instead of "glamorous" or "sophisticated" to describe Makeba's style disrupts the usage of the term as a way to describe a masculinized cool pose often attributed to black jazzmen. For countless young black South African women, Makeba was at the center of the soul style politics emerging from the black jazz and art community in Johannesburg. By wearing her hair short, Makeba was turning a punishment into a transgressive and stylish hairstyle for modern women. *Drum* magazine commemorated Makeba and her signature style on the cover of the 1957 issue dedicated to "the stars of jazz."[16]

When Makeba was rising to fame in the late 1950s, advertisements for products such as Apex skin lightening cream were commonplace on the pages of *Drum*. The beauty culture in South Africa in the late 1950s was largely dependent upon the international circulation of skin lighteners and hair straightening elixirs marketed across the anglophone African diaspora.[17] Many of these products were manufactured in the United States (and to a lesser degree in the United Kingdom) and marketed to black South African women using images of glamorous local black celebrities.[18] This established beauty culture circuit that linked black women on both sides of the Atlantic helped set a global market for soul style in the mid-1960s. Remarkably, companies would sell products such as Afro Sheen and Afro wigs to the same women, illustrating that an "African" appearance could be purchased and could be put on and taken off at the consumer's whim. But long before soul style became commonplace among Africana women, Makeba consciously adopted an image that celebrated "natural" beauty.

Makeba's stance on makeup and other beauty enhancements won her favor with those who associated modern beauty culture with whiteness. She preferred not to wear makeup because the global market still catered to white women. Makeba stated, "Of course there's nothing non-African about makeup. . . . But today, ladies' makeup is manufactured by white companies for whites. It does not suit the color of our skin. A black girl looks as if she is wearing a mask. Her face is a different shade from her neck."[19] In other words, the makeup "mask" looked like a second layer of skin that detracted from instead of enhanced black women's beauty. Makeba's own sense of style was rooted in her understanding of herself as a black South African woman. Though her sentiments were far from representative of all South African women or African women, antiapartheid activists read Makeba's statements on natural beauty as pro-black and anti-imperialist. Her style linked her to the burgeoning antiapartheid movement even before she publicly spoke out against legal segregation.

Because Sophiatown was a hub of black cultural production and black politics, the South African government decided to raze the bubbling cultural epicenter and disperse its residents. In the summer of 1955, more than 2,000 Johannesburg police entered Sophiatown armed with guns to forcibly remove its multiracial residents and relocate them into racially segregated townships. Black residents were moved to the cluster of South

Western Townships that residents called Soweto.[20] People opposed re-settlement because they would lose many of the freedoms they had enjoyed in Sophiatown (including property ownership) and would have to rebuild all of their cultural institutions. Soweto was also farther from downtown Johannesburg. Under the Immorality Act (1950), those who had formed intimate relationships with people of different races would see their families divided as coloureds and South Asians were resettled in different townships. Sophiatown residents took to the streets to protest the government's relocation plan. They chanted "Ons dak nie, ons phola hier" (We won't move) in Flaaitaal, the township slang mostly used by men that blended English, Afrikaans, and Zulu.[21] From 1955 on, the government forcibly moved more than 50,000 blacks from Sophiatown to Soweto. Sophiatown was razed, removed from maps of Johannesburg, renamed Triomf (Afrikaans for "triumph"), and rezoned as a "whites only" neighborhood in the early 1960s. The protests against the dismantling of Sophiatown were a critical step in the antiapartheid movement that helped shine an international light on what was happening in South Africa.[22]

Miriam Makeba became the world's window into Sophiatown and the violence of apartheid when she appeared in American director Lionel Rogosin's docudrama *Come Back, Africa* (1959). Rogosin smuggled two hand-held cameras into South Africa to shoot the film, which used a cast of amateur actors and local celebrities to reveal the horrors of apartheid to liberal audiences in the West.[23] Rogosin filmed primarily in Sophiatown amid the government's forced removals. The film centers on Zachariah, a black man of Zulu heritage who leaves a famine-stricken rural village for Johannesburg to seek employment in order to care for his family. He moves to a black township and settles into the urban community, with its lively nightlife and thriving underground economy. There, Zachariah comes face to face with the paradox of apartheid: because he does not have a job, he is denied the employment pass needed to work outside of the township, but without the pass, he cannot leave the township to secure a job that pays a decent wage. Instead, he has to cobble together several odd jobs within the township to help make ends meet. Zachariah's wife, Marumu, has to make the difficult decision to work full time as a live-in domestic for a white family in the city. Makeba's nightclub scene serves as a lighthearted counterpoint to the film's message of despair. Dressed in one of her signature off-the-shoulder sheath dresses, she entertains the men in her small entourage. As Makeba sings, she begins dancing and winding her small waist rhythmically to an a capella backing from the men in the nightclub. The film concludes after Zachariah is arrested while trying to visit Marumu at her employer's house. Once he is released from jail, he returns home only to learn that Marumu has been murdered by a local gangster. Makeba's brief scene speaks to the simultaneous pleasure and violence of black life in South Africa.[24]

The themes and imagery of *Come Back, Africa* were featured prominently by black-oriented publications in South Africa and the United States.[25] It was through this type of media that ideas about blackness, Africanness, and modernity were exchanged and debated. Because of her celebrity status in South Africa and her growing international audience after *Come Back, Africa* was screened at several European and American film festivals, Makeba became a symbol of the growing unrest in South Africa's black townships. For the children of Sophiatown who came of age in Soweto in the mid-1960s, soul style became the marker of their militancy. Over the course of the 1960s, the style lost many of its Western points of reference and celebrated local textiles and black ethnic sewing and embroidering techniques. Makeba's image resonated with them, as it did with progressive African Americans who were equally concerned with black freedom and cultural autonomy.[26]

Black Americans' Fascination with African Style

While black South Africans were remixing North American and European fashions, African Americans were looking to Africa for models of black style and modernity. Miriam Makeba became central to these swirling conversations on fashion, beauty, and liberation once she moved to England and then to the United States after the success of *Come Back, Africa*. She arrived in the United States at a moment of cultural and political change that was heightened by growing interest in the African freedom struggle. At that time, many Africans came to the United States on diplomatic assignments or to attend college or, in Makeba's case, to launch a career in entertainment. Situating Makeba's early career in the United States within the broader conversation about Africa in the black American press reveals why soul style in the United States was envisioned as being an African-derived style (in contrast to its usual framing as African American). It also reveals African Americans' vexed relationship to Africa and the ways in which it led to cultural misrepresentations of Africanness, evident in media coverage of Makeba's shows.[27]

Ebony devoted its February 1960 issue to the cultural and political implications of the African presence in America. The year 1960 was a pivotal one for activism on the continent; thus it comes as no surprise that the black press trained its gaze upon the women and men of Africa's diverse countries. On the cover of the February issue, Guinean president Sekou Toure appeared wearing a "Western" suit and tie in navy blue. But he paired the suit with a variation of the karakul cap commonly worn by Muslim leaders in the Middle East.[28] Toure, who was descended from precolonial African royalty, and other African leaders adopted the hat as a sartorial way to express their independence from Western Europe. Together, the "Western" suit and the "Eastern" cap spoke to the hybridity of early soul style and the notion that modern African fashion should reference both its pre- and postcolonial styles, the traditional and the Western. Inside was a feature story on Toure's travels through the U.S. South as he met with young black leaders of the sit-in movement. The black press was also interested in the purchasing habits of Toure's wife, Hajia Andre Toure. The *Chicago Defender* wrote that while in Washington, D.C., the "poised . . . pretty brown-skinned" Mrs. Toure purchased an expensive "white beaded French purse," positing her as an arbiter of global fashion and elegance.[29] The African president's journey represented a moment of diasporic unity between southern African Americans and West Africans and a shared interest in black opulence.

Three months later, *Ebony* ran a cultural piece on West African highlife, a genre of music and dance that the article touted as "Africa's hottest export."[30] The article featured images of West African diplomats and their wives, who had come to the United States to represent their newly independent countries, demonstrating the highlife dance. The description of the dance read: "Just shake your body, shuffle your feet and occasionally shout 'freedom' and you are doing one of the hottest new dances introduced in America since Ghana received its independence."[31] For *Ebony*'s African American readers, highlife was a shining example of modern, postcolonial African culture, a dance of liberation that someone of African descent needed no training to perform. The dance conveyed that freedom was about the body. Symbolically, it was a rhythmic means through which African Americans could (re)connect with their believed West African roots.

The women in the highlife spread, who were dressed in West African printed garments, became the faces of African fashion and culture. Embodied notions of freedom were centered on the freedom to adorn the body on one's own terms. Spreading this message, the highlife article became the medium through which black Americans could see the dressed African body. The diplomats' wives were stylishly appareled in luxe *bubas* (loose-fitting blouses with long sleeves), *lapas* (skirts that are wrapped and secured around the waist), and *geles* (material that is intricately styled and tied around the head) in bold prints. Their images in the pages of *Ebony* forced its readers to confront an image of Africa and its people that was drastically different from the simulacra of bare-breasted African women and African men dressed in loincloths that appeared in *National Geographic* and Hollywood films. In the wake of independence, the future of West Africa was projected on the dressed bodies of African women and men. In this moment, fashion became a powerful display of African modernity. Designers such as Nigeria's Shade Thomas-Fahm returned home in 1960 to launch the fashion industry in their native countries. Thomas-Fahm studied at London's Central Saint Martins College for Art and Design. After graduation, she opened Shade's Boutique in Lagos, where she sold her original designs that used traditional textiles including Ankara-print jumpsuits, *aso oke* dresses, embroidered culottes, and hand-beaded shoes. Thomas-Fahm recalled that her soul style fashions were ahead of their time: "At the time Nigerian women wore imported dresses; they thought African wear was their mothers' thing." Yet she quickly found an audience in women like the diplomats' wives who appeared in *Ebony*.[32]

Makeba represented a vision of African style and modernity that was visibly different from what passed for traditional African dress. She did not wear traditional Xhosa or Zulu dress and was neither African royalty nor a diplomat's wife. Makeba embodied the "everyday" woman. She stood for life in the townships, a freedom that was still in process, not one that had already been achieved, as was arguably the case in Ghana, Nigeria, and Guinea. She was a curiosity to members of the U.S. Left, such as Lionel Rogosin and Harlem-born singer-activist Harry Belafonte (of Jamaican and Martinican descent) who were making connections between South African apartheid and Jim Crow in the U.S. South. For them, Makeba was an eclectic musical talent who represented a population whose voice was often absent in conversations about apartheid.

Belafonte saw Makeba as a potential ally in the continuing cross-diasporic fight for political, social, and cultural freedom. Makeba was a voice of hope and a new model of beauty for women of African descent in the Americas. As an African everywoman, she had the potential to represent an African womanhood that existed outside of tropes of primitivism and lasciviousness that had been used to mark Africana women's bodies as nonnormative. Though at the time most African American women's interest in Africa was nothing more than a fleeting fascination, Belafonte was committed to using his platform and celebrity to advance the careers of other Africana artists.[33] And as a seasoned performer, he had the foresight to see the direction the music and fashion industries were heading. But despite being a brilliant trend forecaster, he was not altogether certain how to market Makeba's African-derived performance of femininity, which was not tightly bound to prevailing African American notions of propriety.

When Makeba arrived in the United States in late 1959, she continued to wear her signature stage attire, and Belafonte merely supplied her with the resources she needed to launch her career in the West. After seeing Makeba perform in London, he worked diligently to secure her travel visa to bring her from England, where she was living with her partner Sonny Pillay, a South African singer of South Asian descent. Belafonte orchestrated a soft launch consisting of a few high-profile appearances that kicked off with her debut on the *Steve Allen Show* in Los Angeles in November 1959. Recalling those early years, Makeba told the *Chicago Tribune*, "When I came [to the United States] I had nothing. [Belafonte] put things together for me. Musicians, clothes to wear on stage and someone to write down my songs, and the band that played during the Steve Allen Show." From her stage costume to her song selection, Makeba's performance was similar to that in *Come Back, Africa*. She appeared onstage wearing her signature short hairstyle and a strapless pink sheath dress. She sang "Into Yam," a playful, upbeat song about loving a man despite the fact that he is no good, which she also sang in Rogosin's docudrama.[34] For those who had not seen the film, Makeba's performance would have been a lively introduction to South African jazz, which was considered "folk" or "world" music in the United States. The show was a success; the audience and critics alike responded well to Makeba's eclectic sound and her earnestness during her interview with Allen. After her appearance in Los Angeles, Makeba moved into a hotel in Greenwich Village on Eighth Street while she was booked for long-term engagements that Belafonte had secured for her at the Village Gate and the Vanguard.[35]

Makeba acquainted herself with Greenwich Village, which had some similarities to the artistic community of Sophiatown. By the late 1950s, Greenwich Village had a reputation as the "crossroads" where black and white artists "could explore the vicissitudes of hip life."[36] Artists, musicians, poets, cinematographers, intellectuals, and music industry headhunters congregated in the few blocks that made up Greenwich Village.[37] The "Elephant Walk" was a strip of cafés and bookstores that held regular poetry readings, which were frequented by those hoping to encounter real-life beatniks. Coffeehouses such as the Hip Bagel, bars such as Cedar Tavern, and community centers such as Judson Church were social gathering spots. Delaney Street Museum and Reuben Gallery held performance art exhibitions, and Café Cino, Café La Mama, and the Open Theater presented off-off-Broadway shows. The artists, intellectuals, and musicians who lived in Greenwich Village also helped to create a fantasy of racial, gender, and sexual harmony that obscured its history of racialized violence and de facto segregation.[38] Despite the palpable racial tensions within the Village, many young African Americans born after the Great Depression who refused to be bound by Jim Crow were attracted to this new bohemia. The African Americans of this generation were more willing, and more able, than their parents to cross racial, social, cultural, and geographical boundaries. The legal collapse of Jim Crow emboldened them to define themselves and their raced bodies on their own terms. Writers Lorraine Hansberry, Claude Brown, James Baldwin, and A. B. Spellman; poets Calvin Herndon, David Henderson, Ishmael Reed, and Lorenzo Thomas; musicians John Coltrane, Ornette Coleman, Thelonius Monk, Marion Brown, Archie Shepp, and Sunny Murray; and painters Bob Thompson and William White moved to and through Greenwich Village.[39] Belafonte and Makeba used the reputation of the Village to help bolster Makeba's career once she was signed to RCA Records in 1960.

Makeba's new team, which pivoted around Belafonte, had to figure out how to package her in a manner that rendered her legible to the black and white American audience that frequented the Village. Though Village dwellers were often more progressive than most Americans, they too had narrow and often problematic images of African women. Makeba entrusted Belafonte, whom she affectionately called "Big Brother," with the task of guiding her career. Belafonte and the team at Makeba's new record label, RCA, decided to amplify her exoticness through her music, having her continue to sing her "click" songs, a diminutive term that white South Africans and Americans used to mimic the sonic traits of the Xhosa language. Yet they opted to alter her hair and stage costumes to fit a more palatable, bourgeois image of African American beauty. Makeba was a seasoned performer in Africa, but she was treated as a new artist in the States. And it was very common for new artists to be heavily subjected to the record label's vision for the artist's brand. Therefore, on most things, Makeba deferred to Belafonte's knowledge of the American music scene, the cultural landscape, and black American ideals of beauty and fashion.

Belafonte commissioned costume designer John Pratt to craft what would become Makeba's "trademark" style in America. Pratt was a seasoned white Canadian man who was likely chosen because he was married to and designed costumes for African American dancer Katherine

Dunham, famous for her brand of modern dance that drew upon Afro-Caribbean and African dance traditions. In other words, Belafonte and the team felt Pratt had experience designing elegant costumes for black women with curves who needed to be able to move comfortably while they danced onstage.[40] The cover art on Makeba's 1960 and 1962 albums, *Miriam Makeba* and *The Many Voices of Miriam Makeba* respectively, featured the singer in long, conservative gowns that were designed to "tame" her Africanness.[41] These gowns, made out of Indian silk in color combinations like rust and gold or foam green and sea blue, tacitly conjured stereotypical images of the exotic while stifling the youthful, sexy, urban feel that Makeba's ready-to-wear township garments projected.[42] In America, the twenty-seven-year-old was marketed as a mature, elegant supper club chanteuse. This was an attempt to make Makeba fit into African American norms of respectability. It also repositioned her as a singer who represented the African American elite. Makeba liked her new glamorous costumes and the image of wealth and success they conjured, which was understandable for a woman who had experienced extreme poverty before becoming an entertainer. She was less thrilled about the changes Belafonte and crew made to her hair.[43]

Makeba's short, natural hair was an affront to African American women's sensibilities. While there were a few radical activists, avant-garde models, college students, dancers (including Pearl Primus), and musicians who were wearing their hair natural in 1960, most black women were wearing their hair processed. In the U.S. context, natural hair was read as African; therefore, women who wore the style were labeled as "other" regardless of their nationality. Makeba's hair was the marker of her racial difference from potential white fans, and it was a marker of cultural difference for potential African American fans. Her hair was deemed a problem that could be fixed by straightening. Belafonte wanted to make Makeba look like singer-actress Diahann Carroll, the latest model of black middle-class respectability. He had her go uptown to Harlem to have her hair pressed and curled at an upscale salon owned and operated by socialite-entrepreneur Rose Morgan, ex-wife of boxer Joe Lewis. Morgan was a stylist to the stars who was often featured in *Ebony* and *Jet* magazines.[44] It is unclear how familiar Makeba was with press-and-curl styling. Some black South African women straightened their hair, but the townships had no real public beauty shop culture like that which existed in the United States. There, as in the British Caribbean, most aspiring beauticians who learned straightening techniques acquired this knowledge while visiting the States.[45] Makeba liked being pampered by Morgan, but after seeing her reflection in the mirror she cried, "This is not me. . . . I'm not a glamour girl. I'm just my natural self." For Makeba, glamour achieved through wearing certain clothing was acceptable because it did not physically alter her body. But glamour by way of a physical transformation represented something artificial and fake that went against her beauty politics. She instantly washed her hair to bring back its "short and wooly" texture in an attempt to regain power and control over both her own body and her professional branding.[46]

Though Makeba's decision to wear her hair natural was likely motivated by more personal reasons than political ones, *Drum* lauded her natural beauty as a rejection of American excess. In a 1960 article titled "Miriam in New York," *Drum* published an image of Makeba at Morgan's salon with the tagline "first trip to [the] beauty salon." She is looking at her hairstyle in the mirror, which appears to be unstraightened, and the caption reads "[She] seems to be pleased with the result." There is no mention of the hair straightening incident. The article continues, "Her trademark is simplicity, in contrast to the gimmicky approach of many American singers."[47] By juxtaposing "simplicity" with "gimmicky," the text places natural Africanness in tension with Western imperialism, symbolized by skin lighteners and hair straightening tools. That same year, Makeba garnered two major endorsement deals in South Africa, becoming the face of Vaseline Blue Seal and President Giant cigarettes. Her advertisements, which ran regularly on the pages of *Drum*, framed her as a local natural beauty who made it big in the United States. Noticeably absent were her new American evening gowns. Instead, she was featured the way hometown audiences remembered her, with her off-the-shoulder sheath dresses and short natural hair. The President Giant advertisements included a special message "From America's New Star Discovery" in which Makeba assured South Africans that despite her newfound international fame, which felt like "a dream," she remained "the girl from Mofolo" (a township in Soweto) who was still humble enough to "stop for a moment and remember the people who helped me get here."[48] The ads helped Makeba build her career in other parts of Africa where *Drum* was distributed, making her the style icon of Sophiatown and the voice of grassroots politics in Soweto.

In contrast, the black press in the United States constructed Makeba not as a humble hometown beauty but as a beguiling African seductress. In a 1960 *Ebony* magazine article titled "Belafonte's Protégée" that ran just two months before *Drum*'s piece on Makeba's trip to the hair salon, *Ebony* described Makeba's stage show: "When she moves into a number, her body sways with controlled intensity. Hips waving sensuously, eyes flashing, hands and shoulders weaving."[49] This comment praises black women's sensuality, highlighting Makeba's body as a site of pleasure, but at the same time the remark is rendered through a language of othering. American journalists often had no nonobjectifying language through which to articulate the artistry of Makeba's performance. Hip gyrating was linked to sex and youthful rebellion in the American context, whereas in the African and Caribbean contexts it was a regular element of the dance culture. The Harlem-based *New York Amsterdam News* review of the "Xhosa tribeswoman['s]" show at the Village Gate even sexualized Makeba's performance of traditional South African labor songs: she "comes on in khaki trousers, a loosely tied shirt and black boots to do a burlesque type dance called 'the boot dance.'"[50] Burlesque shows evolved over the course of the twentieth century from humorous parodies played out in theatrical performances to risqué song and dance numbers that often included a striptease. But the boot dance was neither a parody nor a striptease. It was a series of rhythmic hand and foot patterns that originated among South African miners. Because South African authorities had banned blacks from using drums, the miners used their boots to make rhythmic sounds, which served as a secret language or code that allowed them to communicate with one another without having their messages intercepted by the overseer. The black press's inability to interpret Miriam Makeba's performance style in any way other than through the lens of sensuality is indicative of African Americans' own fetishization and fear of Africa and its cultures. The *Ebony* writer assured readers of their safety by pointing out that Makeba was "under the personal surveillance of Harry [Belafonte] himself." The use of the term "surveillance" invoked Americans' fear of a foreign enemy, constructing Harry Belafonte as a friend of the black middle class who had the authority to police the African singer's actions.[51]

Younger people in New York City had a different response to Makeba's natural African beauty. Trinidadian-born activist Stokely Carmichael first encountered Makeba's image on the cover of an album he purchased when he was in high school in New York City. The day after he heard Makeba's music on Symphony Sid's radio show, Carmichael went to the local record shop and placed an order for her record. The album cover image of Makeba reflected a new type of blackness that Carmichael found unfamiliar but attractive. Recalling the day the album arrived, he wrote in his autobiography:

When it came, I could scarcely believe my eyes. The owner of that incredible voice was young and absolutely beautiful. Her rich, smooth brown skin seemed to glow. Her strong yet delicate features were those of a classic Xhosa beauty. And, the beauty of the African woman, she wore her hair natural. The only other female artist I knew who did not fry her hair was the magnificent Odetta, whom I had seen in the benefit concerts she frequently gave in support of the Southern struggle in Montgomery. Now here came Makeba, just young, impossibly beautiful, and natural.[52]

By placing these two black women singers in conversation with each other, Carmichael traced the parameters of soul style that were forming in the United States from elements of both U.S. southern and African cultures. For Stokely Carmichael and his cadre of young activists, natural hair was a political symbol of the emerging Black Freedom movement.

Soul Women, Gender, and Style Politics

While black audiences in the United States were grappling with Makeba's image, she and other women in the Greenwich Village artistic community were publicly challenging normative notions of femininity by claiming Africa as the origin of black style and beauty. Nina Simone, Odetta, and Abbey Lincoln, who formed friendships with Makeba and one another, became the arbiters of soul style before it morphed into a global trend. Significantly, they shifted the center of the conversation from one focused on black masculinity to one that was women-centered.

Nina Simone moved to Greenwich Village in 1958, where she joined the community of activist-entertainers who helped her find her own voice as an activist and protest singer. Born Eunice Waymon in Tryon, North Carolina, in 1933, she adopted the stage name Nina Simone to keep her mother from discovering that she was singing "the devil's music." That name quickly became a stage persona. She emulated pictures of French actress and chanteuse Simone Signoret, wearing elaborate wigs and dramatic eye makeup. Her sound, which drew upon her classical training and her days as an organist in her minister-mother's church, layered Bachian fugues with gospel rhythms.[53] Simone was booked regularly at jazz venues in the Village after she received critical acclaim for her cover of "I Loves You Porgy," featured on her album *Little Girl Blue* (1957).[54] Initially there was nothing overtly political about her music or her stage persona, but by 1961, Simone began to develop ties to Africa and to the Black Freedom movement.

A fortuitous encounter with Miriam Makeba in late 1961 offers insight into Simone's early imaginings of herself as an African woman. Simone met Makeba after one of her shows at the Blue Angel nightclub in midtown Manhattan. Simone remembered that "after only a few minutes we felt like we'd known each other all our lives."[55] Part of their feeling of kinship came from the transnational circulation of their music. Makeba informed Simone that she had heard Simone's music on the South African radio station in the late 1950s and had wanted to meet her ever since. Simone's image was also circulated in *Drum* throughout the 1960s.[56] Similarly, Simone recalled, "I loved [Makeba's] music the moment I heard it."[57] They felt like they were part of the same black musical tradition.

Simone remembered, "It was her attitude I liked more than anything; she was so straightforward in what she said and thought, and at the same time so relaxed, so African."[58] Simone's description of Makeba as "so African" is significant, given that the two met shortly after Simone's first trip to Africa. Simone had traveled to Lagos, Nigeria, with Odetta and several other American jazz singers to participate in the 1961 Dinizulu Festival held by the American Society for African Culture. Founded in 1957, AMSAC was the U.S. branch of the International Society for African Culture, which began in Paris in the early 1950s. The organization aimed to connect artists, intellectuals, and writers throughout the black Atlantic world in order to promote a greater appreciation of African cultures, which had been devalued by colonial authorities.[59] Simone's experience in Nigeria was transformative, and she began to reshape her stage persona during the trip. Recalling her arrival in Nigeria, Simone wrote in her autobiography, "I knew I'd arrived somewhere important and that Africa mattered to me, and would always matter."[60] Though she still performed in the United States wearing straight-haired wigs and Western-style garments, during the Dinizulu Festival she dressed in local West African garments. She was also photographed by her good friend Langston Hughes in her downtime frolicking on the beach in a polka-dot bikini and a straw hat with her natural hair peeking out underneath.[61]

When Simone met Makeba after her return from Nigeria, she was already rethinking her own connection to Africa and African women. Given Simone's budding African consciousness, it is likely that Makeba's performance of womanhood felt legible to Simone. Makeba likely also provided Simone, a woman with a full nose and lips and dark skin, with a new way to articulate and celebrate her blackness. In Simone's imagining of the African diaspora that connected her with Makeba, the two women had more similarities than differences. "We liked the same food, drinks, men, jokes, clothes—you name it."[62] This soul connection between Makeba and

Simone was based on deep feelings. It was romantic in some ways, but for many African Americans in particular this sense of belonging was central to the process of making an African diaspora and becoming modern black cultural agents. Over the course of the 1960s, Simone began to frame herself as a diasporic subject culturally, politically, and musically as she engaged with other black women such as the folk singer Odetta who were active in the global Black Freedom struggle.

Simone's good friend Odetta had been performing in the Village since the early 1950s. Odetta Holmes, who was born in Birmingham, Alabama, in 1930 and raised in Los Angeles, began singing in her local church choir as a young child and enrolled in classical music lessons at Los Angeles City College when she was thirteen. From 1949 to 1950, the classically trained singer toured with the Los Angeles production of *Finian's Rainbow*. While playing dates in San Francisco, Odetta spent her days off in the bohemian community of North Beach, where she immersed herself in folk music and culture.[63] After learning a few blues ballads such as "John Henry," Odetta purchased her first guitar, which she named "Baby," and booked gigs at popular folk dives, including the Tin Angel and the hungry i. To supplement her meager earnings as a performer, she worked as a domestic in Los Angeles. After developing a fan base among San Francisco's North Beach community, Odetta moved to Greenwich Village at the urging of veteran folk singers Harry Belafonte and Pete Seeger, who helped her book dates at the Blue Angel in midtown Manhattan.[64] Once she arrived in New York City, her career skyrocketed. As one of the few black women of the folk music revival, she found that her style attracted attention.

Odetta used ethnic clothing, which was in vogue in Greenwich Village, to create a silhouette that suited her large frame. Though many women in bohemian milieus wore conventional clothing, the culture welcomed creative, eclectic dress, including women wearing men's slacks, blazers, blue jeans, and caftans. The flexibility in style options for bohemian women appealed to Odetta, a self-proclaimed "big-boned" girl. "I started developing my style when I was in high school," she recalled in a 1989 interview in the *Seattle Post Intelligencer*; "I was large, and I was shy about my body. So I dressed in black, thinking that would make me look smaller. But then I added caftans and scarves."[65] The caftan became Odetta's signature garment. As with most popular African garments, the caftan was designed to accommodate and accentuate a larger, full-figured body. Geometric shapes and patterns were strategically placed to show off women's buttocks, breasts, and hips because a full, curvaceous body was a sign of power, wealth, fertility, and health in most parts of Africa.[66]

The caftan was read differently on Odetta's thick black body than on the bodies of her white peers who also wore the style. Though folk musicians tended to be less adorned than women in other genres such as pop music, the beauty norm within the community was predicated on whiteness and thinness. Singer Joan Baez, who was of Mexican and Scottish descent but was read as white, epitomized this aesthetic ideal. Baez had long, thin limbs, equally long and straight hair, and olive skin. As she popularized a folk balled called "Come All Ye Young and Tender Maidens," Baez herself became the model of the young maiden. Girls across the country began growing their hair long to resemble Baez.[67] Nonetheless, Baez considered Odetta her idol, even though she described her as "big as a mountain and as black as night."[68] Baez might have chosen to use this language to capture the essence of Odetta's formidable presence, yet her language, which would have been considered disparaging by many African Americans, speaks to the ways in which racial prejudice, even on the part of white liberals, was closely bound to normative constructions of the body. Odetta, though, was invested in celebrating an African beauty and body ideal despite the prevailing norms in the industry.

During her performances, Odetta linked the U.S. struggle to liberation movements in Africa. Remembering these early days of her career, Odetta stated, "In the country, things were really coming to a boil. Those who were interested in the injustices and getting things fixed became aware of Odetta and her folk songs. So they would invite her to perform for them whether it was a demonstration or amassing monies."[69] Odetta recognized that African Americans were connected with a diasporic struggle for black self-determination and that she could use her music to raise awareness of the cause. She recalled, "I do know there were many times I embarrassed especially we [sic] African Americans when I talked about slavery or mentioned something about Africa." Yet she persisted because she saw a need to break from what she considered "Hollywood's version of Africans," which caused black people to be ashamed of their cultural roots.[70] She used her concerts and stage costumes to make explicit connections between the fight for civil rights and the cultural liberation of Africana people.

More than her African caftans and her size, it was her short, natural hairstyle, a style that people began calling "the Odetta," that placed her at the center of debates about black beauty in the African American community.[71] Early in her career in California, Odetta started wearing her hair in a short, natural style. Her hair was shorter than the rounded halo style that would become known as an Afro, yet it was longer than Miriam Makeba's closely cropped do. In this early period, such fine distinctions between types of natural styles were lost on most African Americans. The fact that it was unstraightened was enough to spark debates about whether or not the hairstyle was befitting to a well-heeled African American woman.

African American activist Carlie Collins Tartakov's first memory of Odetta was a discussion her aunts had about the singer's hair. One aunt contended that the hairstyle was unbecoming of a respectable African American woman. The other aunt, Helen, countered, "Wouldn't it be nice if we hadn't 'bought into' the Europeans' conception of what is beautiful? If we could just wear our hair any way we wanted?" At the time, young Carlie, who had been raised to believe it was "an embarrassment for us to let other people see us without some disguise of our hair," thought, "Maybe Odetta's African. Why else would she wear her hair that way?" In the American imaginary, unprocessed hair was synonymous with African-ness, even though African women across the vast and diverse continent wore their hair in a variety of straightened and unstraightened styles. By the late 1960s, as Tartakov went off to college, she began to understand and respect her aunt Helen's perspective, started wearing her hair natural, and avidly followed Odetta's career.[72] The link between natural hair and Africanness helped to propel Odetta's brand of soul style as transgressive and resistive while also defining its contours as African.

Like Odetta and a growing cadre of politically conscious black women, singer Abbey Lincoln was invested in using African fashion and beauty aesthetics to liberate women of African descent across the diaspora. Although she was born in Chicago in 1930, by the early 1960s Lincoln lived and worked in New York City with her husband, drummer Max Roach. The two were deeply involved in grassroots political work and heavily invested in cultural politics. Lincoln was one of the main people who bridged the early soul style scene in Greenwich Village, which was smaller and mostly made up of musicians and writers, with community organizers in Harlem, who were instrumental in propelling this Africanized soul style out into the diaspora. Lincoln was also a founder of the Cultural Association for Women of African Heritage (CAWAH) in the early 1960s. They chose the name in part because the acronym "sounded exotic" and seemed to mimic an African word.[73] The organization comprised teachers, dancers, musicians, and writers, including Lincoln's good friend writer Maya Angelou, many of whom had traveled to Africa. The women of CAWAH worked closely with other black groups in Harlem, helping to support, raise funds for, and bring awareness to black civil rights organizations. CAWAH was best known for "exploring the cultures of the African diaspora."[74] Its activities included encouraging black women to wear natural hairstyles, sponsoring African-inspired fashion shows, and speaking out before the United Nations against the assassination of black leaders such as Patrice Lumumba by the agents of neocolonial powers.

Lincoln's African-derived aesthetic politics and musical innovation were seen as a threat to the music elite. She brought her politics to the sonic space of the 1960 album *We Insist! Max Roach's Freedom Now Suite*. Roach and his collaborators envisioned a black liberation movement that expanded beyond the boundaries of the United States, as evidenced by song titles such as "All Africa" and "Tears for Johannesburg." The songs incorporated a variety of genres with sounds not yet classified by music critics. As the only woman on the album, Lincoln used the music to illustrate the varied ways that black women were fighting against racial and gendered oppression. Her vocals on "Triptych: Prayer/Protest/Peace" defied normal jazz vocals and scatting techniques as "words were replaced by hums, chants, and sighs" that crescendoed into "screams, roars, screeches, and pants."[75] Lincoln's work on *Freedom Now* "transformed Lincoln's reputation from a supper club chanteuse to a 'social singer.'"[76] Now branded as defiant and radical, she was virtually blackballed by the mainstream music industry for most of the 1960s. Though it would not be until the 1970s that Lincoln would record again, she continued to speak out about African cultural politics. Lincoln and her female contemporaries were instrumental in developing a language for the style politics and politically engaged music they were creating in the early 1960s.

The Language of Soul

Though political singing was lucrative, at the time there was no generally accepted name for the package of music, dress, beauty aesthetics, and politics associated with Nina Simone, Odetta, Miriam Makeba, and Abbey Lincoln. They were listed under various genres, which most of the performers considered arbitrary labels that music executives and music critics developed to market their music to consumers. The growing buzz around this political music culture helped to introduce the language of soul. Although this new language was a spontaneous development, it was soon pushed by record label executives who wanted to find a catchy way to market this style, which involved natural hairstyles, nonconformist fashions, political activism, and innovative musical forms that drew from African and African American folk traditions. Jazz record labels including RCA, Blue Note, Prestige, Columbia, and Riverside all capitalized on Africana people's desire for an aesthetic that represented their roots. Words like "soul," "funk," and "ethnic" became part of a vocabulary used to describe "black" and "African" people. This moment should not be seen as one solely driven by market tastes, however. Label executives were also feeling pressure from artists who were becoming more engaged with the movement and building lucrative careers as political singers.

In the late 1950s and early 1960s, the term "soul" was attached to a specific style of music, dress, and politics in ways that it had not been before. Soul-jazz was the name given to this aesthetic by record label executives. Soul-jazz used techniques from gospel and rhythm and blues, harkening very explicitly to black vernacular or folk traditions of an earlier era.[77] A subgenre of hard bop that was more rhythmic and harmonious, it made excellent dance music. Record label executives saw dollar signs with the potential crossover success of soul-jazz, which bridged jazz, R&B, and pop music and would appeal to teens and college students. Through their music, so-called soul-jazz artists were bringing words like "soul," "groove," and "funk" into an idiom that had previously been defined by words like "cool," "hep," and "cerebral." The popularity of soul-jazz helped to take the term "soul" outside of the black community into the mainstream. The language of soul offered modern updates on terms such as "gutbucket," "dirty," "gutter," and "alley," which had been used to describe the "earthy flavor" that had always been in the "blood stream of jazz."[78] Jazz masters of various instruments, including "Cannonball" Adderley, Oscar Brown Jr., Lou Donaldson, Horace Silver, Bobby Timmons, Gene Ammons, Eddie "Lockjaw" Davis, Stanley Turrentine, Jimmy Smith, and Shirley Scott, were among the pioneers of soul-jazz. A host of albums in the late 1950s and early 1960s either directly used "soul" in the title or conjured up the feeling of down-home folk culture, including "Lockjaw" Davis's *The Cookbook* (1958), Jimmy Smith's *Home Cookin'* (1959) and *Back at the Chicken Shack* (1963), "Cannonball" Adderley's *What Is This Thing Called Soul* (1960), Oscar Brown Jr.'s *Sin and Soul* (1960), Bobby Timmons's *Soul Time* (1960), Shirley Scott's 1961 releases *The Soul Is Willing* and *Soul Shouting*, Lou Donaldson's *The Natural Soul* (1962), and Freddie Roach's *Mo' Greens Please* (1963). Though soul-jazz has not gained the long-term success or recognition of other jazz subgenres, it was instrumental in introducing a new language that moved beyond the jazz community. As soul went mainstream, it was also touted as an expression of black masculinity, often marginalizing black women's roles in developing the look and sound of soul.[79]

By 1964, RCA recognized that such fervor could be translated into a profitable package and re-signed Miriam Makeba. Between 1960 and 1964,

Makeba had become an outspoken singer-activist. Initially, she was hesitant to be vocal about her political stance against apartheid because "my whole family is in South Africa, and they will have problems if I do something to displease the authorities."[80] Shortly after the Sharpeville Massacre on March 21, 1960, when sixty-nine peaceful protesters were gunned down by South African police officers, Makeba and Belafonte toured the U.S. South speaking out against Jim Crow and apartheid. One of their stops was a rally in Atlanta with Martin Luther King Jr.[81] In 1963, Makeba toured without Belafonte. She also appeared before the United Nations to advocate "a complete boycott of South Africa" in support of the decolonization movement.[82] RCA realized that Makeba could represent the African soul aesthetic and that she had the political bona fides to make her credible. They marketed her as "the voice of Africa." Clad in African-inspired garments and headdresses, the thirty-something Makeba was no longer a supper club chanteuse for the elite; she was an icon of the global movement for black freedom. Recalling this time, Makeba wrote, "The excitement of the Nationalist Movement in Africa has spread to the United States, and more and more there is an interest in things African. I find myself right in the center of this interest."[83]

Women soul singers and writers brought black women's issues to the fore of their liberation politics. Writer-activist Lorraine Hansberry, who lived in the Village with her husband, Robert Nemiroff, advocated a women-centered initiative within the global movement. Hansberry's essay "This Complex of Womanhood," which ran in *Ebony* magazine in August 1960, argued that black women should use the platform created by the civil rights movement to break free from the fixed roles and stereotypical images that had been assigned to their bodies. To Hansberry, redefinitions of womanhood were "inextricably and joyously bound" to the fight for liberation in Africa and Asia. She concluded, "In behalf of an ailing world which sorely needs our defiance, may we, as Negros or *women*, never accept the notion of—'our place.'"[84] By joining the larger struggle for black and brown liberation, women of the burgeoning soul generation played a crucial role in constructing the image of a modern, liberated woman of color. During the close friends' numerous conversations, Hansberry encouraged Nina Simone to join her and other black women such as Odetta in the struggle to liberate not only the race but women as well. Simone recalled that her conversations with Hansberry were never frivolous, because "it was always Marx, Lenin, and revolution—real girls' talk" when the two women got together.[85]

Nina Simone heeded Hansberry's charge, penning her first political anthem, "Mississippi Goddam!," in 1963 in response to the murder of four black girls in Birmingham. Through lyrics like "I don't trust you anymore / Keep on sayin' go slow," Simone criticized moderate activists and government officials whose broken promises to the black community led to the brutal murder of black children, including Cynthia Wesley, Denise McNair, Addie Mae Collins, and Carole Robertson, who were killed in the bombing of the Sixteenth Street Baptist Church in Birmingham earlier that year. The song was also critical of integrationist approaches to reform. "Mississippi Goddam!" was banned on many southern radio stations, supposedly for the use of the word "goddam" in the title, though it was more likely due to the song's virulent attack on the southern racial order. A South Carolina distributor returned a crate-load of "Mississippi Goddam!" albums cracked in half.[86]

To be sure, political singing came with its set of perils. Remembering her appearances at numerous Congress of Racial Equality (CORE) and Student Nonviolent Coordinating Committee (SNCC) events in the early 1960s, Simone wrote in her autobiography that "those shows were a mixture of excitement, pride, and cold, cold fear."[87] At a concert at Miles College in Birmingham in August 1963, white segregationists threatened to kill Nina Simone, Johnny Mathis, Joan Baez, and other performers if they even stepped on the stage. Choosing to ignore the threats, Simone performed an "ululating rendition" of "Brown Baby" that had "thousands cheering to the skies."[88] That same year, Simone believed she was targeted by the CIA. Agents went to Juilliard and the Curtis Institute in Philadelphia, where Simone briefly took private lessons, to question those who had known her in the early 1950s, including her former instructor Vladimir Sokoloff, asking if they believed she was a threat to national security. Others of her activist friends, including Miriam Makeba and Stokely Carmichael (who began dating around this time), Pete Seeger, and Paul Robeson, were also under heavy government surveillance.[89]

Despite its risks, being a popular activist-entertainer was lucrative. Odetta recognized the racial and gendered implications of her newfound success as well as the ways in which the civil rights movement gave her a platform that catapulted her career beyond Greenwich Village and North Beach. "I certainly wasn't on the radio," she recalled, attributing her virtual invisibility prior to the upsurge in civil rights activism to race; "if I was white, looked like a dog, and had only a fraction of what I have going on[,] I would've been out there!"[90] Record label executives often paid DJs to throw away records by black R&B singers so the studios could promote their white pop artists, who sang less soulful covers of the R&B songs.

The practice was called "paying to play," and these payola schemes ruined the careers of many talented black singers who could not get the exposure needed to launch their careers. Though most R&B artists chose not to publicly support the Black Freedom movement out of fear of losing their mainstream audience, Odetta quickly discovered that her reputation as a singer of the civil rights movement enabled her to gain visibility:[91] "I believe . . . that the civil rights movement gave me my career; it certainly made it viable for folks to see me. There was no other way a black girl singing folk songs about injustice during that time period was even going to gain an audience."[92]

Songs like "Mississippi Goddam!" helped to reshape the nature of protest music, making the genre more commercially viable. Early movement protest songs, or "freedom songs," were church hymns designed to be sung en masse. Nina Simone and others introduced a new repertoire of protest songs.[93] Unlike the freedom songs or the music on *Freedom Now*, which seemed abstract and foreign to many listeners, these new protest songs had groovy beats and catchy lyrics. Simone's fan base continued to grow, and she won over more black listeners, especially students who were active in organizations such as SNCC and CORE (which also had a large nonstudent membership). Young activists adopted "Mississippi Goddamn!" and "Brown Baby" as movement anthems. Nina Simone recalls, "During the 60s, I was told that every SNCC group played Nina Simone recordings. They played my music because they knew where I was coming from, my message was the same as theirs. They were inspired by it."[94] Recognizing that progressive students with disposable incomes bought albums, record labels were open to recording protest songs and speeches. For example, in 1963, the black-owned soul label Motown Records, which dubbed itself the "Sound of Young America," inked a deal to distribute Martin Luther King Jr.'s "I Have a Dream" speech.[95]

Although protest singers such as Miriam Makeba, Odetta, and Nina Simone maintained the image associated with a perceived nonmaterialistic, bohemian Greenwich Village culture, by 1963 these soul women lived in upscale neighborhoods and had the money to purchase expensive material goods. Simone bought a gray 1960 Mercedes-Benz convertible with a red leather interior, acquired a matching red hat, and "put the roof of the Mercedes down and cruised around the Village for hours, looking so fine."[96] After her divorce from her first husband, a white man named Don Ross, Simone purchased a fully furnished six-bedroom apartment on the twelfth floor of a high-rise building at 415 Central Park West. Nina Simone's apartment had a large bathroom, plush carpeted floors, pastel-colored

walls, a piano in the living room, and a live-in housekeeper. Other prominent activist-entertainers such as Duke Ellington, Max Roach, Abbey Lin-
coln, and Olatunji also lived in the building. Simone's new fiancé, Andy
Stroud, an African American man who had worked as a police officer in
Harlem before becoming Simone's manager, lived at 392 Central Park
West, in the same building where Odetta had an apartment. Around the
same time, Miriam Makeba moved from her basement apartment on
Eighty-Second Street to a luxurious apartment not far from Nina Simone
and Odetta, in Park West Village on Ninety-Seventh and Central Park West.
Soul music pioneer Ray Charles lived on the twentieth floor of the build-
ing, and jazzman Horace Silver and actor Brock Peters were also Makeba's
neighbors.[97] Abbey Lincoln lived in a "luxury penthouse apartment" on
Columbus Avenue on the Upper West Side.[98]

The soul women were earning top dollar in royalties, endorsement
deals, and club appearances. By 1964, Nina Simone had an endorsement deal with Crest toothpaste that in today's dollars paid $150,000 for
a single print advertisement. She received another $150,000 in royalties
from Bethlehem Records, under whose label she released two albums.[99]
In the early years of her career, Miriam Makeba earned "a mere $18,000
(in today's figures) per week," which *Sepia* writer Richard Cabrera claimed
was still "more than the average South African earns during an entire year
of hard labor."[100] Considering that they were not megawatt stars singing
in pop music categories, these earnings were impressive. In 1964, Makeba
noted that "Nina Simone and I get just about the best salaries that anyone
has been offered at the popular Village Gate."[101] Though Odetta has said
little about the amount of money she made early in her career, she was
one of the highest-grossing folk music singers in the early 1960s, regularly
playing top venues such as Town Hall and Carnegie Hall, as well as large
auditorium concerts, college campus shows, and major civil rights movement events such as the March on Washington. While Odetta and other
folk singers often waived their appearance fees when playing civil rights
movement events, the fact that they were able to do so speaks to how
much money they were making.[102]

Acknowledging the lavish lifestyles that women of the movement were
living by the mid-1960s is not an indictment or a means to question their
legitimacy. The amount of money they were able to command provides
evidence of the growing popularity of soul culture. Moreover, it demonstrates that, even in its early years, soul style was always entangled with
capitalism and the demands of the market place. There were clearly ten-

sions over what this Africanized cultural form represented and for whom and why.

At the same time, the equation of soul culture and resistance had significant implications, as many of those who were a part of the Greenwich Village milieu were tied to grassroots political movements in Harlem and in the American South. As a result, ripples of soul and the language of soul traveled and spread as members of the soul generation, including Abbey Lincoln, LeRoi Jones, and Lou Donaldson, connected with Black Nationalists in Harlem. The next chapter examines how these soul-jazz artists in particular teamed with Black Nationalist modeling troupe Grandassa to export this Americanized version of African culture and beauty to other parts of the African diaspora.

In 1962, Blue Note released soul-jazz saxophon-
ist Lou Donaldson's album *The Natural Soul*.[1] The
recording showcased the bebop-turned-soul-jazz
artist's bluesy, more soulful side. Unlike previous
albums that featured Donaldson on the cover, the
focal point of *The Natural Soul*'s cover is a dark-
complexioned black woman with a short-cropped
"natural" hairstyle (figure 2.1). Her head is tilted in a
charming, playful manner, and her smile is cool and
inviting. Hers is not a sexy pose; her conservative
black blouse and simple drop earrings, instead, communicate an air of confidence wrapped in a youthful vibrancy. There is nothing particularly African
or militant about her clothing, nor is her gaze that
of the stereotypical angry black radical that colors
the white American imaginary. But the unprocessed
state of her hair speaks volumes about black women's
beauty politics in the early 1960s and what it meant
to be "modern," "natural," and "soulful" in the age
of the burgeoning global Black Freedom movement.
The model is Helene White, an original member
of the Harlem-based Grandassa modeling troupe.
Sponsored by the African Jazz-Art Society (AJAS,
pronounced "a-jazz"), Grandassa was known for its
"Black is Beautiful" slogan and black cultural nationalist politics.[2]

White and the Grandassa models are a key link
between grassroots activism in Harlem and the burgeoning transnational soul marketplace. The previous chapter delved into the ways in which soul
singers in Greenwich Village created a sonic and political language through which soul could be mass
marketed. This chapter examines the same time
period in a different New York City neighborhood to

2

HARLEM'S "NATURAL SOUL"

Selling Black Beauty
to the Diaspora in the
Early 1960s

Figure 2.1.
Lou Donaldson,
The Natural Soul,
Blue Note Records,
1962, with Grandassa
model Helene White
on the cover.

demonstrate how young Black Nationalists helped make soul style cool for everyday black women. Focusing on AJAS and the African Nationalist Pioneer Movement (ANPM) offers a window into how these groups, made up of African American men and women and the children of Caribbean immigrant parents, were envisioning "Africa" as both a homeland and a model of black beauty and pride. At the time, AJAS and the ANPM described their style of adornment as African, meaning they were making efforts to link the styles they were wearing to specific ethnic groups and countries in Africa. As AJAS used its ties to Abbey Lincoln and others who were part of the soul-jazz music scene to export images of the Grandassa models throughout the diaspora, their look became known as soul style. The stories of these seldom-studied organizations deepen our understanding of the importance of beauty and style in their political platforms and protest strategies and of the ways in which the marketplace and the grassroots influenced one another.[3]

The role of beauty and style as markers of black modernity were popular topics for debate among activists within the U.S. Black Nationalist community and beauty columnists in the United States and abroad. At the crux of the issue was natural hair, hair that had not been altered by chemicals or heat, along with African-inspired garments. There was no consensus about whether these two forms of adornment were markers of black modernity or a liberated black world, even within nationalist circles. Soul style was born out of these contested transatlantic conversations. For the Grandassa models in particular, soul style became emblematic of one's ability to "think black," or express a pan-African worldview.[4] Their style politics simultaneously upheld and complicated exoticized notions of the African body as a site that was pure, authentic, and untouched by the racial amalgamation produced by New World slavery. As the models rose to international prominence, this American vision of African blackness became the image of soul style as a brand.

Wigs Parisian Comes to Harlem in 1963

Harlem, a neighborhood in uptown Manhattan, was a crucial nodal point in the transnational milieu that connected black people in the United States, Africa, the West Indies, and Central and South America. The community was a mecca for African-descended people and provided a home to pan-Africanist thinkers, activists, and musicians, including Amy Jacques Garvey and Amy Olatunji (wife of Nigerian drummer Olatunji). Because of its eclectic mix of inhabitants who were involved in a myriad of social and cultural movements such as the New Negro movement, the Back to Africa movement, and the black cultural renaissance, Harlem represented a "vision of brotherhood and sisterhood among African-descended peoples on all sides of the Atlantic."[5] This relatively small community held the key to many people's hopes of a transatlantic unity that could reconnect the genealogical and cultural ties that had been strained or severed during slavery. Although white ethnics and others also lived in the neighborhood, Harlem's reputation since the 1920s endowed it with a black identity. But while Harlem symbolized a fortified black American racial pride that harkened back to the African continent, its black residents did not share a unified vision for black liberation or of black beauty.[6] The ANPM's protest against the white-owned shop Wigs Parisian in the summer of 1963 illuminates the intra- and interracial class and gender politics related to beauty and black economic autonomy.

Wigs Parisian stood out amid the sea of buildings with African names such as Lagos Bar, Zanzibar, and Africa Square. The store's owners, Mike Cherney and Edward Levine, had established a thriving clientele at their flagship Wigs Parisian store in downtown Brooklyn, across from Mays department store on 577 Fulton Street. The Brooklyn store catered to white ethnic women, but it would also have had some African American clients, given the diversity of shoppers in downtown Brooklyn. In 1963, Cherney and Levine decided to expand uptown, presumably to tap into Harlem's predominantly black consumer base, moving into a shop on 151 West 125th Street. The Harlem shop was likely Cherney and Levine's first venture into a majority-black consumer market, and it coincided with a larger moment when white companies realized there was money in advertising and selling goods to black Americans. They hired local women of color to work in the store and began running advertisements in the local black newspaper.

Wigs Parisian's ads in the Harlem-based *New York Amsterdam News* focused on the ease and range of styling that wigs could offer black women.[7] Though their intended clientele was black, the cartoon drawings in Wigs Parisian's ads depicted women with conventional European features who were merely shaded to appear darker. It is likely that Cherney and Levine simply tinted images from the ads targeting their white customers in Brooklyn. In the eyes of many Black Nationalists, the ads upheld white beauty through thin facial features, showing that white business owners in black communities had no desire to create ad campaigns that celebrated black women. But most Harlem women were seemingly unoffended by the ads, as hundreds of black women gathered outside of Wigs Parisian's Harlem store to take advantage of the free wig giveaway announced in the advertisements. "We're Giving Away 1,000 Wigs" read one ad that ran once weekly throughout the month of August, leading up to and immediately following the opening of the Harlem store. The free wigs were described as a "wonderful break" for women who were "fashion conscious."[8] The catch was that the black women who obtained a "free" wig had to pay to have it maintained by one of Wigs Parisian's stylists for an unstated price.[9] Yet for many black women, the offer was alluring because in the early 1960s high-quality wigs cost, on average, between $100 and $300.[10]

Around the world, wigs and hairpieces were growing in popularity among young black women because they were markers of modern sophistication and style. The women who shopped at Wigs Parisian were part of a transnational beauty culture circuit. Black women in the United States were experimenting with wigs as a way to look modern. For example, Diana Ross and the Supremes, who epitomized innocent, mainstream American girl charm, wore wigs to symbolize the elegance and sophistication that Motown Records represented. Inspired by the singers, models, and actresses of the day, women of all races on both sides of the Atlantic flocked to salons and wig stores asking for the latest styles in wigs and hairpieces.[11] There was much debate throughout the African diaspora about the place of wigs and skin lighteners. In most cases, black women who wore wigs did so not to be white; rather, they were trying to be on trend. The problem was that most of the trends were set by a beauty and fashion industry that lauded whiteness. Thus, most of the black women who worked as models in the global fashion and beauty industries up until the late 1960s had fair skin and straight hair. So emulating those women meant emulating a particular beauty image.

The international popularity of wigs coincided with African Americans' growing interest in black fashion models and beauty pageant queens who were integrating the European fashion industry. *Ebony* magazine ran a series of articles that addressed how the beauty and fashion industries in seemingly racially tolerant, cosmopolitan cities such as Paris were beginning to recognize the beauty in brownness—albeit lighter shades of brown on models with thin facial features and processed hair.[12] In 1960, Alexandria, Virginia, native LeJeune Hundley, whom *Ebony* described as "tan, tall, and terrific," became the second woman of color to win the Cannes Film Festival's "Miss Festival" title. Hundley, who could pass for white, was becoming the toast of southern France. "Amber-brown" Helen Williams, America's "most successful negro model," won contracts with Christian Dior and Jean Desses in Paris. According to Williams, Paris was "the capital of style and sophistication."[13] Some within the African American community considered the integration of the European fashion industry a major victory for blacks. Yet the insistence upon light-skinned beauty reified colorism within the black community and linked modern black beauty with fair skin and straight hair.

Wigs Parisian tapped into this vision of cosmopolitan brown beauty. The store's owners hired local Harlem celebrity Doris Chambers, a model and beauty pageant queen, to set a standard of glamour for the women entering the shop. Chambers had just won the Miss Beaux Arts Pageant, which was sponsored by socialite-activist Mollie Moon's elite Urban League Guild and the F&M Schaefer Brewing Company and was one of the most elite events among New York City's black high society. The contestants were called "Cleopatra's Daughters," and the pageant was designed to showcase the women's outward beauty. Cleopatra's Daughters strove to emulate not only historical images of the North African queen but also images of the women whom mainstream America had chosen to represent Egyptian elegance, including singer-actress Lena Horne, who inspired Max Factor's first makeup foundation ("Light Egyptian") for black women, and white actress Elizabeth Taylor, who played the title role in the 1963 film *Cleopatra*. In other words, these black socialites were drawing upon an ancient African culture that was perceived as prestigious and powerful but was not sub-Saharan. In Egypt, dark skin and natural hair were markers of lower social standing. For centuries, wigs had been a symbol of superior class status and royalty. Ancient Egyptian pharaohs and their royal families wore wigs that symbolized their high status, while their slaves and servants were required by law to wear their own natural hair. The Miss Beaux Arts Pageant sponsors were invested in a vision of Africa and African beauty that was not linked to darker skin tones and kinky hair. Chambers brought the cosmopolitan glamour celebrated by Moon and the Urban League Guild to Wigs Parisian's 125th Street customers.[14]

The ANPM Protests Wigs Parisian

The ANPM's brand of beauty was in direct contrast to the principles of African beauty upheld by the Urban League Guild and Wigs Parisian. ANPM was a neo-Garveyite organization founded in 1941 by Carlos Cooks, a man of Afro-Caribbean descent born to a middle-class family in the Dominican Republic. Like Marcus Garvey's Universal Negro Improvement Association, of which Cooks had been a member, the ANPM upheld three core tenets: racial purity and race pride, economic autonomy and self-help, and independence from European colonialism.[15] To promote its ideal image of beauty, the ANPM founded the Miss Natural Standard of Beauty contest, which was held annually on August 18, during the organization's Marcus Garvey Day Celebration. The 1963 pageant occurred around the same time that Wigs Parisian opened on 125th Street.

The ANPM's "natural" beauty pageant had a similar format as the Miss America pageant, featuring bathing suit, evening wear, and question-and-answer segments. The contest was created to highlight local black women who would have been marginalized in pageants such as the Miss Beaux Arts competition. "Natural" was shorthand for the concept of racial purity—the idea that one's "black blood" had not been tainted by race mixing, which had often resulted from the rape of black women by white men—that was believed to be evidenced by dark skin and kinky, tightly coiled hair. Miss Natural Standard of Beauty contestants were dark-complexioned in order to represent the beauty of blackness in its imagined purest form. But the concept of a natural beauty was complicated, as indicated by the fact that most people of African descent in the Americas were of mixed race. The ANPM was inadvertently encouraging a standard that most black women's genetic makeup prevented them from attaining.[16]

The structure of the pageant indicates that the ANPM believed naturalness could also be performed. It is this performance of naturalness that allowed the ANPM to overlook the legacies of racial amalgamation and choose the candidate who looked and acted the most "black." In contrast to mainstream beauty competitions, Miss Natural Standard of Beauty contestants had to compete with their hair unprocessed and could wear no makeup. They had to answer questions about black history and were evaluated on their level of black consciousness. The overall aim of the pageant was not to deconstruct femininity; indeed, the ANPM was invested in most normative notions of feminine propriety. Rather, the organization wanted to establish dark skin and natural hair as the markers of feminine beauty instead of the blonde-haired, fair-skinned beauty standard celebrated in mainstream society.[17] The ANPM believed that European notions of beauty brainwashed black women into buying products like wigs in a futile effort to look white.

The ANPM boycotted shops like Wigs Parisian because they exploited black women's desires to be beautiful. In 1963, a band of male and female ANPM protesters marched outside of Wigs Parisian in the August heat, the protest reflecting the movement's three-pronged approach to black liberation. ANPM adherents believed that one of the ways in which white America exploited the black community economically was through its promotion of European beauty standards, which black women were not born with but could purchase in the form of wigs and skin bleaching creams. In other words, by destroying the black woman's image of her own natural African beauty, shops like Wigs Parisian were complicit in the larger colonial project that sought to keep Africana people economically, culturally, and socially oppressed. To combat white exploitation, ANPM promoted the concept of consumption as a form of identity politics through Carlos Cooks's "Buy Black" campaign. Since the 1940s, the ANPM had endorsed the public condemnation, embarrassment, and corporeal punishment of African Americans in the Harlem community who refused to buy at black-owned stores.[18] It is unclear if and how these acts were carried out, but the tactics seemed to become less violent and more practical by the 1960s. At its most basic level, the campaign stressed that a black woman could illustrate her ability to "think black" by purchasing and consuming beauty products produced by and for black people. Wearing one's hair natural was both a form of cultural self-expression and a way to abandon reliance upon hair products such as straightening pomades and wigs (often manufactured by white companies) that reinforced white hegemony.[19] In its efforts to topple the Wigs Parisian empire, the ANPM sought to strike a blow against the cultural imperialism that fueled negative constructions of black womanhood.

Wigs Parisian co-owner Mike Cherney considered himself an economic friend to the black community. Cherney told a *New York Amsterdam News* reporter covering the protest that approximately 15,000 people were employed by the wig industry, 90 percent of whom were black. This percentage is likely exaggerated, and those blacks who did work in the industry were almost always low-wage workers, not business owners or creative directors. He claimed that his goal was to help the African American and Latin American women on his staff—Oberia Martinez, Bette Bullock, and Muriel McClelland—earn a living wage.[20] The protest made the women worry that they would lose their jobs. Wigs Parisian's owners may have been able to stand any financial blows caused by the protest; it was the women who worked for them who were in the most precarious financial situation. From the ANPM's vantage point, though, Cherney could never be a friend to the black community because his store modeled a colonial infrastructure that exploited low-wage-earning laborers, and his brand was deeply entangled in racist ideals of beauty.

The ANPM launched its protest to push back against Wigs Parisian and to promote its African beauty politics. The signs the protesters carried spoke volumes about the organization's viewpoint. The ANPM was critical of black women who considered the store's offer a financially savvy investment with real beauty advantages. One sign read, "WANTED 1000 Misfits for a 'Giveaway' Program APPLY WITHIN!"[21] Another, "We Don't Want Any Congo Blondes," visually communicated the inherent contradiction by depicting deep ebony–complexioned women with large, full lips, like the so-called Ubangi women of Chad and the Central African Republic, wearing blonde and red wigs.[22] ANPM protesters were rejecting colonialism and empire, which revealed itself not only through the forced control of African people but also through the development of businesses that drew upon imperial names, imagery, and notions of beauty. As indicated by the references on their signs to the Congo, a Belgian, francophone colony, and the Zulu people, who had been colonized by the Dutch, British, and Portuguese in South Africa, Rhodesia, and Mozambique, the ANPM likened the exploitation of black women consumers to a form of neocolonialism that propagated imperial notions of beauty and racial difference.[23] Its platform stated that the ANPM "denies all standards of beauty that do not represent the vibrant characteristics of the African race."[24] Ideal ANPM beauties were black women who honored their heritage by wearing their hair natural.[25]

As the Wigs Parisian protest continued into September, it exposed the rifts within the black American community over self-styling. The demonstration developed into a picket war between wig protesters and wig supporters. The wig supporters were largely black women who wanted to defend their right to wear wigs and some black men who preferred wigs to short, natural hair. It is unclear whether they were part of a rival local organization or were sent to the store by an outside agency to raise the intensity of the protest. The fervent battle between wig protesters and wig supporters was an intraracial fight not only over the significance of natural hair but also over the ideological framework for representations of blackness and black womanhood. Black women's hair had always been "a highly sensitive surface on which competing notions of 'the beautiful' are played out in struggle."[26] From the ANPM's perspective, the beauty of the black woman was tarnished by wearing "some dead cracker's hair or horse tail."[27] While the organization's signs singled out black American women who preferred to wear blonde and redheaded wigs, signs carried by wig supporters were equally provocative.[28] "NO man wants a woman who looks like his *Brother*!" read a sign worn by a male wig supporter. In other words, feminine beauty achieved through the artifice of wigs was better than short, unprocessed hair because natural hair was regarded as unfeminine.[29] This sign was reflective of responses that black women with short naturals received within the African American community. Actress Cicely Tyson recalled negative reactions to her "little boy" hairstyle in the early 1960s: "Once I was in Washington and was virtually attacked by a group of middle class ladies, 'bourgeois Negroes' as we call them. They said I was 'hurting' the Negro image in America. A woman's hair should be long and straight in this country."[30] Other signs simply affirmed black women's right to choose styles that made them feel beautiful. "If it looks good, wear it," one poster read, rejecting what it considered reverse cultural elitism.

New York Amsterdam News writer Thomasina Norford humorously described the social violence of the protest in one of her articles. She opened her September 14 piece on the protest by calling up the names of the "battle of the Bulge," the "battle of Normandie [*sic*] Beach," and the "battle of Bataan in the Philippines" and jokingly surmising that these famous battles were "minor" compared to the "battle of the wig pickets."[31] Though Norford's article invoked humor, black women were the objects of ridicule on both sides of the debate in ways that could have been emotionally damaging. No negative images of white women were presented on the signs. The protest became an attack on black women and their hairstyle choices, shaming them for either wanting to wear a wig or wanting to wear their hair natural.

This local protest was indicative of international debates in the black press about black women's hairstyles. During the month the ANPM launched its protest against Wigs Parisian, *Negro Digest* ran an article titled "Should Black Women Stop Straightening Their Hair?" The story featured comments by *Lagos Times* columnist Theresa Ogunbiyi, who opined that traditional African modes of hairstyling and adornment were stifling for Nigerians, particularly the women. She argued that Nigerians "carry this national pride thing a bit too far," wearing their hair in plaits in the workplace often "to the detriment of our Country's progress." For the popular Nigerian beauty writer, in a modern society, "traditional" or ethnic hairstyles had to be effaced for the benefits of modernity, which included comfort and ease of care for modern working women with "never-a-moment to spare." Ogunbiyi represented a transnational black female voice that opposed the natural on the grounds that it was not modern. Her stance was considered assimilationist by some of her countrywomen and countrymen and may have also been problematic for many cultural nationalists in the United States whose vision of an independent West Africa was one that celebrated precolonial African cultures. It might have also shocked many African Americans who believed that all African women wore their hair natural. But Ogunbiyi's statements reflect the fact that many African women found local cultures to be stifling for women because they bound them to traditional gender roles at a moment when they wanted to be urban women who earned their own money, decided if and when they wanted to get married, and styled themselves according to the latest global fashion trends.[32]

Even some women in the United States who self-identified as Black Nationalists pointed out the contradictions within the community over natural hair and beauty. In "Hot Irons and Black Nationalism," which ran in *Liberator* in the summer of 1963, activist Eleanor Mason argued that black women in parts of precolonial Africa used to "burn" their hair with metal irons to give it a straightened appearance, not to look white but as a form of self-expression and group affiliation. Linking hair straightening to an early African beauty ritual allowed Mason to establish hair straightening as authentically black. She pointed out that over the years, hair straightening had become part of the rites of passage that bonded black girls to their mothers and sisters. In other words, straight hair, too, had a place in the community- and identity-building process that African Americans were hoping to facilitate by embracing African cultures. Mason's analysis of hair straightening affirmed Africa as an important cultural homeland for African Americans but challenged Black Nationalists' narrow aesthetic scope in positing natural hairstyles as the only viable choice for modern, liberation-minded black women.³³ Mason concluded that a woman should be given the choice to decide how she should physically embrace and embody her blackness because the "apparents [*sic*] of servitude" for one might be liberating to another.³⁴ In other words, though some might see straightened hair as an obvious sign of bondage, other black women might find it liberating.

Long after the ANPM's protest against Wigs Parisian fizzled that fall, the debates over natural hair continued. Wigs Parisian remained open and still drew a black clientele, but the protest helped to call attention to the politics of soul style. Though the African-inspired look was far from popular in the early 1960s, it was gaining more international attention. The black press was instrumental in circulating news about local events such as the Wigs Parisian protest and debates over natural hair. Print media also became a space where black women had the authority to speak as experts on these topics, enabling them to shape how people understood black women's hairstyling choices. And as the black press was reporting on the translocal and transnational politics of natural beauty and hair, black models, fashion designers, and boutique owners were carving out a niche market for soul style across the diaspora. The print media and the burgeoning informal soul style fashion network complemented one another and were critical to the success of the Grandassa models.

The Grandassa Models and Black Style Politics

In the frenzy of the natural hair debates, a group of younger, more culturally oriented ANPM activists sought a less divisive approach to promoting black pride. Brothers Ronnie and Cecil Brathwaite, of West Indian descent, attended the 1961 ANPM's Miss Natural Standard of Beauty contest. That year, a young black woman named Clara Lewis won the competition. Lewis was a Harlem native with dark skin and thick tresses that she often wore in a kinky bun. The Brathwaites were dismayed upon seeing Lewis the following Sunday when she came to receive her $100 prize and was no longer wearing her hair natural. There were a variety of possible reasons why Lewis had opted to wear her hair straightened that day: perhaps her mother made her wear it straightened for church. Whatever the case, the brothers were still shocked. It was not surprising to them that most black women outside of Black Nationalist circles wore the more widely accepted straightened styles. What surprised the Brathwaites was that even a woman within the movement would not feel confident enough to wear her hair unprocessed once she left ANPM events. Many black women in

America who wanted to go natural found that family and friends—like the pro-wig protesters—ridiculed them relentlessly for wearing their hair unstraightened in public. For example, former *Jet* magazine associate editor Helen Hayes King remembered that when she went natural in the early 1960s, the remarks from members of her predominantly black community on Chicago's South Side were crueler than those of whites, with friends giving her the "have-you-gone-crazy" stare and some even being bold enough to ask if she had in fact lost her mind.[35] Safe havens for black women who wished to go natural were few and far between, even in progressive communities like Harlem and the South Side of Chicago.[36]

With their newfound revelation, the Brathwaites decided to shift the focus of AJAS to more explicitly concentrate on style and adornment politics. The organization, founded by the Brathwaites and five other friends from the School of Industrial Arts (now the High School of Art and Design) in Manhattan, gained popularity in the Bronx and Harlem during the late 1950s by collaborating with soul-jazz acts such as Lou Donaldson to promote awareness of African-derived black music and dance forms. Though they maintained their ties to the jazz world, AJAS members decided to contribute to the growing activism and discourse surrounding natural hair and its role in the fight for black freedom. Emphasizing culture and race pride, the collective aimed to create a cultural-political space where Black Nationalists and non–Black Nationalists could interact and communicate, believing that a less adversarial relationship between Black Nationalists and the broader black community was crucial to the advancement of the Black Freedom movement as a whole. They also recognized that the older producer model, which relied upon blacks making their own goods to sell or barter within the community, had worked for Garveyites earlier in the century but was not as effective with the post–World War II generation, whose members reveled in their freedom to pay for leisure and entertainment, which often meant spending money outside of the black community.[37] In light of these two realizations, AJAS employed the talents of its members to create a culturally based activist strategy that promoted performance as identity.

AJAS envisioned a modeling troupe that wore African-inspired fashion while embodying Black Nationalist beauty principles. Using the resources of AJAS member and model Jimmy Abu, the Brathwaites began recruiting women for their modeling troupe. They named the group Grandassa, drawing from the name "Grandassaland" that Carlos Cooks used to describe the lush beauty of the African landscape. In the early years, the Grandassa models represented Cooks's imagined Africa and the specific type of Black Nationalism in which he was invested. Along with ANPM pageant winner Clara Lewis, the original Grandassa models were Rose "Black Rose" Nelms, Helene White (the woman on the cover of Lou Donaldson's album *The Natural Soul*), Priscilla Bardonille, Wanda Sims, Mari Toussaint, Esther Davenport, Beatrice Cranston, Jimmy Abu, and Frank Adu.[38] The models shared a certain ideal of African women's appearance, which celebrated the race purity ideology that undergirded AJAS's black cultural nationalism worldview. They ranged only slightly in complexion, from medium brown to dark chocolate; most had full lips and noses; and all wore their hair in styles that highlighted its kinky texture. Physically, the models linked naturalness and blackness to a fuller figure. While none of the female Grandassa models were plus size, none had the waif figure of 1960s British supermodels Jean Shrimpton and Twiggy. Black and white Americans had different perceptions of ideal body types. African Americans, as in others parts of Africa and its diaspora, generally preferred women's bodies with noticeable hips, stomach, thighs, and breasts, seeing a connection between size, healthiness, and sensual appeal, and though there was not a universally accepted body type among African Americans, the Grandassa models reflected the perceived desire for the fullness of black women's bodies. The Grandassa models were not trying to integrate the white world of haute couture; they were creating a new industry driven by black fashion and "natural" models.

AJAS and the Grandassa models had to convince everyday black women that African fashions were cool. Many black Americans linked soul style to Africa. Because most African Americans, particularly those who lived outside of major East Coast cities, had accepted the notion that Africa was a primitive place covered by jungles, they did not see such clothing as aspirational. AJAS had to rebrand Africa in the American imaginary. It did so by focusing on fashion in various African cities across the continent, linking the clothes worn by Grandassa models to those popular in vibrant cities such as Lagos, Accra, Dar es Salaam, and Nairobi. They used fashion to demonstrate that urban dwellers in Africa were not unlike urban black folks in the United States. AJAS organized fashion shows that featured the latest hairstyles and apparel popular throughout the African diaspora in an effort to appeal to fashion-conscious, leisure-minded African Americans of various political and class backgrounds. The group called it "edutainment"—striking a balance between education and entertainment—that connected personal grooming to an African-based history and cultural aesthetic for black youth.[39]

Style and performance had long been an integral part of black consumer culture and strategies for racial advancement. The first black fashion magazine, *Ringwood's Afro-American Journal of Fashion*, was published in 1891. Catering specifically to a female audience, the magazine showcased the latest fashions from Paris and also featured articles on racial uplift and black clubwomen's efforts. *Ringwood's* would have appealed both to the free black population and to recently freed slaves who used clothing as a symbol of their freedom, which allowed them to fashion a liberated identity. Fine clothing was expensive to procure and therefore something that many African Americans could not afford. But they could and did make their own garments. During slavery, bondwomen used their earnings to buy fabrics in bright colors that they would use to create garments to wear to church. Vibrant colors and prints were part of the rural southern black style tradition, as they were in Africa.[40] Enslaved women seamstresses likely chose bright colors because they were vastly different from the muted-tone garments they had to wear when laboring. Bright Sunday clothes allowed them to distinguish their worshipping body from their working body. Because their wardrobes were largely restricted under slavery, both by mandates of their owners and by the nature of their labor, after emancipation many former bondwomen and bondmen continued making and wearing flamboyant outfits full of color. Their liberated style drew inspiration from the fashions that their white counterparts were wearing but also incorporated elements that represented their own heritage and aesthetic perspective.

In the early twentieth century, black Americans began exhibiting their style innovations in formal shows, appropriating department stores' fashion showcases as a model for their own style shows.[41] The idea of strolling down a runway dressed in custom-made clothing was not an unfamiliar concept to African Americans. When enslaved women and men wore their brightly colored finest to church, they paraded from the plantation to the church house. The fashion parade became a popular custom among the enslaved, which endured in the postbellum years. In the World War I era, the concept of the Sunday parade and the department store style show were melded, resulting in a cultural phenomenon that became popular in black communities throughout the country. In places such as New York City, New Orleans, Pittsburgh, Louisville, Chicago, and Kansas City, these shows ranged from small local events to fashion extravaganzas. Churches, fraternal and sororal orders, and colleges and universities all held their own fashion shows. The shows were typically linked to the black middle class and served as coming-out affairs for local debutantes and aspiring models. Fashion shows gave elite African American women an opportunity to perform their respectability and to create class delineations between themselves and blacks of the poor and working classes. In other words, the shows reflected a middle-class black culture predicated on the consumption of goods. There was also an emphasis on black women making their own items, which is significant because as soul style grew in popularity, black women became designers of these goods, both as do-it-yourselfers and as ready-to-wear and haute couture designers across the African diaspora.[42]

In the 1960s, black fashion shows became more countercultural in nature and celebrated transgressive style politics. Youth in the mid-twentieth century built upon the earlier styles, recognizing how transgressive such garments as the zoot suit were. Their youth fashion aesthetic flourished outside of mainstream fashion currents, made popular by informal fashion networks and by magazines such as *Sepia* that featured four-page editorials on rising Afrocentric fashion designers, including the New Breed and Palmer Brown. Ethnic fashions that subverted the mainstream mold were labeled "anti-fashion" by the mainstream fashion world. The pejorative term "anti-fashion" not only disqualified those who were not white or elite from participating in the mainstream fashion world but also suggested that blacks' racial and class status meant they could not be arbiters of style and taste. The industry labeled as anti-fashion those undesirable garments that would not be accepted by the fashion world, even though mainstream designers would often steal these so-called anti-fashions and sell them under their own labels. But in spite of backlash from the mainstream fashion industry, black subversive styles assumed a life and industry of their own, and black fashion shows such as those held by AJAS featuring the Grandassa models became a vehicle to exhibit and promote street fashions that were inspired by black urban life across the African continent.[43]

In its inaugural show, AJAS brought its Black Nationalist politics to the runway, demonstrating a new form for the street fashion show. The Grandassa models entertained a packed house on January 28, 1962, at Harlem's Purple Manor, premiering their show named "Naturally '62: The Original African Coiffure and Fashion Extravaganza Designed to Restore Our Racial Pride and Standards" (often shortened to "Naturally"). The Naturally show was meant to "prove to the world that 'Black is Beautiful'" by promoting natural hairstyles and soul fashions as tools of liberation. Drawing upon its resources and ties to the jazz and performing arts world, AJAS recruited actor Gus Williams to host the show. Popular soul-jazz singer and activist Abbey Lincoln, who also wore her hair natural, cohosted, modeled, and offered commentary, while her husband, jazz drummer Max Roach, provided the musical accompaniment.[44] Publicity photos of the Grandassa models in their African-inspired garments and natural hairstyles offer a sense of their runway fashions. The models wore dresses with intricate patterns and prints that lent an ethnic feel. The basic dress silhouettes were made more striking by the addition of peplum waistlines (a flounce that extends over the waist and accentuates curvy hips) and bell, A-line, or puff sleeves. The women accented their garments with large hoop earrings, chunky bracelets, and kitten-heeled mules and sandals.[45]

AJAS aimed to create a show that centered fashion as a communal experience, using it to tell a different narrative of black women's bodies. Such street fashion shows had an element of spectacle, as had the earlier class-based fashion extravaganzas and beauty pageants. Yet shows like these encouraged crowd participation, becoming a form of interactive entertainment. AJAS's shows were accompanied by music, usually popular songs that allowed audience members to clap along as the models swayed rhythmically down the runway. The models choreographed their movements, often incorporating a series of turns and poses that drew cheers and shouts from the audience. At these more countercultural fashion shows, there was an exchange between the models and the audience, which AJAS believed had the potential to unify the black community.[46] AJAS envisioned clothing as an instructional tool that could be "used to tell a story the wearer thought most compelling."[47] Walking with their heads up and chests lifted as they strutted down the runway, the Grandassa models demonstrated a "dignified body posture," showing how proudly black Americans should walk in their African garments.[48] Their clothing could also be used as "armor" that women could put on to defend their own honor and dignity. Grandassa models used clothing to signify their roles as freedom fighters. By wearing African-inspired garments, they were communicating their support of a liberated Africa and symbolically expressing their hope for black freedom and social, political, and cultural independence in the Americas.[49]

The Naturally show's hosts discussed the politics behind the models' "African" hairstyle choices. The Grandassa models' hairstyles were diverse, and the models claimed to have researched the hairstyles, tracing them back to a particular African country or region. Helene White's short-cropped natural was considered "a traditional hair style of South and West Africa," Clara Lewis exhibited a "Zulu style," and Priscilla Bardonille's neatly coiffed hair, which was pulled into a massive Afro puff on the crown of her head, was an "Amharic hair style" from the North Central region of Ethiopia.[50] Associating their hairstyles with a particular place helped them orient their audiences to Africa while authenticating the Grandassa models and the brand of African soul style they promoted. It is not clear where they did their research to learn about these styles, but they do appear to be based on local hairstyles. Their differentiation between the various types of natural hairstyles was significant because at the time, African Americans were largely collapsing these styles into the category "African." But the Grandassa models' neat typology of "African" hairstyles was predicated on a belief that there was one main hairstyle worn by women of various African ethnic groups. Moreover, it did not take into account that urban African women were veering from so-called traditional hairstyles and opting for wigs and straightened hairstyles, which created a whole new set of options for African women's hair.[51]

Though the troupe was mixed-gendered, it was the women, with their "exotic" African-inspired natural hairstyles, who garnered the most curiosity, criticism, and fanfare after their fashion show debut. Some black men were initially skeptical of the appeal of natural-haired, dark-complexioned women. Ronnie Brathwaite recalled one man telling his brother, Cecil, "You mean you're gonna put some nappy headed black bitches on stage to model?"[52] Like the male wig supporter who claimed that no man wanted a woman who looked like his brother, many other men of African descent—presumably, even some male Black Nationalists—relied upon sexist language to voice their disbelief that women with kinky hair and dark skin could be beauty ambassadors or even entertaining to watch. Despite their skeptics, the Grandassa models garnered a cult following, mainly among black women from a variety of political and class backgrounds, of different complexions, and with various hair textures. Journalist Helen Hayes King, who was not a Black Nationalist and who wore her hair processed at the time, remembered the Grandassa models being "very attractive" and how struck she was by the fact that Abbey Lincoln was "no longer ashamed of her hair, which was impressively well groomed." Lincoln's decision to go natural boosted King's appreciation of her own hair, eventually motivating her to cut off her processed locks.[53]

Journalists exoticized the models, describing them using language that referenced black Americans' perceptions of African bodies. Writer Melba Tolliver, who covered the "Naturally" events for the *Herald Tribune*, recalled: "To see the Grandassa models for the first time was stunning. They were so dark their faces had a bluish shimmer, 'blue black' people. . . . You saw them and your mouth just fell open."[54] "Blue black" was a slang term often used by African Americans to describe the complexions of dark-skinned African Americans who they believed had retained strong African features. The term was sometimes employed lovingly, but most often it was a language of ridicule that African Americans used to shame someone for being too dark to be attractive. Tolliver's comments were meant to praise the models for their ability to be African and beautiful simultaneously. Tolliver, who later became a local news anchor for an ABC affiliate, was known around New York City for her natural hairstyle. She won the praise of many African Americans in 1971 when she refused to wear a wig or to cover her Afro with a head scarf when she reported from the White House during President Nixon's daughter Tricia Nixon's wedding. Her favorable coverage of the Grandassa models reflected Tolliver's own beauty politics and political commitments. Tolliver understood that the Grandassa models wanted to make themselves more exotic as a way to rebuff the colorism that they believed most African Americans suffered from.[55]

The Grandassa models used tropes of the exotic to craft their own interpretation of black sensuality. Because white women were regarded as innately morally pure and passionless, individual white women were able to engage in displays of sensuality without compromising the perceived wholesomeness of their group. Black women were not afforded the same moral status. Europeans' fascination with "primitive" black bodies led to grotesque and inaccurate depictions of black women's genitalia in images and art. Black women's sensuality was considered lascivious, a function of their primal nature that marked their raced and gendered bodies. The Grandassa models aimed to disprove these racist and sexist stereotypes by bringing new aesthetic value to black flesh. If black was beautiful, it was also sexy. It was the site of a self-determined pleasure. Their aim was not to dismantle the gaze but to shift the nature of the lens by changing the frame of reference. The models worked within an ANPM framework wherein women adhered to many normative notions of feminine propriety. But they were also using tropes of the African exotic as a way to liberate black women in the Americas from a politics of respectability that kept them from expressing their sexuality in public. To this end, the frame of reference was no longer one of the sexually vulnerable enslaved woman or the tragic mulatta. The Grandassa models were strong, proud African women, the descendants of African royalty, who disrupted the power paradigm of the white male gaze. Soul style was at the center of their performance of the black exotic. By putting on the clothing and hairstyles worn by African women, black American women believed they could be liberated from their own cultural baggage.[56]

AJAS and Soul Style on the International Stage

Because of the popularity of the Naturally shows, AJAS realized that by positioning the Grandassa models as the fashionistas of the emerging soul market, it could move beyond the Harlem community to bring its brand of soul style to this burgeoning international audience. The group diversified its artistic efforts and used the global black print media to expand its grassroots base into a transnational presence. Unlike Carlos Cooks, who banned the press from ANPM functions, AJAS discovered that it could use the black radical media to create a black beauty and style brand that could be emulated throughout the African diaspora. The group moved into a studio space next to the Apollo Theater and added a graphic design element (a photo studio, art production, and a rehearsal space), changing its name to the African Jazz-Art Society and Studios (AJASS). With a professional space and the ability to (re)produce images and logos, AJASS now had the credentials and the means of production to book elite venues that drew larger crowds and to place images of its models in local, regional, and international publications and ephemera.[57] Once AJASS went into mass production, what it called "African" dress in Harlem soon became known as soul style.

Boutique owners and fashion designers used the soul language to build upon the burgeoning soul style fashion network. Boutiques were early sources of ethnic fashions for Black Nationalist women, college students, singers, and entertainers. Fashion boutiques first opened in the 1920s as smaller shops within couture fashion houses, selling less-popular items from the couturier's line. By the 1960s, they sold affordable, trendy pieces and hard-to-find eclectic wares aimed at the youth market across the African diaspora.[58] Shade's Boutique in Lagos, Nigeria, was owned and operated by designer Shade Thomas-Fahm. Singer Miriam Makeba planned to open a boutique in Nassau, the Bahamas, to help build the nation's economy after it gained partial independence from Britain in 1964. She worked with a Trinidadian dressmaker who made clothing in a "Caribbean" style, and from her residence in New York City, Makeba served as the artistic director, supervising production in the West Indies.[59] In Harlem, Ntu (pronounced en-too) Stop opened down the street from Wigs Parisian at 63 East 125th Street in Harlem in the fall of 1963. The owner, James Davis, boasted that his "original designs were imported from Africa" and were meant to "encourage a cultural concept of self." The goods were made from "traditional African designs" yet were "acceptable to western dress."

Though priced for the person on a budget, the items were made of fine materials such as silk, mohair, cashmere, mahogany, bamboo, and rosewood. Davis's clothing encouraged a pan-African concept of blackness: West African dashikis, Egyptian perfumes, South African beads, and Moroccan leather wallets and purses. The air of exoticism in the marketing of the items created a degree of glamour around African fashions that paralleled the allure of French haute couture designers Christian Dior and Givenchy.[60] AJASS hoped to position the Grandassa models as the face of this diverse African diasporic style.

AJASS made inroads into the soul market after it designed several soul-jazz album covers with images of Grandassa models on them. AJASS members already had strong relationships with soul-jazz artists. When Blue Note Records sought to brand soul-jazz, the label took suggestions from its artists and from graphic designer and photographer Reid Miles, who designed most of Blue Note's album covers in the 1950s and 1960s. Miles studied at Los Angeles's Chouinard Art Institute and worked as an art designer for *Esquire* early in his career. His new post at Blue Note was his big career break. Miles was responsible for helping Blue Note develop a graphic style for its album covers that set it apart from the other indie jazz labels of the era. Miles, who was not black or a jazz enthusiast, translated the language of soul into a visual package that could be easily recognized and consumed by Blue Note's hipster audience. It was Miles who worked in conjunction with the Brathwaite brothers to design the covers that featured Grandassa models on them. The covers of Lou Donaldson's *The Natural Soul*, Freddie Roach's *Brown Sugar* (1964), and Big John Patton's *Oh Baby!* (1965) all shared a similar aesthetic and design concept, and Ronnie Brathwaite is given photo credit for all of the covers.[61] Each featured a Grandassa model—Helene White, Clara Lewis, and Brenda Deaver, respectively—and highlighted the model's skin tone, full facial features, and natural hair. The *Brown Sugar* cover in particular played upon Clara Lewis's deployment of the sensual African exotic. Lewis was photographed close up, gazing over her bare shoulder directly into the camera. "Brown sugar" was a metaphor for the raw, sonic goodness on the album and for the sensuality of Lewis's deep brown skin. The viewer was invited to imagine what it would be like to consume Lewis's sweet, delectable flesh. The pleasure derived from both the music and the model's tasty parts represented black desire for the down home, the familiar, the soul (figure 2.2).

The cover of Lou Donaldson's *Good Gracious!* (1963), also shot by Brathwaite, tells a different narrative but conveys a similar message about black

Figure 2.2.
Freddie Roach,
Brown Sugar, Blue
Note Records, 1964,
with Grandassa
model Clara Lewis
on the cover.

beauty and sensuality (figure 2.3).[62] Instead of a headshot, curvy model Rose Nelms is featured in full view wearing a knee-length fitted black sheath dress and her signature medium-length tapered natural hairstyle. She is reading a magazine that has images of women (who might even be Grandassa models) wearing stylish African garments. Donaldson is captured walking past Nelms, staring at her ample derriere. The album's title, *Good Gracious!,* draws upon the awe and sexual excitement Donaldson feels as he gazes at Nelms's body. Her tight sheath dress serves as a thin barrier between her ample flesh and his sexual desire. This imagery offers a visual example of a line from one of Carlos Cooks's speeches about the beauty of Africana women: "As you look at the Black Woman coming toward you with all those lovely shapes and curves it is like looking at the rhythmic waves of the ocean, and when she turns around, wow!"[63] Yet, instead of buying into being the object of Donaldson's or any other black man's gaze, Nelms ignores his gaze and continues reading her magazine. She knows she is beautiful and desirable and recognizes that she has the power to decide if and how she wants to respond to him. By choosing to continue reading the magazine on African fashion, she is demonstrating both her appreciation for soul style and her ability to "think black." The album cover also projects a feminist consciousness in that it positions Nelms in a place of power with the choice to reject unwanted advances.

Figure 2.3.
Lou Donaldson,
Good Gracious!,
Blue Note Records,
1963, with Grandassa
model Rose Nelms
on the cover.

As a body of work, the AJASS-designed series of Blue Note covers positioned the Grandassa models as soul style ambassadors. Over the course of the 1960s, album covers evolved from mere protective covers to artwork. The "jackets," as they were often called, were an inexpensive form of cultural ephemera that, presumably, blacks of all socioeconomic backgrounds could afford. By owning a copy of a soul-jazz album with a Grandassa model on the cover, working-class blacks could participate in the cultural revolution, even if they could not afford a piece of artwork. Because of their cultural significance, album covers were circulated throughout the African diaspora as collectors' items that people hung on their walls. While it is difficult to track exactly how, where, and at what volume the albums were circulated, it is clear that featuring the Grandassa models on Blue Note covers helped AJASS spread its vision of African blackness outside of the United States. They did not have the level of exposure or name recognition that Abbey Lincoln, Nina Simone, Odetta, or Miriam Makeba had, but they possessed a different type of cultural capital.[64]

National and international publications used the models as arbiters of black Americans' fashion tastes and as cultural authorities on the Black Freedom movement. In July 1963, Rose Nelms, who also worked as a hairstylist in Harlem, penned an article titled "Natural Hair Yes, Hot Irons No" that ran in *Liberator*. Nelms, who was also featured on the cover of the issue, rearticulated the Grandassa models' notion of black consciousness, charging readers to accept "our original standard of beauty by strongly refusing to look like or act like anyone other than ourselves."[65] Just as the Grandassa models were rebranding Africa for black Americans, they were rebranding black Americans for Africans. That same year, Herbert Managatheri, editor of *African Pride* magazine, which was published in what was then Northern and Southern Rhodesia (now Zambia and Zimbabwe, respectively), visited the AJASS headquarters in Harlem and decided to feature the models in his magazine. He ran three consecutive feature stories on the Grandassa models; the first and third had images of Grandassa models on their covers, and the second featured Abbey Lincoln on the inside of its cover. Managatheri, who also edited eleven other regional newspapers in Rhodesia, began using photos of the Grandassa models to set the standard for African American beauty and fashion culture, countering the image of African American women in the mainstream U.S. black press, which Brathwaite claimed projected a superficial "candy lipstick" and "hot pants" image of blackness. In other words, fashion could either be used to convey what Brathwaite considered to be the frivolity of black life or a more politicized black consciousness, which he believed Grandassa projected.

Flamingo magazine, a West Indian publication with headquarters in London, featured Grandassa model Brenda Deaver on the cover of its 1965 Nigerian edition, wearing her signature Afro bun with a piece of kente cloth draped over her shoulder (figure 2.4).[66] *Flamingo* was a lifestyle magazine targeted to Afro-Caribbeans in the islands, as well as to those who had migrated to England. By the mid-1960s, it was circulated in West Africa and regularly published an "African" edition for its readers on the continent. Each issue featured an African or Afro-Caribbean model on the cover. Deaver went from being the model on Patton's *Oh Baby!* cover to being the face of soul style in the diaspora (figure 2.5). Deaver's selection as the cover model for the Nigerian issue is both peculiar and telling: black American visions of African beauty and style had become the norm by the mid-1960s. It also marked a shift in soul style, from it being understood as African in origin to it being an African/African American hybrid whose contours were defined by blacks in America.

Their growing international popularity helped AJASS legitimize the Grandassa models as cultural icons of the radical Black Freedom movement and of soul style more broadly. In explaining why the Grandassa models gained international acclaim, AJASS founder Cecil Brathwaite told a *Muhammad Speaks* reporter, "People were ready, the time was right."[67]

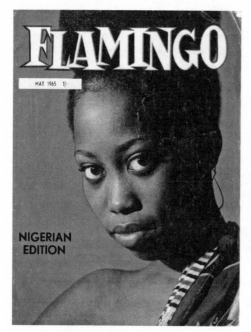

(left) Figure 2.4. *Flamingo* magazine, May 1965 "Nigerian Edition," featuring Grandassa model Brenda Deaver on the cover. Courtesy of the Black Cultural Archives, London, England.

(right) Figure 2.5. Big John Patton, *Oh Baby!*, Blue Note Records, 1965, with Grandassa model Brenda Deaver on the cover.

But as the 1960s passed, the models were not able to sustain media attention. Grandassa models were featured on only one more album cover, Freddie Roach's *All That's Good* (1965), and had a photograph run in an August 1970 issue of *Ebony*. They did, however, continue to have a strong grassroots presence, which in many ways helped to preserve their image as a group for and by the people and not as one wrapped in the trappings of capitalism. Part of the decline in their mass media popularity was due to the reality that once soul style became hypervisible, Grandassa no longer had a corner on the market. In AJASS's early years, most black Americans did not have a sense of what "African" attire looked like, and Grandassa provided them with a vision. But by the early 1970s, soul style was everywhere, and anyone could purchase African-inspired clothing and perform their soulfulness and their black consciousness. Thus, the early 1960s marked a moment in which Grandassa had the political power and cultural cachet to shape soul style, forecasting the cultural politics that were on the horizon as well as the world's growing interest in the soul market.[68]

AJASS's entry into the marketplace was critical for the making of soul style. To be sure, the soul market at this time did not look like it did in the late 1960s and early 1970s, when soul was a mere tag line used to sell a host of products, from Afro Sheen to Lee jeans. But this moment in the early 1960s should not be trivialized. It marked a time when grassroots organizations could engage with and shape the market with a large degree of autonomy because they had not yet caught the attention of multinational corporations. It reveals the ways in which soul style and Black Nationalist politics were entangled in the consumer market. The market at this time was largely driven by blacks across the diaspora, although white small business owners such as Wigs Parisian's Levine and Cherney also realized that there was money to be made in black hair care. Small mail order companies started carrying ethnic wares, challenging black boutique owners' corner on the market. As the style became more popular, local artisans who made their own textiles occupied a smaller part of the market as big fashion houses and department stores began mass-producing cheap imitations of local African and Asian prints. Since most of this means of production, even in the informal soul style fashion network, was concentrated in the West, soul was beginning to be seen as more of an American construction.

Because of the efforts of black women in uptown and downtown New York City, the style helped to revalue Africa by celebrating African modes of adornment. The heart of the capital power to drive the narrative of soul style both in the black print media and in the emerging informal black fashion network was really seen as coming from the United States. Having the power to shape the narrative, manufacture cultural products, and circulate them around the globe ensured that soul style would be recognized as an African American product, despite the fact that many women initially wore the style because they found something liberating in the ways that they perceived African woman as being able to adorn their bodies. In their eyes, African women were not as bound as they were by politics of colorism and respectability.

In many ways, these were seen as problems of the urban North. While northern blacks were debating natural hair politics and protesting white cultural and economic encroachment in their communities, blacks in the South were fighting the vestiges of Jim Crow segregation. Beyond the Nation of Islam, many of the Black Nationalist organizations such as the ANPM did not gain sustained political momentum outside of the region. But the southern Black Freedom struggle garnered national attention as young people faced police attack dogs, billy clubs, and water hoses in their struggle to integrate lunch counters and public transportation. The young people who were on the front lines of the southern struggle were interested in the politics of style, but their soul style looked quite different. The next chapter examines how southern black college students defined soul and changed the dress codes on their campus because of their political commitments. The southern struggle moves us into a different phase of soul style that is based upon the imperative to dress casually as a marker of one's politics.

On a humid July evening in 1963, George Raymond, director of the Madison County, Mississippi, voter registration drive, announced to the small crowd gathered at the Freedom House, "I want you to meet one of my co-workers. She's going to spend some time with us here in and around Madison County. She is a real soul sister." The young woman Raymond spoke of was Anne Moody, a student activist from Tougaloo College. In Raymond's eyes, Moody had earned the title "soul sister" by being "beaten and kicked all over Jackson," participating in the "bloody sit-in" and all of the other demonstrations in the Tougaloo-Jackson area, and being arrested "four or five times." As daunting as this list of qualifications for being a "soul sister" sounds, Moody was not alone, as hundreds of young black women became active in student-led organizations like the Student Nonviolent Coordinating Committee to fight for their rights as black women and for the rights of their communities.[1]

Though we might think of a soul sister as an urban revolutionary in the late 1960s, this image has roots in the southern struggle. The black press was instrumental in constructing representations of a church-based civil rights movement that was tied to black middle-class respectability, Christian values, and feminine propriety. But while many SNCC activists upheld some of these practices, others were consciously deconstructing them. The SNCC soul sister typically wore her hair natural, donned unisex denim overalls and other casual clothing, and risked her life to advance the Black Freedom agenda by confronting segregation in the South. Such attire was central

3

SNCC'S SOUL SISTERS

Respectability
and the Style Politics
of the Civil Rights
Movement

to SNCC women's self-presentation as a signifier of political radicalism and an alternative definition of gender.

This chapter explores why young SNCC soul sisters abandoned their "respectable" clothes and processed hairstyles in order to adopt jeans, denim skirts, bib-and-brace overalls, and natural hair. I argue that their modification of clothing and hairstyles was initially a response to the realities of activism, but eventually natural hair and denim became a uniform for SNCC. The women used the uniform to consciously transgress a black middle-class worldview that marginalized certain types of women and particular displays of blackness and black culture. SNCC women's clothing represented an ideological metamorphosis that was articulated through the embrace and projection of real and imagined southern, working-class, African American cultures. SNCC members believed denim had the potential to unite the young activists with the poor and working-class members of the communities they helped to organize. Moreover, the women used the SNCC "skin" to advance their own women-centered agenda that redefined the roles women could and would play in the movement, on their college campuses, and in the broader society. In the context of the early 1960s, the SNCC uniform must be seen as more than simply adornment to cover the body; it was a cultural-political tool used to create community and to represent SNCC's progressive vision for a new American democracy.[2]

As they solidified their radical new identities, many SNCC women began to evolve a new brand of soul style, drawing inspiration from international fashions in the diaspora and from other soul sisters who popularized casual clothing on their college campuses. Although the SNCC skin may not seem at first glance to have much in common with the prominent fashions of the Black Power era or of the Grandassa models, the women who wore it were central to the continual evolution in soul style. They also signified a larger shift toward dressing casual that college students were instrumental in initiating. Thus, this chapter follows SNCC's soul sisters as they moved between the field, where they labored as activists, and their campuses, where they were engaged in a different kind of cultural revolutionary work. In doing so, it tells a larger history about how the world's focus on the U.S. southern struggle had a lasting influence on soul style, making it less African and more southern black in inspiration.

SNCC Women and the Respectable Body

In 1960, a wave of student protests swept through the South as critical masses of black women and men integrated lunch counters in stores such as Woolworth's and Davidson's. From Greensboro, North Carolina, to Rock Hill and Orangeburg, South Carolina, to Nashville, Tennessee, young black college-educated women from institutions like North Carolina A&T University, Claflin College, and Fisk University courageously withstood heckling and blows from white segregationists who adamantly refused to relinquish the power that the system of Jim Crow segregation bestowed on them. Among these activists were women, including Debbie Amis Bell, Diane Nash, Ruby Doris Smith Robinson, and Anne Moody, who would assume prominent leadership roles. Wanting to harness the students' energy and develop their organizing skills, veteran activist Ella Baker planned a meeting at her alma mater, Shaw University (the first black college in the South) in Raleigh, North Carolina, to rejuvenate the student-led movement that had begun to disband after the first round of sit-ins. Having spent years waging war against the black male leadership of various civil rights organizations, Baker understood firsthand the need for change. And, more important, she realized that the students needed the freedom to craft their own activist ideologies, without the heavy-handed guidance of the Southern Christian Leadership Conference, which was made up mostly of black ministers. Held April 16–18, 1960, the retreat at Shaw provided the space for student protesters to define a core set of values, principles, and tactics. It was from this meeting that SNCC was born.[3]

SNCC was formed at a time when discussions about the efficacy of the politics of respectability were at their peak. As the quest for citizenship rights intensified in the wake of the *Brown v. Board of Education* decision in 1954, the performance of respectability became a critical aspect of the black organizing tradition. After *Brown*, White Citizens Councils formed to uphold white supremacy. They sought to delegitimize African Americans' demands for citizenship by (among other strategies) attacking the moral character of black women. Some black women believed that through a public performance of respectability they could counter attacks against their character. And although they were often denied prominent leadership roles within civil rights organizations, many women activists believed that they could play an important symbolic role in the Black Freedom movement. Leaders of the major civil rights organizations asserted that dressing "modestly and neatly as if you were going to church" was crucial to the movement's success.[4]

The relationship between the image of modesty that represented respectability and the injunction to dress as if one were attending church dated back to the nineteenth century. Many black women fought for racial uplift, employing the "politics of respectability" as a strategy to fulfill Victorian norms of womanhood. This performance was achieved through the clothes black women wore and the ways they styled their hair, along with speaking standard English, reciting biblical scriptures, and knowing how to correctly set a table and pour tea.[5] After the collapse of slavery, northern white missionaries Harriet Giles and Sophia Packard founded Spelman College (originally named Atlanta Baptist Female Seminary) in Atlanta, Georgia, to serve as a moral training ground for former bondwomen whom whites had deemed inherently immoral. Embodying and enacting the brand of womanhood that Spelman and other black colleges across the South espoused became a way for black women to publicly articulate their moral rectitude in order to disprove the racist and sexist stereotypes that portrayed African American women as innately promiscuous and wanton. Black women activists and educators such as Ida B. Wells and Anna Julia Cooper used the black press as a medium through which they could fight to both challenge and define respectability on their own terms, dictating notions of proper dress for themselves.[6]

At the turn of the twentieth century, black women college students were dressing to assert themselves as refined, professional women. As figure 3.1 shows, female students wore clothing that covered much of the body, including long skirts or dresses and long-sleeved shirtwaist blouses in white or pinstripe. This was the typical outfit worn by women who had jobs outside of the home, from teachers to factory workers. Their hair was straightened and neatly pulled into buns or French twists, and accessories such as gloves, hats, and post earrings lent a sense of refinement and sartorial elegance that could distinguish a woman with professional training from a working-class woman. In the interwar period and beyond, fashions evolved, but respectability remained central to both the curriculum and the institutional culture at historically black colleges.

Given African Americans' conscious employment of respectability as a political tool, it is no coincidence that these principles of respectable dress, hygiene, and etiquette were reinforced in women-centered spaces. In the mid-1950s, black women's colleges were supplemented by charm schools designed to teach skills that would help them enter middle-class society, such as proper hygiene, posture, beauty care, and personal style.[7] Although black college women's hemlines became shorter and their hair was allowed to hang loose, respectable attire still included nylon stock-

Figure 3.1. Four Atlanta University students seated in front of a campus building, circa 1900. Their long skirts, shirtwaist blouses, and accessories suggest that they were in training to become women of the professional class who worked outside of the home. Courtesy of the Library of Congress.

ings, cardigan sweaters, skirts and dresses, pearl necklaces, and modestly heeled pumps. Though black college women were encouraged to be civically and professionally minded, they were supposed to maintain a healthy respect for authority and for the male head of their household. These class, civic, moral, and gender standards were communicated in the performance of church-endorsed modesty and middle-class aesthetics.

Many African American activists in the late 1950s consciously constructed the civil rights movement as a fight for the black middle class. Black ministers were recognized as natural leaders of the movement and arbiters of others' morality, though it was actually churchwomen and clubwomen who spearheaded most protests and boycotts. Using Christian rhetoric helped African Americans depict segregationists as amoral and ungodly. By maintaining their dignity and Christian values, even against the brutality of billy clubs, attack dogs, and water hoses, African Americans aimed to expose the savagery of white segregationists and of segregation itself as it denied "well-behaved" African Americans their full citizenship rights. Religious movement rhetoric also contained traces of long-standing intraracial, class-based tensions, as the black middle class sought to set the standards by which they could uplift the black community as a whole even as they used markers of respectability to distance themselves from the poor and working-class African Americans whom they, along with whites, perceived at best as unkempt.[8]

The emphasis on respectability performed through wearing one's "Sunday best" and having neatly pressed hair created a complicated body politics for young women activists. Movement leaders and many of the students heralded the "respectable" body as politically effective because it was a direct affront to Jim Crow–era depictions of black womanhood that included the hypersexual Jezebel and the argumentative Sapphire.[9] Young black women activists were urged to invest political and aesthetic value in their Sunday-best appearance. The well-groomed student activists "projected a safe, middle-class image that played well before the news cameras."[10] White segregationists, who were often the same age as the student protesters, responded by throwing food and drinks at the young women of SNCC who sat defiantly at lunch counters dressed in their Sunday finest, with their hair neatly coiffed. Anne Moody recalled her first sit-in at Woolworth's in Jackson, Mississippi, around 1960, during which she, another Tougaloo student named Pearlena Lewis, a black man named Memphis Norman, and later two white activists—the petite, blonde Tougaloo College student Joan Trumpauer and Tougaloo professor Lois Chaffe—among others attempted to integrate the lunch counter.[11] In a violent attack, the women were assaulted with "ketchup, mustard, sugar, pies" by a group of mostly white male college students who were around the same age as Moody and her companions. Moody, who was wearing a skirt and closed-toed pumps, was dragged out of Woolworth's by her hair, which she had painstakingly straightened and curled, and lost her shoes in the struggle. Tougaloo College president Dr. A. Daniel Bittell intervened to rescue the women from the violent mob that had swollen in size after news spread about the events.[12]

After protests like this one, black women like Moody and Lewis had to undergo intense hair and beauty regimens to restore their respectable bodies. Being seen in public with food and aqueous condiments plastered to their hair, which began to "turn" it back to its kinky state, was emotionally overwhelming for black women who had been trained since childhood never to be seen in public with their hair unstraightened. Given the history of racist and sexist stereotypes, which linked black women's immorality to their perceived lack of grooming, the forcible debasement of their bodies was understood as an assault on their respectability. These young activists were taught, at home and at their institutions of higher learning, to feel and project self-dignity through their grooming regimen.

Moreover, many black Americans equated feminine beauty with straight hair, light skin, and conservative fashion, considering these physical attributes signifiers of strong moral character. For some, going out without their hair pressed was associated with ugliness, social unruliness, Africanness, and even manliness. The constant washing, which stripped much-needed moisture from black hair, and the often-painful straightening process required to maintain the respectable look damaged hair follicles and caused much mental and physical anguish. Yet, with every well-pressed dress and perfectly coiled tendril of hair, black women were fighting to regain their dignity and assert their political agency.[13]

The trip to the beauty salon was an important part of the movement experience for black women activists in the early 1960s. Recalling that day at the lunch counter, Moody wrote: "Before we were taken back to campus, I wanted to get my hair washed. It was stiff with dried mustard, ketchup, and sugar. I stopped in at a beauty shop across the street from the NAACP office. I didn't have any shoes because I had lost them when I was dragged across the floor at Woolworth's. My stockings were sticking to my legs from the mustard that had dried on them."[14] Though in her account of the event in her autobiography, Moody does not explain why having her hair redone was her highest priority, her decision was motivated by something much more significant than the vanity of an image-obsessed college student. Beauty shops had long been places of refuge and sisterhood for black women, and during the civil rights movement these spaces came to have an even greater significance. Women activists used the beauty shop as a place in which they could organize and mobilize other women. Through the experiences of Anne Moody and other student activists, we can see how the salon also played an emotionally supportive role in black women's lives. Here young black female activists located a community of women who could assist in the dignity-rebuilding exercise they needed after being demoralized by angry segregationists.[15]

Memphis, Tennessee, native Gloria Wade-Gayles, an instructor at Spelman, shared similar memories of the damage that civil rights activism did to black women's hair and to their emotional well-being. Wade-Gayles remembers that demonstrations and protests in the hot sun, often resulting in confrontations with high-pressure water hoses and police attack dogs, incited in activists not only fear for their lives but also a heightened awareness of their physical appearance. Grueling protests in the summer heat were usually followed by arrests and extended jail stays. Since SNCC practiced the Gandhian concept of "jail, no bail," prisons were overcrowded, and black women would go for days or weeks without having the self-affirming ritual that the beauty shop provided. The degree of emotional distress this deprivation caused was evidenced in a letter Ruby Doris Smith Robinson wrote to her sister from a York, South Carolina, jail, where she was serving a thirty-one-day sentence. "My hair is awful!" Robinson exclaimed.[16] Given that this was her first arrest, she was missing classes, and she was away from home and family, the fact that her hair was important enough to mention in the letter is telling of the degree to which beauty, activism, and emotional warfare were interconnected. It is likely that upon her release, Robinson, like Moody, went directly to a beauty salon. After Wade-Gayles's discharge in 1963 from the Fulton County jail in Atlanta, she went to a beauty shop around the corner from the SNCC headquarters on what is now James P. Brawley Drive (a strip that runs through Clark Atlanta University) to have her hair washed and straightened. The emphasis in the memoirs of black women activists on the impact that demonstrations and jail sentences had on their hair and their self-image reveals an important role that beauty shop culture played in the lives of young women. Though many of these beauticians' names have been lost to history, and most were not on the front lines of the struggle, they helped to carry their sisters' burdens and to restore their sense of self-respect and pride.[17]

While black women activists were struggling with the emotional as well as physical insults of white opposition, police and city governments' tactics for punishing and containing student activists became more sophisticated, and threats against women's bodies became more violent and more emotionally and sexually degrading. During a march held in honor of slain Mississippi civil rights leader Medgar Evers in Jackson, Mississippi, in 1963, Anne Moody, SNCC field secretary Dorie Ladner, and several other women were arrested and locked in a paddy wagon for over two hours. As if being restrained in an overcrowded police vehicle on a hundred-degree June day was not torture enough, the arresting officers turned on the vehicle's heater. Trapped inside the man-made inferno, the women struggled to breathe, sweat covered their foreheads, and their perspiration caused their straightened hair to kink. Sweat quickly turned their clothing transparent and exposed their undergarments. The heated paddy wagon enabled officers to circumvent rules that prevented them from conducting body searches on women. While men were patted down and searched, women often were not, in large part because it was deemed inappropriate for male officers to search female arrestees, and female officers were few in number. Purposefully drenching their captives' bodies in sweat could reveal the items like transistor radios and playing cards that women had learned to stuff in their undergarments and give the officers probable cause for a body search.[18]

This form of gendered harassment exposed everything beneath the women activists' wet clothes. Bras and panties were visible to their male arresting officers, creating an image of sexual availability and inciting fear of the response their near-nakedness could arouse in the officers. Indeed, SNCC women had heard the stories that passed through movement circles of white male officers peering at showering arrestees and even sexually assaulting them. Atlanta SNCC worker Norma June Davis recalled that, after her first arrest in 1961, a white male guard raped the young woman in the bed beneath her in the middle of the night. Hearing the woman's muffled screams as the guard violated her was excruciating for the other jailed young women, who felt powerless to stop the rape. Sexualized arrest tactics created a kind of fear and inflicted a type of emotional damage unlike that resulting from public physical assaults with food and condiments. Rape and sexualized violence were largely about using power to inflict brutal humiliation. Such violence created a feeling of sexual vulnerability that one had to endure alone, which would have been even more frightening than the physical attacks of angry white mobs—which tended to occur when student activists were protesting in groups. Even the strongest and most seasoned of activists were not immune to such feelings.[19]

SNCC members were finding that maintaining the respectable body was difficult and that being respectably clad did not protect them. SNCC women often participated in multiple protests, sit-ins, or freedom rides each week, which made the process of beautification emotionally and financially taxing. Remembering those early days of SNCC, Atlanta field secretary Debbie Amis Bell, from Philadelphia, remarked, "You see a lot of pictures, particularly of young women, with [skirts and petticoats] and bobby socks, which is totally unreasonable if you're going to go on a demonstration."[20] Bell and other women began to realize that the dress code had to be modified. In late 1960, SNCC leaders began rethinking the political efficacy of the black respectable body and the middle-class ideologies that undergirded it. They understood that emphasis on the dignity and "home training" of the black middle class offered no shield from violence and created more distance between middle- and working-class African Americans. They did not forgo all of the ideas about proper grooming that their parents taught them, but they saw those ideas about dress as malleable and situational.

The New SNCC Skin

Once SNCC women left college campuses and cities such as Atlanta for places such as McComb, Mississippi, their outlook on activism and the role of the respectable body rapidly shifted. SNCC's McComb voter registration project, which required SNCC members to canvass rural communities to find people brave enough to challenge discriminatory voting laws, provided a model for activism that the organization developed and modified over the course of the early 1960s. Before McComb, SNCC comprised mostly student representatives from various campus organizations. With the McComb project, SNCC gained field secretaries, many of whom dropped out of college so they could devote themselves to SNCC full-time. Of SNCC's twenty-four members when the McComb project launched in July 1961, only six had been to the founding meeting in Raleigh over a year before, which meant that a tremendous amount of new energy and talent was attracted to the burgeoning group. The people who made up SNCC in 1961 "included some of the most militant and dedicated leaders of the southern student movement."[21] SNCC started using the term "revolutionary" to describe its members and its goal, which was not to overthrow the government but to step outside of previously defined methods of activism in order to achieve freedom for all African Americans regardless of class. Debbie Amis Bell recalled, "There's a saying that 'we are soldiers in the army,' which we used to sing, and I think that characterizes exactly our identity."[22] This imagery suggests that SNCC women like Bell believed they were called into battle to fight for the freedom of the black community. It also symbolized their belief in the power of a collective body. Like an army, SNCC needed a new uniform that could represent its unity, and denim became part of the uniform that symbolized SNCC's revolutionary army.[23] All clothing is a "skin" that takes on various meanings in different social settings.[24] Once SNCC women had more direct contact with black sharecroppers, they began adopting the clothing, or the skin, of the local organizers. Often, the local people they lived with gifted these garments to SNCC members. For example, women sharecroppers donated their casual cotton shirtwaist dresses to the SNCC women who worked in their communities (figure 3.2).[25]

Their choice of uniform carried historical, political, and cultural significance. In the early nineteenth century, New England textile manufacturers designated raw denim and other cheap manufactured fabrics such as osnaburg for southern slave owners who bought it in bulk to clothe their bondmen and bondwomen. Often referring to these fabrics as "negro

Figure 3.2.
Freedom School
director Lorne
Cress at her home
in Hattiesburg,
Mississippi,
in 1963. She is
pictured wearing a
lightweight cotton
shirtwaist dress.
These dresses
were commonly
worn by women
sharecroppers and
were often donated
by local women to
SNCC women to
wear when they
were organizing
in the rural South.
Courtesy of George
Ballis/TakeStock.

cloth," white Americans ensured that clothing created social and cultural differences between them and the enslaved. In 1873, clothing manufacturer Levi Strauss began mass-producing denim trousers, which were purchased by miners in California and by sharecroppers in the South. By World War II, denim was a standard uniform for male and female factory workers.[26] In adopting the clothing of wage laborers instead of the attire worn by the middle class, SNCC was consciously producing a politics around social class while also addressing practical concerns. Overalls were the clothing of choice for sharecroppers because they had multiple pockets for carrying farming tools and supplies. The durable fabric could sustain the wear and tear of work in the fields. It was cheap, was easy to clean, and did not require ironing. Moreover, baggy denim pants and overalls allowed a free range of movement that aided farmers as they got on and off tractors, horses, and mules. SNCC women likely found the overalls practical for many of the same reasons that farmers did. SNCC member Judy Richardson remembered, "You could put on jeans and they got dirty but they didn't look dirty. So given that we weren't washing at the frequency we should have and doing the wash [regularly], it became very efficient to wear what we wore."[27] The multiple pockets enabled organizers to carry flyers and leaflets inconspicuously. Like sharecroppers, SNCC activists maintained long hours in the "field," canvassing rural communities in an attempt to enlist African Americans to register to vote.[28]

To be sure, wearing overalls would have required some adaptation for many women who were fashion-forward and loved to wear clothes that framed their shape. Ruby Doris Smith Robinson, who was from a middle-class family in the Summerhill section of Atlanta, followed all of the fashion trends. She had a classic Hollywood hourglass figure: small waist, round hips, and large, shapely legs. To accentuate her curves, she often wore sweaters paired with A-line skirts and wide belts that flattered her tiny waistline. Her sister Mary Ann recalled that Ruby Doris had "very expensive taste. Very! She wore nothing cheap. She couldn't stand cheap clothes, and cheap shoes she would not put on her feet."[29] Yet Robinson and other SNCC women discovered that movement life changed many of their middle-class perspectives. "Something happened to me as I got more and more involved in the movement," Anne Moody remarked in her autobiography. "It no longer seemed important to prove anything. I had found something outside myself that gave meaning to my life."[30] Like Moody, in giving to the movement, SNCC women were gaining a new perspective, and a new way of dressing reflected their budding ethos.

Some SNCC women were adopting natural hairstyles for both personal and political reasons. As Debbie Amis Bell remembered, "The natural hair was new. But a lot of us had adopted the style, first of all because we could not have afforded to do anything else other than that."[31] Women who had devoted themselves to the movement full-time often had very little money for food, much less to get their hair done. Trips to the salon became a luxury that many considered frivolous, given their regular encounters with sexualized violence. "Some of us were very bedraggled," Bell reflected; natural hair "was not becoming to us, but we thought our message was the most important thing and not our looks."[32] In other words, their political aims trumped aesthetics. But for others, natural hair was indeed a political choice. SNCC field secretary Joyce Ladner wanted to wear her hair natural to "emulate Abbey Lincoln and Odetta."[33] Ladner, who was a student at Tougaloo College, envisioned the natural not as a simple response to being unable to get her hair done but as a style in its own right that expressed her aesthetic politics as well as her commitment to organizing. Women such as Lincoln made natural hair hip for young activists.

Gloria Wade-Gayles's transformation from processed to natural hair came after a four-day stay in a North Carolina jail cell with a poor, dark-complexioned woman with thick plaits in her hair who had been accused of murdering her abusive husband.[34] Wade-Gayles learned much about her cellmate, and when she was released she decided to go natural:

> An activist with straightened hair was a joke, really. The right to tout the movement gospel of self-esteem carried with it the obligation to accept and love one's self naturally. Our appearance had to speak the truth before our lips stretched to sing the songs. Never again, I decided, would I alter my hair. In its natural state, my hair would be a badge, a symbol of my self-esteem and racial pride. An act of genuine bonding with black women who were incarcerated in jails all across America and those who were in psychological jails.[35]

Wade-Gayles's statement that hair had the power to bond black women was telling. Judy Richardson recalled that this shift in self-presentation among SNCC women was an inherently political "outward manifestation that we had broken from the traditional norms. . . .We don't abide by segregation and we're trying to get economic equity. . . . The outward way we do that is the hair and the dress."[36] Though SNCC women were arriving at their decisions to wear their hair natural for a variety of reasons and at different times, they were forming a sisterhood based on a shared notion of black womanhood that transgressed the politics of respectability. Gradually, many SNCC women began going natural, associating the style not only with radical politics but with a new sense of gender pride in which respectability took multiple expressions. Women like Ruby Doris Smith Robinson, Gracie Hawthorne, Bernice Johnson, Jennifer Lawson, Gwen Robinson, Freddie Greene Biddle, Ethel Miner, Jean Wheeler Smith, Muriel Tillinghast, and E. Jeanne Breaker—most of whom were from elite institutions such as Tougaloo College, Spelman College, and Howard University—were defying their institutions' and their families' expectations for their adorned bodies.[37]

In SNCC's first three years, the denim and natural hair soul style look emerged unevenly among the organization's ranks, but by 1963 the SNCC skin was members' unofficial uniform. When Judy Richardson left Swarthmore College to join the hundred other members of SNCC's paid staff in

1963, denim and natural hair were the standard. Richardson was schooled by white veteran SNCC worker Penny Patch about the organization's aesthetic politics before she joined. Patch, who had just returned to Swarthmore after the Freedom Rides, told Richardson, who at the time religiously straightened her hair weekly at Miss Preleau's Salon in Tarrytown, New York, "You're going to have to stop frying your hair. Nobody has straight hair."[38] Though most of the organizers from other local organizations (especially the older women) still wore their hair straightened, Richardson found that Patch was correct: most SNCC women did not. Some SNCC women chose to maintain their press-and-curl style and did so by having a friend press their hair for them, either in their dorms or in the Freedom House. Patch's admonition, however, is indicative of the degree to which the unadorned look among SNCC women had become an integral part of the SNCC skin.[39] Though Richardson did not say she was bothered by being told how to wear her hair, many African American women and men within SNCC were growing weary of the white volunteers (most of whom were new to the movement) who felt they had a major say in the organization's direction in everything from political strategy to dress and adornment. The SNCC skin was a defining attribute of who they were, how they believed the activist body should be styled, and the political and aesthetic value they placed on their look.

The Performance of Class and Gender

For many of SNCC's members who came from privileged backgrounds, the first time they encountered poverty and realized some of the fallacies in how they were trained to think about their class status occurred during their political work. Even those who had not grown up with much but whose college experiences had created a disconnect with their working-class roots had to readjust to life among the poor and working classes.[40] By consciously adopting the SNCC skin as a political strategy, SNCC women were placing themselves at the center of intraracial class tensions among movement organizations. As SNCC further distanced itself from the respectable body and the class politics it represented, some members became more aware of the tensions between and among movement organizations.

Judy Richardson, a leader of the Greenville, Mississippi, campaign, remembered that organizers earned the respect of members of the local NAACP because they did not come into the community dressing like outsiders.

We were not organizing the southern black middle class, whatever that was. We were organizing sharecroppers. So you didn't want to come in looking like you were coming in from the NAACP national office. Now there were those who did, but the thing is, the people [whom the local community] most respected were those from the local NAACP, people who did not dress like the national [NAACP officials]. One of the main reasons that the local NAACP people really worked with us and sheltered us and helped us to understand what it was that they needed [regarding] help organizing was because we assumed that they were intelligent in a way that the national [NAACP] did not. . . . Local people saw that we were of them, and I think they accepted us in a way because we were not standing around in suits and ties.[41]

Richardson's observations about dress expose a long history of class tension within the black community.

Many middle-class African Americans both in the South and in the North associated the rural laboring body with a moral laziness, ignorance, and a backward way of life. For example, before Martin Luther King Jr. became the pastor of Dexter Avenue Baptist Church in Birmingham, Alabama, his seat was occupied by Vernon Johns, a minister and civil rights activist who supplemented his income by farming. Unlike King—who was college-educated, wore fine suits, spoke with an air of erudition, and had a fair-complexioned wife—Johns, who had also been well educated at Oberlin College and the University of Chicago, wore overalls while selling his produce in the city. His comfort in wearing denim in public spoke to a close tie with the soil. To his congregants, however, it symbolized a lack of education and refinement, resulting in many clashes over issues of class and respectability.[42] SNCC women who consciously chose to wear casual clothing were exposing the problematics of class stereotypes related to dress and the body. As they worked to mobilize black southerners across often staunchly held class lines, SNCC women navigating this terrain had to learn southern social cues and mores about dress politics. While there were some sartorial miscommunications between SNCC and various subgroups within the broader community, SNCC activists were clearly rejecting elements of the respectable activist body and creating their own militant political and cultural posture that revalued the rural laboring body.[43]

Though Richardson and others believed that denim-clad SNCC members were well received in rural communities, the reception of SNCC's sharecropper style was actually quite mixed. Some local residents felt the same way about SNCC as the Dexter church congregants had felt about

Vernon Johns, stating that "anybody wearing old work clothes couldn't be about very much."[44] C. C. Bryant, head of the Pike County, Mississippi, NAACP chapter, "worried that some of the organization's workers looked sloppy and unkempt."[45] Many poor people themselves associated share-cropper clothing and other forms of working-class attire with a past of poverty and oppression that they wanted to leave behind.

South African singer Miriam Makeba, who dated and eventually married SNCC leader Stokely Carmichael, was critical of his and his SNCC comrades' adoption of the clothing of the impoverished. Makeba, who grew up poor in a township outside of Johannesburg, felt that Carmichael, who had no personal experiences with black poverty, viewed poverty through a romantic middle-class lens. Makeba believed that only a person of privilege would think it proper to wear the clothing of the working class as a form of social rebellion: "When I was growing up, we were poor. But we were clean, and we took great pride in the way we dressed and looked. Stokely and his American friends, who are not poor, dress like vagabonds. Stokely wears dirty jeans and torn jackets. . . . Tattered clothes means that a person identifies with the masses. . . . Hey, Man, I grew up with the 'masses.' We were not proud of our poverty."[46] Makeba and her South African peers were careful to dress in stylish, clean, freshly pressed clothing as a way to maintain their dignity under apartheid. Makeba interpreted SNCC's denim uniform as a hipster approach to activism. By mocking the way in which Carmichael used the term "the masses," she implied that Carmichael and his peers did not fully understand its class implications. Carmichael likely used the term "the masses" to situate SNCC at the vanguard of the movement. But for Makeba, since Carmichael had the privilege of putting on and taking off the denim uniform as he saw fit, he was ignoring the reality that truly impoverished people did not have such a luxury.

Activist James Charles Evers recalled being so poor as a child growing up in rural Mississippi that the only decent clothes his family had were reserved for Sunday, when they went to church. Once he and his younger brother Medgar Evers returned home, their first act was to remove the nice Sunday clothes and put on their old, dusty denim jeans. From Evers's perspective, denim was synonymous with the poverty of his youth, and as an adult, he could not bear to put on the clothes that he associated with a background he worked so hard to overcome.[47] Debbie Amis Bell remembered a conversation she had with her father, who was a member of the Communist Party in Philadelphia: "In the discussions I had with my dad, who was an activist, he said that workers always hated [their denim uni-

Figure 3.3. Protesters at the 1963 March on Washington, dressed in their "Sunday best." The women wear skirts, dresses, pearls, and modestly heeled pumps; the men are in slacks, blazers, dress shirts, and ties. In addition to class politics, their clothing also upheld normative notions of feminine and masculine propriety. Courtesy of the Library of Congress.

forms] when they're not on the job, so as soon as people got off of their shift, they would shower and change into their nice clothes. . . . I always wondered if people took offense to us usurping their work clothes, but I never heard anything of that sort."[48] Bell's memory of this conversation provides an example of the varied and complex meanings that denim had for different segments of the black community.

SNCC women used casual clothing to make a statement about their gender politics. The Ladner sisters, Joyce and Dorie, even wore their denim to the March on Washington, where old-guard civil rights organizations were attempting to project the respectable black body to the American public (figure 3.3). Images of the sisters clad in their denim overalls did not appear in mainstream publications. For example, Johnson Publishing Company, which published *Ebony* and *Jet* magazines, produced a special issue on the March on Washington, *The Day They Marched*. It featured photographs of numerous black women—including activists Daisy

Bates and Rosa Parks, entertainers Diahann Carroll and Lena Horne, and some ordinary participants—adorned in dresses, cardigans, pearls, pillbox hats, and gloves with their hair straightened and neatly styled. Joyce and Dorie Ladner, with their natural hairdos and denim overalls, stood in stark contrast to these women (figure 3.4).[49] Anne Moody expressed shock and awe at her peers' willingness to wear their denim skirts and jeans at the March on Washington, recalling that she was "the only girl from Mississippi with a dress on. All the others were wearing denim skirts and jeans."[50] To be sure, there was diversity of thought and disagreement among women about the degree to which they should promote a women-centered political agenda. But they were clearly using dress to challenge conventional constructions of gender.

Denim overalls in particular provided an androgynous self-presentation that reinforced women's political aims. Casey Hayden notes that the women of SNCC, both black and white, created a laboring identity for themselves as "organizers" as a way to challenge the idea that women were not equal partners in the movement.[51] They were deconstructing the notion that men were natural leaders, demonstrating that women could literally and figuratively "wear the pants" in the public sphere. Yet, as the men stopped getting haircuts and let their hair grow longer and the women started cutting their hair short and wearing it natural, both the men and the women pushed back against the performance of masculine and feminine propriety that respectability politics hinged upon. SNCC women and men were helping to lay the groundwork for a soul style that resisted normative constructions of gender and respectability. Though these performances did not, in and of themselves, fundamentally alter the gender politics within and beyond the Black Freedom struggle, they point to emerging conversations about clothing and what we would today term the "queering" of the gender line.[52] Members of the African Nationalist Pioneer Movement, who promoted natural hair and African clothing in New York City, were still deeply connected to more normative performances of femininity and masculinity. Conversely, SNCC women and men were showing a range of gender performances and gendered presentations of style.

Soul Style and the Politics of Dress on Campus

For black women in the twentieth century, new ways of "displaying their bodies" presented the "possibility of personal liberation" from their assigned place in American society.[53] Though these activists held diverse

Figure 3.4. Joyce Ladner at the March on Washington, wearing denim overalls and sporting a short-cropped, natural hairstyle. Johnson Publishing Company did not feature images of the denim-wearing women of SNCC in its coverage of the march. This is a rare image that likely did not run in any local papers of the day. Courtesy of Ivan Massar/TakeStock.

views on the soul sister's role in the movement, they were defining a new vision of black womanhood in which black women had choices. College campuses became places for them to perform their new notions of black womanhood. SNCC members began to wear denim in urban centers such as Atlanta, where SNCC's national headquarters was located. Ella Baker, who had become a political mentor and mother figure for the young women and men of SNCC, tried to school them on how to use the denim uniform most effectively. The SNCC skin helped to create a public identity for the group, particularly among Atlanta college students. "You were identified almost immediately when you were walking down the street that you were a worker in the civil rights movement by what you were wearing," Bell recalled.[54] SNCC members wore denim on campus to recruit students for demonstrations. During a SNCC meeting around 1963, Baker had a discussion with young women and men—present were Ruby Doris Smith Robinson, Judy Richardson, Bobbi Yancy, Jim Forman, Julian Bond, and several others—about their use of denim. Baker encouraged them to be strategic about when, why, and for what end they wore their denim attire.[55] Though SNCC members had begun to understand and question the class politics within the black community, Baker pointed out that they would have to "break through the pseudo-sophistication of college students and you can't do it in overalls."[56] By telling SNCC leaders that they could not effectively mobilize college students while wearing denim, she was not telling them to abandon the strategy altogether but rather to understand that it was politically savvy to know when to put on and take off the uniform.[57] Baker, herself a daughter of the South, was trying to teach SNCC women and men how to be fluent in the cultural politics of multiple communities in order to behave in ways that gave them cultural capital in each environment. SNCC members continued to use denim as a uniform, but field secretaries were allowed to set a loose dress code for the SNCC soldiers under their command. For example, Gwen Robinson, who headed the Laurel, Mississippi, project in 1964, instructed her staff not to wear shorts in the streets and to adopt "generally modest dress."[58] The relaxed dress requirements gave SNCC members freedom to choose when to wear denim.

When Baker advised the students on how to make the SNCC skin a more useful tool for recruitment, she had a good point. But the use of denim had become a powerful sign of the ways in which the energy of youthful rebellion could be channeled in a fruitful political direction. By adopting the clothing of working-class people, SNCC was harnessing the progressive potential of the student sit-in movement and making it even more radical. Not only were SNCC activists forming cross-class alliances that they might not have been able to forge otherwise, but they were consciously and subconsciously creating a new political and aesthetic value for black activists and for the black body. This shift was particularly important for SNCC women who used the uniform to advance the cause of their gender as well as of their race. By drawing upon the history of the oppression of black women laborers' bodies, SNCC women were redefining what a black female body could look like in the mid- to late twentieth century. SNCC women's adoption of denim overalls and skirts was an important, yet vexed, intervention that reflected a budding form of black feminism.

Women activists brought their politics to campus and challenged college dress codes. Until the mid-1960s, college administrators had the legal right to act as the parental figure for students under a policy called in loco parentis. Administrators used dress codes as a strategy to encourage conformity. SNCC members Norma June Davis and Lana Taylor Sims recalled that at Spelman College, it was mandatory for women to wear stockings, not socks, and they were not permitted to go barefooted.[59] SNCC field secretary Gwen Robinson began wearing her hair natural around 1962, during her first year at Spelman. "After I appeared on campus with my new Afro," Robinson recalled, "I was called into the dean's office" and told that she was "an embarrassment to the school" because "all Spelman women were expected to be well-groomed."[60] Dress codes were seen as restrictive because they were tied to other rules designed to police and contain women's bodies. For example, women had stricter visitation and curfew policies than men. Men were expected to dress nicely, but they did not have to worry about their garments being too short, too tight, or too revealing. They also were not ridiculed as harshly for their hair. With such strict rules about proper dress and adornment for women, any infractions against these mandates constituted an act of defiance. Activism around dress codes is an understudied aspect of SNCC's legacy that dates back to SNCC mentor Ella Baker's college years in the 1920s. One of Baker's first acts of protest was against a dress code at Shaw that prohibited students from wearing "fancy, colored, or silk hose." She penned a letter to the school administration, and Baker and her peers presented their argument to the dean of women. It was a long battle, but Baker and her comrades won the fight four years later when the dean lifted the ban on silk stockings. Baker understood why the young women of SNCC were fighting for the freedom to wear more casual clothes on campus, and she also knew that such forms of embodied activism could spark a more radical consciousness among college women.[61]

SNCC activist and educator Howard Zinn remarked that when he arrived to teach at Spelman in 1956, the students were largely adhering to the college's code of conduct, and there was no sign that a movement could spark there: "The campus was quiet. The city looked quiet. My students were quiet." Despite this surface calm, impulses toward social and cultural activism were circulating underneath as more students were joining the movement, often without the knowledge of campus administrators. "And then in a few years," Zinn continued, "this quiet campus exploded and the adjacent campuses exploded."[62] Not only was the student movement growing and gaining media attention, but students in the Atlanta University Center, like their peers across the country, were wearing more casual clothing, including denim jeans and skirts, loose-fitting shirts rather than blouses, and athletic wear with team logos. These students were now seasoned activists who knew how to organize and protest. Pushing back against dress codes became an effective way to gain more power and autonomy on campus. While Spelman and Morehouse remained two of the more conservative colleges in the country, their students made noticeable changes in their wardrobes, which became even more pronounced in the late 1960s.[63]

SNCC women carved out a social and cultural space for themselves within the changing milieus of their campuses. Debbie Amis Bell, who was organizing from the SNCC headquarters in Atlanta, her sister Cynthia Amis, who was a student at Spelman, and some of Cynthia's peers who were active in the movement made their own denim skirts. Bell recalled, "Most of the women wore jean material. . . . I had made myself a couple of denim skirts and jeans we would wear."[64] Joyce Ladner remembered that most women owned only one or two denim skirts or overalls, so most of the time they wore casual "street wear" that consisted of more casual skirts, jackets, and athletic gear.[65] Street wear, too, spoke to their desire to dress more casually as a way to reject the middle-class politics surrounding adornment. SNCC women's interpretation of the new activist female body forged a sisterhood that espoused an ideology and political aesthetic that countered normative notions of female beauty. White SNCC member Mary King remembered that most of the women in SNCC, regardless of race, dressed "plain" and "wore little or no makeup, cut one another's hair, and had no possessions or clothing worth mentioning."[66] This unadorned style was in distinct contrast to the respectable body of the early sit-in years when, Debbie Amis Bell observed, women were reluctant to wear natural styles that were perceived to mar the respectable body and to damage racial self-esteem.[67]

As street wear became more popular among young people, SNCC women developed differing ideas about their relationship to the fashion world that was adapting to college students' casual style. Bell stated, "I don't ever remember any discussions of frivolous things like [fashion]. . . . Even in [campus] housing, I don't remember us discussing anything about clothing or cosmetics."[68] Others definitely attached a style politics to their political attire. Ladner recalled, "We were young people who were growing and developing and trying on different kinds of styles and personas." Having an investment in movement work did not mean they had no desire to be well groomed or on trend. "Doing movement work did not mitigate against keeping one's hair well groomed or being well groomed," Ladner stated. "Black people cared about how they looked because we were raised that way. It would have been a slap in my mother's face had I gone around half kempt. Poverty was no excuse."[69] The stylish Ruby Doris Smith Robinson never wore denim, but she did wear skirts made out of burlap. She also purchased several West African garments during SNCC's trip to Senegal and Guinea in October 1964. The fashion-conscious Robinson must have welcomed the colorful burst of dramatic African-inspired pieces into her unadorned SNCC wardrobe. Like youths in other parts of the world who were wearing the garments of other ethnic groups, such as saris, caftans, kimonos, and gaucho pants, Robinson loved blending African accessories with her burlap skirts, sandals, and other ethnic fashions. She had her natural hair cornrowed to resemble her West African peers' hair. A 1965 image of Robinson and her two sisters shows them standing in line, each wearing long earrings that dangle to the collarbone.[70] African-inspired earrings were an appealing accessory because they allowed black women to make a subtle statement about their cultural politics while they maintained and projected their femininity. SNCC women's mixing and blending of African-inspired fashions such as the caftan and dangling earrings made of metals, wood, and exotic fibers grew in popularity over the course of the 1960s, becoming a visual shorthand for women who were soulful, in touch with their southern and West African roots, and committed to a global struggle for black liberation.[71] Whether they wanted to or not, SNCC women were becoming style icons.

Because of the sartorial crosscurrents on campus and beyond, SNCC's casual style was lauded in the media as part of the dress of a generation. As the world turned its eye toward the U.S. South and as celebrities joined the Black Freedom cause, Greenwich Village bohemian culture overlapped with that of southern black activists. SNCC women's embrace of denim and other ethnic clothing was part of a larger trend across subcultural pockets like the countercultural artistic spaces of the Village. Folk singers such as African American Odetta and Mexican-Scottish Joan Baez were also wearing caftans, pedal pusher jeans, and rebozos that created a striking visual tableau that appealed to American youth. Photographs of denim-wearing SNCC leaders such as Bob Moses, Stokely Carmichael, and James Forman at marches with Joan Baez, James Baldwin, and Martin Luther King added to the charismatic aura surrounding the young activists. Publications such as *Look* ran stories about white women who ventured south from northern colleges to volunteer for the massive voter registration drive in Mississippi in 1964, known as Freedom Summer.[72] Those who arrived wearing low-cut blouses, heavy makeup, and ornate earrings soon received a sartorial baptism into SNCC's mode of dress.

Seasoned civil rights activist Bayard Rustin pushed back against the mythology of SNCC that was symbolized by its clothing. He told a crowd of SNCC members at Howard University in 1963 that white students should "stop putting on blue jeans and packing off to Mississippi."[73] For Rustin, the power of revolution was not in the white students adopting the SNCC skin but in their mobilizing working-class whites in the North. Photographs of SNCC members, along with people's personal stories of political and sartorial conversion, mythologized SNCC in the press and branded its members radical celebrities. Even members of SNCC became critical of the group's style, believing that the unadorned look was becoming political pastiche, a cool, hip look—perhaps even a "status symbol," as SNCC leader John Lewis put it—for socially conscious youth.[74]

Though SNCC members did not call their clothing "soul style," a burgeoning soul market linked expressions of black freedom with new fashion aesthetics. SNCC was borrowing from Nina Simone, Abbey Lincoln, Odetta, and Miriam Makeba, who were performing for movement benefits. SNCC's expression of soul style and its political aims in the early years differed from that of New York City Black Nationalist groups such as the Grandassa models, mostly because SNCC was not espousing a fashion aesthetic that revolved around Africa. SNCC was more invested in placing political value on the experiences of working-class black farm laborers. This style refocused attention on the customs and cultures of the rural South. In soul-jazz music, there was a reverence for the U.S. South as well, and the cultural impetus of the U.S. struggle began to shift south in the early 1960s. As the image of the wholesome, nonviolent student protesters changed after 1965, the SNCC denim uniform came to represent revolutionary politics.

In the mid-1960s, activists from civil rights student organizations such as SNCC abandoned the nonviolent, integrationist strategies reflected in slogans like "Freedom Now" to embrace a more radical political approach symbolized by the mantra "Black Power." SNCC member Willie Ricks led protesters across Mississippi in June 1966 shouting, "Black Power for Black People."[75] Ricks urged blacks not only to fight for their rights but also to reclaim their self-dignity, using the term "black"—which had previously been used to denigrate African Americans—to communicate a sense of pride and collective action. Black was also a term that became a part of the language of soul used by jazz musicians. Ruby Doris Smith Robinson, Joyce Ladner, Gloria Wade-Gayles, and other SNCC women had expressed their own form of Black Power for years, choosing to wear their hair unprocessed and to dress in the clothing of sharecroppers to reclaim agency over their bodies and to connect with their southern roots. SNCC's public articulation of Black Power gave these women's actions a degree of militancy far more radical than many would have imagined in the organization's earlier years under the guidance of the Southern Christian Leadership Conference. Though Willie Ricks, a lesser-known member of SNCC, had stirred the crowd with his cries of "Black Power," he did not garner much media attention. When SNCC leader Stokely Carmichael addressed the crowd using the phrase, however, the media immediately began publishing stories on SNCC's radical turn.

Ruby Doris Smith Robinson was present in the crowd gathered outside of the Greenwood, Mississippi, jail when Stokely Carmichael, who had just been released, told the crowd, "What we gonna start saying now is Black Power."[76] Robinson was still wearing the natural hairstyle that she had adopted in the early 1960s. Although this style had its own history and politics, it became linked to the new, loosely defined concept of Black Power. The growing interest in Black Power and the increased visibility of SNCC women in the media led to rearticulations of the nature of black womanhood and black women's roles in the movement more broadly. Diverse pictures of black women activists' lives were brought to the fore in the media. Between 1965 and 1970, women of SNCC forged their identities as radical activists. Despite differences in the lived experiences of these women, the stories highlighted particular characteristics that gave shape to a national soul sister image. Even though Robinson would succumb to a battle with cancer in 1967 at age twenty-five, her presence that day signaled a shift of "soul sister" from a regional term used within movement circles to describe women activists like Robinson and Anne Moody in the early 1960s to a term commonly used in the black urban vernacular in the 1970s.

The diversity of outlooks among the soul sisters of SNCC inspired other college-age women to join the ranks of the radical student movement. Kathleen Cleaver particularly admired Diane Nash, Gloria Richardson (a prominent leader in the Cambridge, Massachusetts, SNCC chapter), and Ruby Doris Smith Robinson, whose personal stories struck a chord with her. Like Robinson, Cleaver was from a southern middle-class family, and she had lived in Sierra Leone and Liberia when her father accepted a job with the Foreign Service. Feeling impelled to emulate the soul sisters' commitment to the Black Freedom movement, Cleaver left Barnard College in 1966 to take a post as the secretary of the New York office of SNCC. She joined SNCC as it was shifting from an organization with a Christian-based, direct nonviolent approach to one that advocated self-defense and encouraged blacks of all religions to empower their own communities. "About two weeks before I joined SNCC," Cleaver recalled, "'Black Power' replaced 'Freedom Now' as the battle cry."[77] Angela Davis, who was active in the civil rights movement in New York City, also came from a southern middle-class family. Growing up in the "Dynamite Hill" section of Birmingham, Alabama, a predominantly black enclave that was often firebombed by white segregationists, Davis was no stranger to black community organizing. Her mother, a teacher, aided in the campaign to free the Scottsboro Boys and was an active member in the Birmingham NAACP, even after the organization was barred by local officials in the 1950s.[78] Though Davis's parents tried to shield her from the turmoil in their community, the seed of activism was planted, and she ventured north to attend Elizabeth Irwin High School in New York City and later Brandeis University in Waltham, Massachusetts, where she moved through various civil rights organizations. Kathleen Cleaver, Angela Davis, and a host of other women embarked on their own cultural-political journeys that transformed the media image of the soul sister from an organizer in the rural South to an urban revolutionary.

The following chapter explores the development of soul style once it gained national prominence in the late 1960s and early 1970s. I demonstrate how the threads of soul style in New York City and those in the U.S. South in the same period wove together to produce a style that was an amalgamation of these expressions. The natural hairstyle that SNCC women were popularizing became the Afro, and denim and dashikis became popular fashions that black women and men wore as symbols of racial pride and protest in the Black Power years. As the 1960s passed, the campus became a hypervisible space in the marketing of soul style, making a U.S. vision of blackness commodifiable and college students the perfect consumers and models of soul style. Black college students were a source of inspiration for global fashion designers who followed the campus fashion trends presented in the media.

Just in time for the new academic year, *Essence*, the self-proclaimed "Magazine for Today's Black Woman," ran its first "College Issue" in August 1973. The cover of the inaugural issue featured two young black women sporting denim, hoop earrings and multiple rings, and the intricate cornrows with large colored beads popularized by celebrity soul sisters such as Miriam Makeba and actress Cicely Tyson.[1] The special issues were designed to glamorize life on black college campuses, and the highlight of each was the seven-page fashion spread featuring student models from historically black schools such as Spelman College, Atlanta University, Hampton University, and Morgan State University. The fashion editors informed readers on all of the hottest fashion and beauty trends. Other articles included dorm room decorating suggestions and advice on how students could use hot plates and other small appliances to prepare their favorite soul food dishes, such as chicken-flavored Rice-a-Roni, broiled cheese franks, zesty pork and beans, and custard cups for dessert.[2] *Essence*'s chic, intelligent college student was a role model for teenagers and a symbol of racial progress for the older generation. This constructed image of black women's college experiences offers us new ways to interpret soul style in the era of Black Power.

Collegiate spaces became important sites for soul style innovation and cultural discourse about blackness. African Americans' enrollment at both mainstream and historically black institutions in the United States increased from 434,000 in 1968 to 727,000 in 1972, with approximately 80 percent attending predominantly white institutions (figure 4.1).[3] This increase in the black presence on campus

4

SOUL STYLE ON CAMPUS

American College Women and Black Power Fashion

Figure 4.1. Indiana University Bloomington students in the Black Culture Center, June 1976, dressed in a manner that was popular among African American college students during the Black Power era. The women wear natural hairstyles, head wraps, large hoop earrings, and denim skirts. The men are also casually attired in jeans, hooded sweatshirts, sneakers, sunglasses, and African-inspired beaded necklaces. Courtesy of the Indiana University Archives Photograph Collection.

coincided with the peak years of the Black Power movement, when images of gun-toting Black Panthers, large Afros, and African-inspired attire were hypervisible in the media. These broader cultural and political crosscurrents influenced dynamics on campus. Black college students became more radical, moving beyond personal protests against the administration's strict dress codes to organizing takeovers of administrative buildings to demand affordable tuition, equal access to campus housing, and the creation of black studies programs. My mother, Amye Glover, already a self-proclaimed black feminist and amateur fashion designer, headed to college at Indiana University Bloomington in 1972. Although narratives of white students' participation in the counterculture are ubiquitous, the countless black women like my mother who innovated with soul style have been marginalized.[4]

Recognizing young black women as the vanguard of soul style and American fashion culture in the early 1970s complicates the oversimplified narrative of soul's shift from "grassroots" to "mainstream" popularity. Many histories of this era consider corporate America's intervention in the soul culture market the moment when soul lost its political power. But as I have demonstrated, soul style had always been entangled with corporate interests as well as movement politics; thus, the 1970s did not mark a moment where soul suddenly became devoid of political meaning. Instead of merely treating this era as one of corporate co-optation, this chapter focuses on the forms of embodied activism that black college women engaged in daily as they moved through and beyond campus spaces. A misplaced emphasis on soul's entry into the marketplace has overshadowed the significance of the transitional period during which black women used their vibrant soul style fashions to contest racism on campus and one-dimensional constructions of black womanhood in the popular press. Between 1968 and 1972, soul style was visible yet considered "edgy," in large part because the fashions were not yet mass-produced. Young black women created their own interpretations of the styles worn by their favorite black celebrities. As they stitched garments that blended their vision of African attire with Western silhouettes and black southern flair, these college women, who often called themselves soul sisters, remixed the language of soul that had been used to market soul-jazz music in the late 1950s. The result was the popularizing of the term "soul style" itself, as well as others such as "radical chic," "Afro look," and "Soul Power," used to describe their race-conscious fashions.

Breaking from the grassroots/corporate binary also allows for a new interpretation of how soul style became American. The soul style of the 1970s was a product of the cultural-political chafing resulting from black women's notions of the socially conscious and chic soul sister and mainstream America's version of her as an Afro-wearing criminal. As black youth, and black women in particular, fought to define their blackness on their own terms, they held soul culture as a product of the long history of black presence in the U.S. South, which white America was itching to steal just as it had already done with the blues, jazz, and other forms of black expression. By rooting soul in a black southern experience, they were shifting its origins story to one that was more American-centered. In the early years of soul style, it was about identifying with a body and style politic that was African in origin. While most students continued to see Africa as a motherland and drew inspiration from African prints and modes of adornment, they also celebrated homegrown manifestations of beautiful blackness. Although there were some who were advocating that blacks return to Africa, student activists were largely focused on employing the political tactics of the so-called Third World to liberate themselves from the oppressive U.S. regime by creating their own community structures.[5] As soul style became hypervisible in the global fashion marketplace, this construction of American blackness was exported to other parts of the black world in more pronounced ways than it had been in the early 1960s, when the Grandassa models were the faces of the "Black is Beautiful" movement.

Soul Style in the Age of Black Power

The sartorial and political contours of soul style were transformed as Americans' focus on the Black Freedom movement shifted in the late 1960s from the rural South to the urban North and West Coast. Although the women of the Student Nonviolent Coordinating Committee were not the sole influence on black women's changing aesthetic tastes, they helped to modify ideas about dress on college campuses and influenced the burgeoning student movement.[6] Understanding the soul connections between the SNCC women, who dressed down in denims in the early 1960s, and the soul sisters of the 1970s, who dressed up in dashikis and printed maxi dresses, illuminates soul style as it reached the apex of its popularity in the United States. This distinction between dressing down and dressing up is significant because it reveals just how much casual dress had become an accepted part of youth culture.[7] As the fashion market catered to young people's desire for street wear, dressing down became a cool way to dress up in the latest trends. The Black Panthers' uniform represents the ways in which soul style sat at the intersection of casual and well groomed.

Soul style garments became the uniform of Black Power organizations such as the Black Panther Party for Self-Defense (BPP), linking the style with urban radical activism. The BPP was founded in 1966, in the aftermath of the Watts Riots. The organization's leaders, Bobby Seale and Huey P. Newton, both college-educated men, were committed to mobilizing the "lumpen proletariat," the disfranchised and disorderly men and women who they believed were most marginal to the capitalist system and thus were inherently revolutionary.[8] BPP leaders aimed to meet the needs of poor blacks in urban areas—many of whom were involved in various aspects of the underground economy, as drug dealers, gang members, and sex workers—whose concerns were not being addressed by middle-class-oriented civil rights organizations. Although the name of the BPP suggests that its membership was all black, Panther Ericka Huggins recalled that there were Latinos, Asians, Armenians, and "two or three white women and men" in the organization. The Panthers "believed that if people really wanted to fight for justice on behalf of all oppressed people, which was our perspective, then if they weren't coming with a lot of guilt and shame and fear, or they wanted a husband or a wife, then fine."[9]

The Panthers borrowed much of their political ideology and symbols, including their Black Panther emblem, from the southern movement. Stokely Carmichael and other prominent SNCC leaders briefly joined the Panthers and helped guide the burgeoning organization. The BPP developed a political strategy that built upon Carmichael's Black Power philosophy. The Panthers' elaborate ten-point platform included grassroots community initiatives such as defending the community against police brutality, providing free breakfast and educational training for students, and offering health care for the economically disadvantaged (figure 4.2).[10] Panther chants such as "All Power to the People" and "The Revolution Has Come, OFF THE PIGS!" accompanied media images of the Panthers raising the Black Power fist in the air as a sign of protest and solidarity. Like the shock troopers of SNCC, who dressed in a denim sharecropper-inspired uniform, the Panthers adopted a paramilitary uniform that was a hybrid of the military attire of radical leaders such as Che Guevara and Fidel Castro and the black cool styling of "hep cats" in their neighborhoods. Panthers patrolled the streets in black leather jackets, powder-blue turtlenecks or wide-collared shirts, and black slacks or skirts. Their uniforms were practical but also projected a sense of style that would resonate on the street corner or in the nightclub in ways that the earlier SNCC uniform did not. The Panthers were aware of their target audience and knew they needed to look the part in order to appeal to it effectively. Despite the community empowerment aspect of the Panthers' plan, they became most well known for their uniforms and were often constructed in the mainstream media as stylish yet dangerous armed radicals.

College-age people were drawn to the Black Panthers, and Panther chapters sprang up on and around college campuses in cities across the country. Though the class composition of these chapters was varied and diverse, the Panthers' Black Nationalist and aesthetic politics appealed to middle-class college students. For young women and men who had been sheltered by the black bourgeois enclaves of their childhoods, college provided a stark realization that most black people did not live the way that they did. After years of protest, class disparities within the black community were, if anything, even more marked than before. This realization moved many middle-class students to engage in more radical forms

Figure 4.2. Members of the Black Panther Party leading the Revolutionary People's Constitutional Convention at the Lincoln Memorial on June 19, 1970. Although the mainstream media was invested in depicting the Panthers as stylish, gun-toting radicals, their politics were far more expansive, as this photo suggests. Courtesy of the Library of Congress.

of activism and to develop personalities that would suit them for this revolutionary struggle.[11] They migrated from organizations such as the NAACP to the BPP and other Black Power organizations.

The Panthers' membership grew exponentially in the late 1960s. In May 1967, the BPP had a membership of thirty-one. Though its numbers were small, the group had a large impact because its political message of community self-help and self-defense was one that everyone—from college students to gang members, convicts, and single mothers on welfare—could relate to. Black youth were excited to see people who looked like them boldly standing their ground in the face of state-sanctioned violence. Many began emulating the Panthers, whether they were official members of the party or not.[12]

These factors, combined with the fact that the Panthers were one of several revolutionary Black Nationalist organizations operating under the umbrella of Black Power, made their numbers appear larger. FBI director J. Edgar Hoover declared in 1968 that "the Black Panther Party is the single greatest threat to the internal security of the United States" and decreed that 1969 would mark its demise.[13] By the close of 1969, shortly after former SNCC member Kathleen Cleaver joined the party, its membership had swelled to 10,000, with chapters in twenty-six states and several international branches, including a chapter in London that formed independently in 1968.[14]

Hoover's threat against the Panthers acknowledged that the student movement had become more radical over the course of the 1960s. At first the FBI did not consider student groups like SNCC a threat to national security. The FBI file on SNCC reveals that it began surveilling the organization shortly after its inception only to determine the "extent of Communist Party infiltration" and was not worried about its "legitimate activities."[15] Likewise, college administrators were not concerned when students at historically black institutions in the South were politely protesting against restrictive dress codes. But authorities soon realized that the early nonviolent protests served as a training ground for the development of more radical tactics and strategies by which young people could make greater demands for equality on campus and beyond.[16] Members of the Indiana University Afro-American Student Association staged a sit-in on the front lawn of the residence of the university president, Dr. Elvis Stahr, to protest the absence of any black members on a new committee on racial discrimination in student housing. And "several hundred" black students boycotted the annual Little 500 bike race, an IU tradition mostly for white fraternities and sororities, to protest what they believed were "discriminatory membership clauses" among those organizations.[17] Like radical black student organizations, members of predominantly white organizations such as the Students for a Democratic Society were also growing their hair long and wearing tattered denim and other garments, a countercultural style that became associated with their protests against the Vietnam War. Mainstream women's rights and gay rights organizations also used clothing strategically as an outward manifestation of their politics. In this climate of campus unrest, clothing became more closely tethered to movement politics for black and white women and men than it had been in previous decades.[18]

Whether they were part of the movement or not, black youth began wearing soul style as an expression of black pride. Soul style and the black cultural politics it connoted gripped the imagination of black youth from Brooklyn, New York, to Bamako, Mali, who by the end of the 1960s were grooving to soul songs like James Brown's 1968 hit "Say It Loud—I'm Black and I'm Proud." Disassociating blackness from ugliness, they were actively celebrating the beauty of having dark skin and tightly coiled hair. The Grandassa models, who were still performing their "Naturally" shows, pioneered the phrase "Black is Beautiful" in the early 1960s. The concept gained wider traction in the late 1960s and became a critical part of the language of soul (though most who used it had never heard of the Grandassa models). Young people believed they could perform their blackness through their clothing choices. Before long, "soul" and "black" became interchangeable terms that many believed signified upon authentic notions of blackness.[19] The more soul one possessed, the blacker she or he was; the blacker one was, the more soul she or he possessed. The logic followed that if one could have Black Power, that person could also have Soul Power. This popular term was used to amplify the collective cultural, political, and social power of the black community. At the same time, soul style and Soul Power were hotly contested as people clamored to define and defend their claims to blackness. For black women, celebrities such as Nina Simone, Abbey Lincoln, and Miriam Makeba were the embodiment of beautiful, authentic blackness.

Black college women expressed their admiration for these iconic soul sisters while showing off their own soul style. In 1968, *Sepia* magazine ran an article asserting that brown-skinned women were more proud of their complexions and their natural hair than ever before. Earlier than most black publications, *Sepia* recognized that college women were the vanguard of the Black is Beautiful movement. The article noted that Lynn Washington of Howard University lauded Stokely Carmichael, a Howard alum, as her "favorite Negro leader" and Nina Simone as her favorite singer.[20] Gaynelle S. Henderson considered H. Rap Brown "her kind of leader" and the South African jazzman and ex-husband of Miriam Makeba, Hugh Masekela, her favorite musician.[21] The accompanying photo boasted that Gaynelle "beautifully wears the natural hairstyle," with long, African-inspired earrings and a stylish top.[22] No occupation was mentioned for Trenton, New Jersey, native Iris Carter, who was shown wearing her hair natural and sporting large hoop earrings. Iris, described as a "living doll," was "as proud of her race as she is of her pretty hair"; she named Stokely Carmichael her favorite leader and Miriam Makeba her favorite singer.[23]

Nina Simone's brazen personality, urban soul sound, and dark skin and natural hair made her an ideal symbol of the Soul Power revolution. Early in her career, she was styled as a chanteuse, wearing straight-haired wigs and evening gowns. Even after Simone began performing with her hair natural overseas, she was still depicted on her album covers wearing her classic style.[24] Her 1967 album, *High Priestess of Soul*, was the first to reflect Simone's Afrocentric political agenda, depicting the artist in an Egyptian headdress. She followed it with the Grammy-nominated album *Black Gold* in 1969, which featured the anthem "To Be Young, Gifted, and Black." The song was popular among black college students, many of whom were attending schools where they were the only black person in their classes. It remained atop *Jet*'s Top 20 singles chart in the early months of 1970.[25] The album's cover emblematized Simone's message of black pride, featuring a drawing of Simone's face in ebony ink with sheet music streaming across it and a gold Afro with the bold words "Black Gold Nina Simone" super-imposed on it. To bolster sales of *Black Gold* and to tout Simone's commitment to black people, Simone and her manager-husband, Andy Stroud, encouraged RCA Records to purchase "several hundred" gold necklaces with pendants in the shape of the African continent and matching earrings, handcrafted by a Nigerian jeweler, to be sold with the records; they also released promotional pictures of Simone sporting the jewelry.[26] Simone became the voice and then the face of the movement. She recalled, "I was told by [former SNCC leader and Black Panther minister of justice] H. Rap Brown once—and I was highly complimented—that I was the singer of the black revolution because there is no other singer who sings real protest songs about the race situation."[27]

Miriam Makeba solidified her status as a Soul Power icon after she married longtime boyfriend Stokely Carmichael in 1968. Makeba, who gave many black Americans their first introduction to African culture in the late 1950s, continued to release hit songs such as the 1967 dance hit "Pata Pata," which sparked an international dance craze. By the late 1960s, she had traded in her short-cropped natural for cornrows adorned with large wooden beads. Makeba and Carmichael's union signified the marriage of soul style and Black Power and evoked notions of revolutionary femininity and masculinity as well as of African diasporic unity. But shortly after her marriage, venues across the country canceled Makeba's concert dates. She believed that the U.S. government also conspired to ruin her venture to open a fashion boutique in the Bahamas after she and Carmichael were detained in the former British colony because he was flagged as a threat to the U.S. government. After the dissolution of Miriam Makeba's career in the Americas, she and Carmichael moved to Guinea, where they continued to advocate the pan-diasporic Black Freedom movement.

The Afro

The black women who emulated their favorite celebrities' fashions wore soul style on campus as a way to claim social and cultural space for themselves. They were continuously mixing and remixing soul style, producing new names for their look that traveled across the country, gaining popularity as it went. The transformation of the "au naturel" hairstyle to the "Afro" is an example of soul style innovation. The difference between the two styles was not in name only. The au naturel was generally used to describe any unprocessed hairstyle in the early 1960s, from Miriam Makeba's low cut to Odetta's signature crop to Grandassa model Brenda Deaver's bun.[28] Deaver and the other Grandassa models had started pushing the black community toward differentiating among these various hairstyles by attempting to trace their origins to various regions of Africa. It is not entirely clear how the Afro hairstyle came into being or who named it, but it was a specific type of natural hairstyle, recognized by its perfectly round "halo" shape.[29] The bigger one's Afro, the better, because the Afro, more than any other natural hairstyle, became symbolic of one's black consciousness.[30]

Chicago-based black psychiatrist Kermit T. Mehlinger became a foremost public intellectual on the subject of natural hair, writing for such Johnson Publishing Company magazines as *Negro Digest*, *Ebony*, and *Jet*. Mehlinger informed his readers that the Afro was "linked with attitudes toward racial and social conditions."[31] He surmised that, in the late 1960s, beauty still held the same importance in black women's lives, but soul sisters were "stimulat[ing] a new pride in Negro men and women."[32] In the early 1960s, the dividing line was between straightened and natural hair. By the early 1970s, it was about who could 'fro their hair and who could not. Black women and men who wore the style had to have tightly coiled hair. Not all women with natural hair could wear an Afro; those with a loose curl pattern were not considered as black as those whose hair could create the desirable Afro. The Afro hairstyle grew in popularity, first in places like New York City, Los Angeles, and Oakland, but the growing media coverage of the Panthers and the popularity of Nina Simone and other soul singers who sported the style helped to make it popular in the Midwest as well.

Amye Glover started wearing an Afro when she was fifteen, after hearing James Brown's anthem "Say It Loud." Though Brown still wore his hair "conked," or chemically straightened, his music inspired black youth across the country to abandon processed hair in order to celebrate their blackness. Glover was one of many black teens in her community in Cleveland, Ohio, who wore an Afro. When she moved from Cleveland to attend a predominantly black high school in downtown Fort Wayne, Indiana, almost no students, male or female, wore the style. Glover was one of a handful of black women in a student body of nearly 2,000 wearing an Afro on school picture day in the 1970 Central High School yearbook.[33] Teen girls were reluctant to wear the style, even at the peak of the Black Power movement, because they were afraid that it would diminish their respectability. Most girls considered school picture day an occasion to dress up and show off their good grooming and home training. Glover contended that the Afro "had a stigma" meaning "you're militant"; her peers and teachers believed that she and other women who wore the style were "crossing a boundary." Remembering the stares she received as she walked through the halls of Central High, Glover stated, "It was strange for them to see this big ol' Afro walking around. They had a hard time relating to it." The boys were not held to the same standards of respectability. Far more young black men than women wore the hairstyle, though most—like my father, Herman Ford—still wore their hair relatively closely shorn.[34] The Afro was not popular among black high school students in Indiana in 1970, but it was definitely in vogue by the time Glover went off to college at Indiana University Bloomington two years later (figure 4.3).

The activist-professor Angela Davis inadvertently popularized the hairstyle, making the Afro a permanent part of the soul style lexicon. Davis's 1970 arrest and subsequent trial brought black women's experiences on college campuses to the fore. She had already made national news in 1969 when Governor Ronald Reagan forced the University of California's Board of Regents to fire her from her post as an assistant professor of philosophy because of her membership in the Communist Party USA. A judge ruled her firing unconstitutional, and Davis was reappointed.[35] The following year, guns registered in her name were used in a fatal courtroom kidnapping. Davis's occasional bodyguard, Jonathan Jackson, had orchestrated the kidnapping to negotiate the release of his older brother, Panther member George Jackson.[36] Hoover, who had intensified the FBI's violent repression of the BPP, relentlessly pursued Davis, issuing a warrant for her arrest on kidnapping and murder charges. Davis fled the state of California, and the FBI placed her on its Ten Most Wanted Fugitives list, plastering flyers with her image in gas stations, hotels, and convenience stores

Figure 4.3.
Senior yearbook photo of Amye Glover at Central High School in Fort Wayne, Indiana, ca. 1972. Glover was one of the few women in her predominantly black school to sport an Afro on school picture day. Most black high school–aged girls still adhered to a politics of respectability that mandated that they straighten their hair for formal occasions. Courtesy of Amye Glover-Ford.

across the country. The FBI poster featured two photos of Davis, both with an Afro, paired with text that described her as a "light brown, American Negro" charged with "interstate flight—murder, kidnapping" and considered "possibly armed and dangerous." Davis eluded the FBI for two months. After she was apprehended at a Howard Johnson's Motor Lodge in New York City, Davis's supporters quickly formed an international "Free Angela Davis" campaign, producing pamphlets, flyers, and buttons with images of the defiant soul sister on them.[37]

The press ran stories about the Afro-wearing fugitive, sparking a media frenzy over Davis's case, her background, and her Afro hairstyle. Following Davis's arrest, *Newsweek* published a five-page spread on October 26, 1970, that described her as the daughter of a schoolteacher and a prosperous black entrepreneur who had chosen to inhabit simultaneously the middle-class "life of scholarship" and the world of "swelling black consciousness . . . Afro hair-do's, angry slogans, guns, and violent death."[38] The cover had two photos of Davis, one a headshot highlighting her Afro and the other an image of the revolutionary at bay, in handcuffs with her hair primly pulled back. *Newsweek* cast Davis as a femme fatale, describing her as "the most glamorous and provocative fugitive on the Feds' list."[39] The photos accompanying the story portrayed a fashionable and beautiful rebel; one showed a long-legged, miniskirt-wearing, handcuffed Davis striding through FBI offices, flanked by three G-men with matching crisp white shirts, suits, and ties.[40] Panther leader Ericka Huggins claims that Panther women were not concerned with their appearance, and "the best thing we could say about our clothing is that it was clean."[41] Although Huggins may be understating the degree to which style mattered to black revolutionaries, her point that the mainstream media overemphasized the fashion of women like Angela Davis is telling. Davis's clothing became not only a symbol of her turn to radical politics but also a radical chic style to be copied. Davis believed that magazines such as *Newsweek* and *Life* did more than the FBI to characterize her as a sophisticated criminal because they had such broad circulation.

While she was in hiding—disguised in "a wig with straight black hair, long false lashes, and more eyeshadow, liner, and blush than I had ever imagined wearing in public"—Davis said she "confronted my own image" on the cover of *Life*. Realizing that the feature story "gave a rather convincing explanation as to why the pictures should be associated with crime and danger," Davis was "convinced that FBI chief J. Edgar Hoover had conspired in the appearance of that cover story."[42] Davis's speculation that some media outlets and the FBI were in collusion is not altogether implausible, for other events suggested that the FBI was using the media to conflate the images of Panther women, linking them all to criminal acts.[43] For example, Davis's high school classmate Regina Nadelson remembered watching television in August 1971 as San Francisco's WPIX aired a cover story on Davis while flashing a picture of Kathleen Cleaver on the screen. After the commercial break, the reporter apologized for the mix-up, stating, "We showed a picture of Kathleen Cleaver during a story about Angela Davis. We didn't realize how much they look alike, but really they do."[44]

The mainstream media's negative representations of Afro-coiffed black women had serious consequences, even for those who had no affiliation with Black Power organizations. Davis recalled that after she was placed on the Most Wanted list, "hundreds, perhaps even thousands, of Afro-wearing black women were accosted, harassed, and arrested by police, FBI, and immigration agents."[45] Law enforcement officers indiscriminately targeted these women, overlooking the diversity of their skin tones, hair textures, shapes, and sizes—a diversity that many soul sisters aimed to celebrate. They reduced black women to a hairstyle, ignoring their individual traits. A black woman accountant named Taylor, who wore what she called an "Angela Davis Afro" in the early 1970s, believed that Afro-wearing black women were harassed even when the police were looking for black male suspects: "Whenever I would wear my Afro I'd get pulled over by the police because I drove a very sleek car and they always thought from the back of the head that I had to be male a lot of times because we [black women and black men] all wore the same hairstyle."[46] The gender-neutralizing effect of the Afro was relatively new: prior to the mid-1960s, natural hairstyles were worn almost exclusively by black women. The police used the marker of the Afro as a way to deliberately harass black men and women, even if they knew that the person they stopped was not Angela Davis. They were particularly cruel to black women as a way to remind them that they should not expect the courtesy extended to their white female counterparts. But not all women minded being accosted by police. Angela Davis remembered a woman telling her "she hoped she could serve as a decoy," considering it a way she could contribute to Davis's effort to escape the FBI.[47] In the months leading up to her trial, more black women around the globe began wearing Afros.[48]

Davis's acquittal in 1972 was undoubtedly seen as a victory by black college women who knew how often black women were denied justice. Davis's firing and subsequent arrest spoke to the precariousness of black women's positions in society and on college campuses in particular. They could relate to being perceived by their peers as a threat simply because of their race and their gender. Amye Glover went off to college that same year Davis was released from jail. She stated that Angela Davis was a power-ful figure; she "liked her whole style" and particularly "loved her Afro." Though Glover had already been wearing an Afro, Davis gave the style new meaning. Glover was inspired by "seeing this strong woman stand up. And through [incarceration], she remained strong in her beliefs." Glover could also relate to Angela Davis in other, more personal ways. Like Davis, Glover was from a middle-class black family. Her father, Seaburn Glover, a history teacher, and her mother, Bennie Lou, a nurse, were both educated at historically black universities and members of a black fraternity and sorority: Kappa Alpha Psi and Zeta Phi Beta. The Glovers owned a three-story home in the Mt. Pleasant neighborhood in Cleveland, becoming the third black family to live on the block. Like Angela Davis, Amye Glover questioned her class privilege and wanted to take a more active role in empowering her community.[49]

When Glover arrived on the Indiana University campus, she discovered that most of the black women were sporting Afros. In a picture of the Tau

Figure 4.4. Alpha Kappa Alpha Sorority, Inc., Tau Chapter yearbook photo, Indiana University, 1972. Fourteen of eighteen members wore their hair in large Afros, which speaks to the popularity of the Afro in the early 1970s and to how black college women were breaking from traditions of hair straightening as a marker of one's feminine beauty. Courtesy of the Indiana University Archives Photograph Collection.

Chapter of the Alpha Kappa Alpha sorority (AKA), fourteen of eighteen members wore their hair in large Afros (figure 4.4).[50] Founded at Howard University in 1908, AKA was the first black Greek letter sorority. For some, the organization epitomized a version of black beauty that upheld normative, middle-class notions of feminine propriety and respectability, including wearing one's hair straightened and dressing in fine clothing. AKAs were known as much on Indiana's campus for wearing pink and green and chanting "Pretty girls wear twenty pearls" as they were for their commitment to community service. Their choice to wear Afros for the yearbook photo reveals that Alpha Kappa Alpha women were more diverse than the stereotype suggested and also that what was considered beautiful and feminine had shifted. Their black consciousness was manifested in ways their older sorority sisters would never have considered.

Essence and the Fashion-Forward Black College Woman

Essence magazine lauded black college women as legitimate soul style innovators in its special issue on college life, which was a response to the lack of attention paid to black women's particular experiences on college campuses. *Essence* aimed to offer a more nuanced image of the soul sisters who were reshaping campus culture on historically black and predominantly white campuses across the country. When it was launched in May 1970, the magazine had a circulation of 50,000 copies a month. The young publication sought to differentiate itself from other black publications of the day such as *Ebony* and *Sepia* in order to increase its circulation, and the College Issue provided an avenue to draw in new, younger readers. The *Essence* staff tapped into a growing consumer market of black college women who had money to spend and wanted to read stories about their lived experiences and see women who looked and dressed like them. From the beginning, *Essence* translated soul style to a broader audience. It had an image of an Afro-coiffed, brown-complexioned woman on its cover. Feature stories included a piece on "Dynamite Afros" and one on women and the Black Freedom movement titled "Revolt: From Rosa [Parks] to Kathleen [Cleaver]." Similarly, the College Issue brought campus fashions to a broader audience, explaining why they were popular and offering instruction on how to recreate the looks.

Despite the political fervor of the movement, the *Essence* soul sister was not overtly political. The special issue did not include stories on topics related to Black Power, black feminism, or antiwar sentiments. Instead, feature stories focused on subjects such as college preparation for high school students, the importance of the campus library, and the United Negro College Fund.[51] *Essence* opted to use the language of "co-ed" that upheld heteronormative constructions of feminine propriety. The label "co-ed" allowed these women to be seen as leaders, particularly in campus social life, but still as respectable enough to be ideal mates. The co-ed was poised and polished, qualities that would allow her to begin a successful career. She was supposedly nonthreatening and more palatable than a feminist radical. *Essence* constructed its ideal college soul sister and brought her to the black community to be consumed by current college students, college hopefuls and their families, and those who could only dream about having the opportunity to attend college.

The *Essence* soul sister attended a historically black institution, not a predominantly white one. The first three campus issues focused on life at black colleges below the Mason-Dixon line: the schools of the Atlanta University Center with female students (Spelman College, Atlanta University, Clark College, and Morris Brown), Morgan State University, and Hampton University, respectively. Not until 1975 did *Essence* begin including profiles of black women at elite, predominantly white institutions such as Barnard College, Wellesley College, Cornell University, Princeton University, and Northwestern University. Though the highest number of black students were still concentrated at historically black colleges and universities (HBCUs), which were mostly in the South, the proportion of black students attending predominantly white schools in the North, Midwest, and West Coast was increasing. In its commitment to promoting HBCUs, *Essence* was also making a claim about the history of soul style. Although the nation was looking to the East and West Coasts for soul style inspiration, *Essence* was positing black students in the South as the trendsetters. It was not by chance, then, that the inaugural issue was set in Atlanta, not only because there was a consortium of schools all in close proximity to one another but also because Atlanta was the black mecca of the South. *Essence* named Atlanta one of the "ten most popular soul cities" in America.[52] Black Americans were beginning to celebrate their ties to the South, even more than their ties to Africa, and many were engaging in reverse migration back to the South. For *Essence*, soul style was an extension of this rich black cultural heritage. All of the excitement of college life was taking place at HBCUs, with their lively bands, vibrant Greek life, runway-ready fashions, and supportive faculty and diverse course offerings. *Essence* wanted to make black women desire to attend a historically black school.

Essence's soul sister had to be impeccably styled and well groomed. The College Issue's fashion feature was its main attraction. The fashion editors reminded readers that although "so much maturing happens in College," college "means an eye for fashion too."[53] Clothes helped young black women express who they were and who they wanted to be in the world, and *Essence* wanted to guide women from adolescence into adulthood. The spreads showcased the latest fashion trends on campus models. The 1973 issue was themed "Campus '73: Casually Coordinated," demonstrating that even at bourgeois schools like Spelman, it was okay to be casually dressed because casual was the new on-trend look. The fashion editors advised readers, "When shopping this fall, look for sleek-lined, uncluttered apparel that you can mix-match, dress up or down—and personalize them as only you can."[54] Model Debra Oxidine, a Florida native who attended Clark College, was photographed wearing a maxi dress and wooden platform sandals accessorized with an African-inspired beaded necklace and bracelet set.[55]

Style was less about having the most expensive pieces and more about possessing the fashion savvy to know how to arrange the pieces in ways that expressed one's individuality. Soul style was largely a do-it-yourself endeavor that encouraged creativity and innovation. The fashion feature in the 1974 College Issue, titled "Fall in Fly," focused on "mixing the old with the new."[56] Editors informed readers that thrift stores were a soul sister's paradise, suggesting that they shop there for old sweaters, jeans, berets, head wraps, and butterfly-collared shirts that could be paired with more luxurious items such as fur capelets and rhinestones. *Essence* tried to accommodate college women's limited budgets by demonstrating ways that they could be stylish on a dime. In its regular issues, targeted toward upwardly mobile professional black women, the magazine featured an "*Essence* Designer of the Month" column that profiled haute couture designers such as Karlotta Nelson (who sold her garments exclusively at the black-owned Beverly Hills boutique The Gazebo) and model Pat Evans and her design partner Ollie Johnson of the Hired Hands label (who specialized in handcrafted leather garments).[57] In the College Issue, editors focused more on the practice of styling oneself than on performing wealth through wearing haute couture. The emphasis on thrift stores was also significant because, even in the early 1970s, more decadent soul style fashions were harder to find. Most students resorted to pairing available garments such as platform shoes, leather vests, long jackets, and bell-bottoms with African-inspired accessories such as gold and ivory beads, earrings that dangled to the shoulder, cowrie shells, and elephant hair bracelets. If they did not have something that looked or felt "African," they simply renamed items to make them sound black. For example, a simple black beret could be renamed a "soul sister" or "soul brother" beret.[58]

Those college women who had access to black-owned boutiques or mail-order catalogs were among an elite group of campus fashionistas. Black designers such as New Breed, whose garments were worn by Aretha Franklin, the "Queen of Soul," and featured in *Sepia*, were reinterpreting African garments such as dashikis, caftans, boubous, *agbadas* and *djellabas* (which were similar to caftans but from different parts of Africa), *lapas*, *bubas*, and *geles*, designing them in wild colors and fabrics.[59] Their garments were considered haute couture and were priced too expensively for the average college student. Women who lived in major cities had the more affordable option of buying African-inspired looks at black-

Figure 4.5.
Amye Glover wearing
her signature zebra-print
maxi dress and matching
head wrap of her own
design, circa 1972. Glover
made garments that she
felt had an "African flair"
to them. Black women
who could sew became
the fashionistas of their
campuses because they
could make elaborate
soul style looks that were
otherwise hard to procure.
Courtesy of Amye Glover-
Ford.

owned boutiques or shopping at outdoor markets where African textile merchants sold their wares. Those who did not live close to major cities often purchased their clothes from mail-order companies that advertised in black magazines such as *Ebony, Essence,* and *Sepia.*

College women who could design and sew their own garments became the soul style divas on campus because they could piece together more exotic looks. "I designed and made my own clothes," Amye Glover stated, including a zebra-printed halter maxi dress with a matching *gele* (figure 4.5). Her skills enabled her to participate in the latest trends without spending too much money. She remembered traveling from Indiana University back to Cleveland to purchase exotic fabrics that were not available in the small college town. Her clothes "always had an African flair to them" because she selected fabrics that were "loud and bright like the colors over in Africa." She was particularly fascinated by Miriam Makeba's clothing: "I loved to see [Makeba] in her garments and head wraps . . . and her music, just hearing the music, that was more jazz, slower movements, modern, but still had that flair of Africa . . . my image of what Africa was."[60] Ultimately, no matter where *Essence* soul sisters were purchasing their clothes, the message was that it was imperative that they "style out," or dress very well, on campus.

Essence's special College Issues projected an image of black beauty that was not tethered to a specific set of political or cultural beliefs about straightened versus natural hair. Aware of the volatile debates about colorism within the black community, *Essence* was careful not to marginalize or elevate any one segment of the black community. The student models had a range of complexions and wore a variety of hairstyles, including Afros, relaxers, and cornrows: "Today's black coed—cornrowed, afro'd, sleeked or straight hair—is in search of a greater self-awareness."[61] In the inaugural issue, Spelman student Cooki Stephens, a fair-skinned woman from Michigan, sported a strawberry blonde natural while her classmate, a dark brown–complexioned woman from Pennsylvania named Vicki Harvey, wore her hair in a short, relaxed style. Others, like Georgia native Marilyn Walker of Morris Brown College, wore intricate cornrows. Presenting a range of styles from natural kinky Afros and cornrows to natural looser-curl patterns as well as chemically processed hair interpreted blackness as accessible to all women of African descent.[62]

Essence focused on fashion and beauty without discussing how and why the fashion emerged from strained social relations on campus. Arguably, soul style was even more significant to black women students who were simultaneously invisible and hypervisible on their predominantly white campuses than it was to their HBCU peers. In an *Essence* article titled "Black Coed, White Campus," the assistant dean of the graduate school at MIT, Clarence Williams, and James E. Lyons, the assistant dean of student affairs at the University of Connecticut, asserted that the increased number of black students at white institutions entailed new and often problematic social interactions between white and black students.[63] The administration was regularly at a loss as to how to resolve these conflicts. As a result, black women felt unsupported by their institutions. Quoting a "soft-spoken black woman" who was far from being a "black power militant," Renee Ferguson wrote in the Indiana University *Arbutus* yearbook in 1970 that "being a black student at Indiana University is Hell!"[64]

Interracial interactions in the dorms were a source of tension among female students. The unnamed student in Ferguson's article recalled, "All the girls on my floor were white except me, but there was one other black girl that I met at dinner who lived a couple floors below me. . . .My roommate was white and I got along with her just fine."[65] Other black women

Figure 4.6. Amye Glover (*left*) with a friend in her dorm room in Wright Quadrangle in 1972. Glover, as a self-proclaimed "soul sister," decorated her room with an Angela Davis poster, African-inspired beads that hung from the ceiling, and a bedspread with matching pillows that she sewed herself in the colors of the pan-African unity flag. Glover was the only black woman on her floor. Decorating her room in this way allowed her to transform the space into a safe haven where she and her friends could express themselves. Courtesy of Amye Glover-Ford.

did not fare so well. Amye Glover was assigned to a room in Wright Quad, which she shared with a white woman whom she could not get along with. Glover found it more necessary to assert her pride in her black female identity than she had in the halls of her predominantly black high school. A photograph taken in Glover's dorm room depicts the amateur fashion designer and a female friend sporting large Afro hairstyles (figure 4.6). Glover decorated her side of the dorm room in homage to Angela Davis and the Black Freedom struggle. She commissioned her best friend, Phyllis Ford, to draw a portrait of Davis, which she hung up over her bed next to a large poster of her heroine. She also made a bedspread in the red, black, and green colors of the pan-African flag. From her ceiling she strung wooden beads that gave the room an ethnic feel. Her side of the room stood in contrast to that of her roommate. Glover used the decor to create a space where she felt safe and comfortable while tacitly communicating to her roommate and her roommate's guests that she was militant and would not tolerate harassment.

Social settings also generated feelings of cultural alienation. An unnamed black woman at Indiana University remembered that she could not relate to the music they played at a campus dance: "I couldn't dance to the music, but that didn't matter since no one asked me to dance anyway."[66] As she looked around the large room, she realized that she was the only black person there. Ferguson surmised that this feeling of exclusion was due to the fact that "blacks at Indiana University are isolated from the mainstream of black activism which take[s] place in urban areas." She concluded that it was necessary for blacks to "colonize, seek each other out, and unite in political, cultural, and social endeavors."[67]

Western Kentucky University senior Stephanie Madison argued that finding black friends was not a real solution to feelings of alienation. Madison, whose essay was featured in *Essence*, explained that on predominantly white campuses, school administrators and white students interpreted black students' "hanging together" as needing a "security blanket" because they were incapable of adjusting to the rigors of college life. The larger issue was that "the black coed has comparatively few outlets for her creativity and self expression," Madison contended. "She can complete four years of college in almost total obscurity."[68] Although a few black women joined cheerleading squads, participated in student government, became residential assistants, and were chosen as campus homecoming queens, most had to create their own social activities.[69] Glover chose to follow in her mother's footsteps by joining the Delta Epsilon chapter of the Zeta Phi Beta sorority as a way to build relationships with other black women on campus. Lyons and Williams concurred: "The adjustment concerns of the black female are by far the most profound." The two administrators attributed black college women's lack of integration to the fact that "the Black movement has elevated her to a position never before attained. She knows that black is indeed beautiful" and expected to have the same active social life and positive peer interaction that she had enjoyed at her predominantly black high school and community, which was impossible at predominantly white institutions.[70] Their statement put the burden of integration on black women instead of on the school administration, which had the responsibility to create a climate of inclusivity on campus.

The campus was a battleground for black women like Glover and her Indiana University peers. They saw the Ku Klux Klan easily obtain permits to march through the streets of Bloomington while black students were routinely harassed by campus police simply for congregating in large groups. Feeling herself becoming more militant the longer she stayed on campus, Glover adopted the Black Power gesture. "When I felt like I wanted to protest something somebody said, I just raised my fist," which "sent a silent message."[71] Dorothy Randall, a student at Harlem University, had similar feelings. She believed that soul sisters across America were demanding "self-respect": "When you walk into stores, you no longer feel the clerk is going to be insolent. You have the upper hand and you say, 'I want a blouse.' You tell him firmly what color you want and you don't want no bullshit. It's a whole thing with pride in yourself. You're sure of yourself and no one can tell you a thing."[72] Despite the media's insistence that all revolutionary soul sisters were consumed with gunplay, Panther women showed black women like Glover and Randall how to arm themselves with words, clothing, and hairstyles to project a sense of self-confidence and self-worth.

Soul Style and the Global Fashion Market

By the mid-1970s, the mainstream fashion industry had co-opted the styles of nationalists, revolutionaries, hippies, and radical feminists, creating both haute couture designs and ready-to-wear collections for department stores.[73] There had long been exchange between the fashions of the black community and the mainstream fashion industry, despite the fact that American and European designers continued to treat black fashion as if it was inferior. In the 1970s, however, blackness was in vogue in ways that even the most haute couture designers could not deny. This was in part due to the burgeoning fashion industry in various African countries whose soul style looks were similar to the fashions of black college women. Fashion critics in the United States called this style the "natural look," drawing upon youths' desire to return to a simpler, less adorned way of life. The fashion industry gave clothing items such as denim jeans, which activists wore to emulate the style of the laboring class, an exorbitant monetary value that far outstripped the fabric's manufacturing cost. "Ethnic" wares, too, were sold at inflated prices.[74] The amalgamation of styles from various racial and political communities under the label "the natural look" allowed the clothes to be treated as material culture that was divorced from the bodies of the women who innovated with raw materials. Furthermore, the industry used the term "natural" as one that was race-neutral, which really meant white, dislocating the term "natural" from the varied meanings it had within the black community and to soul. As the cultural value of soul style was propagated across the country, it also became more entangled in corporate America than it had been in earlier years.

A similar phenomenon occurred with the Afro. Leading beauty industry companies such as Directional Wigs and David and David, Inc. partnered with black hairstylists such as Rudel Briscoe and Walter Fontaine of New York City's Coif Camp Salon and entertainers such as Leslie Uggams to mass-produce designer Afro wigs. Tastemakers in the fashion and beauty world called the hairstyle the "Afro look." Adding the word "look" after "Afro" made it a bona fide style to be emulated by the coolest of trendsetters. The wigs allowed women who did not want to give up their press-and-curl or whose hair was too fine to kink up into an Afro the opportunity to perform their blackness through artifice. The Afro wig quickly became a trend among blacks and (though to a lesser degree) whites, becoming what Fontaine rightly predicted would be "the first truly new style this country can export overseas." David and David's "L'Afrique" wig—a name coined by a male Harlem-based, Afro-Haitian hairstylist known as Frenchie Casdulan—was constructed from synthetic fibers, which made the wigs cheaper to produce and export.[75]

The commodification of soul style should not overshadow the ways in which black women responded to corporate America's appropriation of black culture. Although it was clear that Davis and other radical soul sisters were influencing fashion trends, they were also very critical of the capitalist engine that fueled the fashion industry.[76] Black cultural nationalist Ann Cook watched in outrage as she tuned into the television show *Like It Is*, which was airing a segment on African-inspired fashion trends in August 1969. She was dismayed to see that "most of the black models preferred to sell their Blackness to white agencies." She was even more "pained" by the "elaborate fashion show of clothing in African prints and styles." Cook, who had traveled extensively throughout Africa and South America, recognized that there is nothing particularly "sacred" about African cloth, particularly because most of the so-called African material sold in the United States had "never seen Africa," meaning it was manufactured and sold in the States. But she was still appalled by the appropriation of the cloth for Western styles, including "African-print Bikinis," "hip-hugging African-print bell bottoms," and "Moslem long dresses and coats" made from sheer fabrics, which she noted transgressed "Islamic codes" for women. Instead of the models and designers using the fabrics to "purge" such "decadent Western values," the models—who included a West African woman—upheld what Cook termed "White Values in Black Face." Cook was alluding to the history of blackface minstrelsy, when African American stage and film performers, like the white actors who had previously portrayed black characters in the nineteenth century, were forced to apply burnt cork to their faces and turn themselves into caricatures of their black selves in order to entertain white audiences.[77] By using the phrase "white values," she referred to the idea that black women had bought into a Western definition of beauty and style. Thus, the women who wore the clothing were merely "shucking and jiving" for "the man" in much the same way that blacks in the early twentieth century had done. Cook saw the fashion industry's adoption of African attire as a form of racial exploitation. She found that the clothes by black fashion designers embodied "by far the most treacherous of the white values"; they "sold 'Blackness' so cheaply" that their work must be "condemned."[78] Of course, Cook's critique did not take into consideration that African designers on the continent were making similar "Western" designs using local textiles. Model and designer Pat Evans was also critical of the fashion industry. She told Essence readers, "Our own uncanny way of dressing is what gives white America ideas to create new style, they come up to Harlem and check it out then design behind what they have seen." Her stinging indictment of the fashion industry was published in Essence in 1972. Evans was most famous for being the bald-headed beauty on the covers of the Ohio Players' albums Pain (1972), Pleasure (1972), and Ecstasy (1973). The Harlem native shaved her hair to protest the fashion industry's imperative in the 1960s that black models' hair be long and straightened, though she often wore a wig to casting calls because she needed the work to support her family. Evans's wig came off one day while she was trying on clothes for African American designer Stephen Burrows. Seeing her bald head, Burrows encouraged Evans to forgo the wig and make the bald look her signature style. Although Evans was the second-highest paid model (only British model Twiggy made more) at the Stewart Models agency, she said in Essence that "the Black model business is like slave trading—only more refined."[79] Meanwhile, Life magazine was commenting that "Black was busting out all over" the industry, highlighting nearly forty female and male black models who were finding unprecedented success because of "pressure from the civil rights movement." The article stated that in the past, fashion houses wanted only "the most Caucasian-looking black models they could find," but now "they want blackness—Afro hair, discernibly Negroid features, truly black skin."[80] In other words, blackness was a fetish that designers used to sell garments to both black people and whites who wanted to try on black cool. Evans argued that those black models who did get jobs were relegated to a niche market at their agencies, and agencies tended to want only one black model on their rosters at a time. She offered tips to aspiring black models but ultimately concluded that black women "are the original models" because it was their style that white designers imitated, and they should not have to model what white designers had copied from them.[81]

Photographer Ming Smith remembered being conflicted about whether to pursue a career in modeling because of the problematic ways it constructed black beauty and style. Smith, the recently divorced mother of a young son named Kahil, was a graduate of Howard University, where she majored in microbiology and minored in chemistry. She decided to delay medical school and moved to New York City in the early 1970s, where she sought a career that would yield enough income to bring Kahil from her parents' house in Ohio. In Washington, D.C., and New York, Ming moved through black intellectual crowds, and at first she refused to pursue modeling. "My head was not into being a model. I was always more political, into black consciousness and Malcolm [X]. Modeling was capitalist; it was like everything I was against." Once she realized the amount of money she could earn, however, the fair-complexioned, curly-haired Ming gave in— but she kept her modeling career a secret from her activist friends. She recalled, "Now, all of my friends who were really into the Black Power thing, I couldn't tell them I was a model because I was ashamed."[82] Although some Black Panthers had moderated their critique of capitalism, they still considered the fashion industry frivolous.[83]

Despite pushback from some black women, the fashion industry had a captive audience of young people, largely college students, who were willing to spend money to look like the women they idolized. Given the high visibility of soul style, the fashion industry did not need to rely solely on professional models to sell their wares. The images of Angela Davis and other soul sisters were imitated by fashion houses, which since the 1940s had had to pay models and celebrities to endorse their products. Designers would strategically place them at parties and events where the media, socialites, and others who influenced fashion trends in their communities would see their clothing. But because most college students were wearing these looks, they had ready-made billboards walking around campuses.

By the mid-1970s, soul had become highly recognizable to a much broader audience, creating a feeling of authentic blackness that could be mass-produced and consumed by everyone from college students to street hustlers. Attention to the production and consumption of this style, however, has overshadowed the ways in which black college women used soul style to reconstruct problematic images of black womanhood and celebrate the activism of black women as freedom fighters. Uncovering this lesser-told history enables us to understand how black women formed real and imagined communities within the private spaces of their institutions. Moreover, album covers and posters, which were distributed internationally, helped to turn natural hair and African-inspired clothing into forms of cultural consciousness that signified soulful blackness. At the same time, the media constructed images through stories that, though often problematic, depicted black American revolutionaries and the black struggle in the United States. The black press in particular was instrumental in fostering a sense of a united diasporic movement in which all blacks could participate, regardless of their nationality or their political and cultural difference. As soul style gained a national and international following, for some the fashions of bodily adornment came to symbolize the potential unity of Africana people. Travel was a critical aspect of the movement, and narratives of revolutionary activists traveling to other parts of the world framed the public imaginary of a network of radical activists who worked together in their quest for black liberation.

Although the mid-1970s marked a period of declension in soul style's popularity in the United States, it was rejuvenating movements in other parts of the black diaspora. The next two chapters examine what this Americanized soul style looked like and how it functioned when it was exported from the United States to England and South Africa. Chapter 5 focuses on soul style in London.

5

WE WERE PEOPLE OF SOUL

Gender, Violence, and Black Panther Style in 1970s London

On November 15, 1969, violence erupted in front of Desmond's Hip City, one of the first black-owned record stores in the Brixton neighborhood of south London. Desmond's was a soul paradise decorated with album covers of black American and Caribbean musicians and posters of militant leaders and activists. Afro-coiffed black British teens congregated at Desmond's on Saturdays to hear the latest in imported soul, reggae, and soca records, reconstituting their Afro-Caribbean and African heritage on British soil. On this particular Saturday, the London police violently attacked Afro-British youth, including seventeen-year-old Olive Morris and other members of the Black Panther Movement (BPM), leaving several with broken limbs and bloody faces. Usually, the police were not interested in patrolling black cultural venues such as Desmond's when they appeared to be merely small businesses. Once the London police discovered that black teens were using such venues as sites of cultural-political resistance, however, they intervened, often violently. The significance of record stores and other black-operated cultural institutions in Brixton's soul geography illuminates a larger history of racial tension, police violence, and resistance by grassroots black organizers. It was this tension that gave rise to expressions of soul style in London.

Soul and the aesthetic politics it connoted were part of the language used by Morris and her Panther peers. Afro-British poet Khadijah Ibrahiim declared that the 1970s was a "'fro wearing time."[1] Ibrahiim linked black-conscious cultural expressions with the rise of a black British leisure culture among youth; soul symbols such as the Afro created a sense of comradeship, and soul-filled music became a soundtrack to which Afro-Caribbean teens grooved. Black Panther minister of self-defense and security Hurlington Armstrong remarked that the late 1960s and 1970s "were the days of soul" and "we were people of soul."[2] Black youth in Britain wore Afros, bell-bottoms, and Black Panther T-shirts and carried tote bags that sported Black Power patches and appliqué images of guns. In doing so they redefined a black aesthetic and gave new cultural-political value to black bodies in white British society.

"Black" was as much a political affiliation as it was a cultural identity. People of South Asian as well as those of African descent called themselves black in response to the common oppression they faced as nonwhites in Britain. They organized marches and public protests to denounce police brutality and racism in the judicial system and to contest de facto segregation, which relegated nonwhites in London and other cities to the poorest schools and most dilapidated housing. But soul style was culturally black; it spoke to a set of experiences that were specific to people of African descent. The overlap and distinction between the two meanings of black played out in complex and interesting ways in the Brixton neighborhood.[3]

London was a central node in the broader circuitry of cultural-political exchange among African diasporic people in the global fight for black freedom. The emergence of a distinct Afro-Caribbean youth culture in Britain is an example of the ways in which soul style developed in various parts of the black diaspora in similar forms but often with distinctly different social meanings. Soul was not simply an African American expression; it was "raw material" that Afro-Caribbean teens used to "redefine what it meant to be black, adapting it to distinctively British experiences and meanings."[4] London soul style blended African, Caribbean, and African American modes of adornment. Most of the youth who sported soul style had moved to Britain as young children. They lived in working-class communities, and though many of their parents had belonged to the educated, professional classes of the Caribbean and West Africa, they had been forced to give up that status in Britain. This diverse community had widely varying ideas about beauty, adornment, and feminine and masculine propriety that influenced how soul was performed.[5] Unpacking these politics reveals that soul style functioned as a diasporic mode of dress that linked Africana people in "an intricate web of cultural and political connections," binding them together as much through difference as through similarity.[6]

Since the seventeenth century, the British had used terms such as "black" and "coloured" to render people of African and South Asian descent social and cultural "others," emphasizing ethnic features such as hair texture and skin color to rationalize white supremacy.[7] The dominant ideology and practices proliferated by British slave traders, politicians, and historians resulted in the "cultural transmission of racist ideas handed down over generations."[8] In the seventeenth century, Africans were forcibly brought to Britain and its colonies as enslaved laborers. After Britain banned the slave trade in 1777 and abolished slavery itself over the course of 1834 to 1843, thousands of African and Afro-Caribbean slaves were freed. Many stayed and worked for their former masters or on other white-owned plantations; some migrated to different parts of the West Indies as free laborers; still others moved to West Africa to found Freetown in Sierra Leone; and a few moved on their own to British cities such as London. As they dispersed across the British Empire, ideas of racial difference became more solidified. Black migration to Great Britain rose near the end of the nineteenth century as blacks looking for work in the burgeoning maritime industry settled in port cities, including London, Liverpool, Bristol, and Cardiff. The rising number of nonwhite bodies created immense social disparities that were built on racist constructions of blackness. In Britain, "English" was used to connote whiteness (which was distinct from Irishness) and the culture and social norms upheld by the dominant white society. While nonwhites could make claims to British national identity, they could not lay claim to Englishness. Because of the entrenched nature of racism in Britain in the 1920s and 1930s, people of African and South Asian descent organized politically across racial lines, giving their organizations names such as the League of Coloured People as a form of racial solidarity. They used "coloured" as a politicized language that represented their similar and overlapping oppressions.

The massive influx of Afro-Caribbean migrants in Britain from the close of World War II to 1962 set into motion a new phase of the Black Freedom movement in Britain, from which Black Power developed. In 1948, the SS *Empire Windrush* brought to Britain approximately 452 Jamaicans who sought the bountiful jobs that the "mother country" advertised in newspapers across its Commonwealth states as a ploy to recruit laborers to help rebuild the nation after the war. The approximately 238,000 Afro-Caribbean migrants from Jamaica, Trinidad, St. Lucia, and Grenada who arrived between 1952 and 1961 were later identified in the media as the

"Windrush generation." Obtaining jobs largely in the transportation and health care industries, they settled in London, Birmingham, Manchester, Coventry, Liverpool, and Bristol. Students made up another large migrant group. Between the end of World War II and 1961, roughly 24,000 blacks moved to England to attend university, including some 12,000 West Africans, 6,949 Afro-Caribbeans, and 4,645 Indians and Pakistanis. Although the United Kingdom had no formal segregation laws, most of these new black migrants were relegated to neighborhoods on the edge of London that were suffering from extreme urban decay: Brixton, in the southern borough of Lambeth; Notting Hill, in the west-central borough of Kensington and Chelsea; and King's Cross, in the borough of Islington in the city's northern quadrant. They were often denied access to government-supported housing projects, called council estates, and had to live in multifamily houses managed by slumlords.[9]

"Immigrant" became a euphemism for "black," a term the state used in policing its nonwhite subjects. The influx of Afro-Caribbean, African, and South Asian migrants presented a social conundrum for the British government and for the migrants as well. Immediately following the war, the government offered British citizenship to those in its former colonies who joined the Commonwealth. In theory, citizenship entitled Afro-Caribbeans to the same rights as Englishmen and Englishwomen, but the promise of equal citizenship was not put into practice. In 1962, Parliament passed the Commonwealth Immigrants Act to restrict the numbers of people of color entering the country. Racist in its very foundations, the bill essentially marked the bodies of Olive Morris and other children of the Windrush generation as a social problem. The term "immigrant" branded these newcomers as foreigners who did not share the same social or cultural position as white British nationals. While the act did not specifically refer to race, it is clear that people of color from Britain's Commonwealth countries were deemed a potential threat to the state. Government officials used the terms "immigrant" and "black" interchangeably as a coded way to implement discriminatory practices against black youth. Afro-Caribbeans continued to migrate to Britain after 1962, but it was much harder to do so; those who had not been born in Britain, did not already hold a British passport, or were not a dependent of someone who did, had to first obtain an employment voucher from the Ministry of Labour. Members of the Windrush generation who had left children behind had to choose between returning home or finding enough money to have their children brought over before the new law went into effect.

Different citizenship status often led to intrafamilial and community tensions. Families often comprised younger children who were born in London, giving them British citizenship, and older children born in the Caribbean, branded immigrants even if they technically had citizenship due to their parents' status. Parents still made claims to British identity for their non–British born children—particularly once they decided to stay in Britain permanently—demanding that all of their children receive the same treatment from the state. However, these children often had different social and cultural understandings of themselves as black Britons, and these dynamics created tension among siblings.[10] The bill also created a broad racial category that lumped disparate peoples—some of whom would never have considered they had much in common before—into the same group in British society. Although people of color moved and traveled to other parts of the Caribbean, each island had its own national and cultural identity and island rivalries. West Indians harbored prejudices against one another, continental Africans, and South Asians, and vice versa. Yet the state's marginalization of these diverse groups created an uneasy and often confrontational sense of commonality among its black population.[11]

The experience of moving from the Caribbean to England was difficult for many Afro-Caribbean youth, most of whom arrived as elementary school–aged children. Olive Morris was nine when she and her three siblings, Jennifer, Ferryn, and Basil, joined their parents in Brixton in 1962. Like many other migrant children, Morris met younger siblings born in Britain, a brother named Errol and a sister called Yana. The family's cramped quarters in a deteriorating urban area came as a shock to children accustomed to the Jamaican countryside, where they used to swim, fish, and play outside until dusk.[12] Another youth activist, Janet Davis, was born in Grenada in 1957 and raised in Trinidad by a single woman named Millicent, who was a teacher from an affluent family. Davis and "Aunt Millie," as she affectionately called her adoptive mother, moved to England in 1969 when she was twelve. After spending a short period of time in London living among other West Indian families, they moved an hour away to Wellingborough, a rural town in the East Midlands, where Millie found work as a teacher. Although Wellingborough was a far less desirable location than London, Millie was fortunate to obtain this job; most black teachers educated in the Caribbean found that British school systems refused to accept their credentials. Davis, however, was struck by the foreignness of the English countryside. "Coming to England was a huge shock socially and educationally," Davis remembered; "there [was] no color in England." In Davis's mind, both the landscape and the people were drab in comparison to the lush greenery, humid air, and rainbow shades of people in Trinidad, who were often of mixed African, European, and South Asian descent.[13]

The children of the Windrush generation found it difficult to adjust to life in London. Many Afro-Caribbeans, particularly adolescents, did not have a Western concept of racial difference until they became a minority in Britain because Caribbean society was ordered on a color-caste system rather than by a racial binary.[14] Afro-Caribbean youth did associate notions of beauty and affluence with features that were more European, especially fair skin and wavy hair, but they did not draw a simple line between "black" and "white" racial groups. Remembering her own childhood in the Caribbean, where there were various shades of caramel, cocoa, and ebony skin, Davis claimed that being in Britain made her conscious of her race for the first time: "In the Caribbean, there was an awareness of color, but you were still one race of people." In Britain, Davis instantly felt as if she were an outsider, someone who was visibly and culturally different from the seemingly homogeneous sea of white children she encountered daily in Wellingborough. Her feelings of alienation were exacerbated when she began attending a predominantly white school. It was then that she realized "I'm black. I've got thicker lips and the hair on my head is thicker." The constant reminders of this difference meant that it became internalized. "You start seeing yourself as different," she stated.[15]

Hair helped to constitute what Afro-Caribbean teens considered a cultural gulf that superseded the self-image they had developed in their native islands. The hair textures of their white peers highlighted a distinction in grooming rituals that were inextricably tied to different cultural and social practices among blacks and whites. Even as children, they recognized that the elevation of English social practices meant that there was more value placed on the hair texture of their white counterparts.

Beauty politics were also complicated for mixed-race girls born in Britain. Activist Stella Dadzie was born in London to a Ghanaian father from an elite family and an English, working-class mother. Dadzie grappled with her own identity as she tried to reconcile her Englishness and her Africanness as well as her different class realities as she moved between life at the council estate with her mother and life in Paris among the African elite with her father.[16] Dadzie's mother encouraged her to suppress her Africanness with commands such as "Cover your hair" and "Don't go out in the sun." Her mother was attempting to teach her a set of grooming rituals that could preserve her whiteness and protect her from ridicule. Dadzie's mother also made overt statements about her racial identity, such as,

"You're not black, you're coffee-colored."[17] Raising black children in Britain was difficult for white mothers, who often lacked participation in parenting or financial support from the children's father or assistance from their white families, who typically disowned them.[18] In turn, it left young girls like Stella to cope with the paradox of being lighter complexioned with curly hair while also being the embodiment of white fears of miscegenation—a racist term used to describe interracial sex that produced mixed-raced children. At the time, her mother's racial politics seemed odd, especially after Dadzie traveled to Ghana to meet her father's family, which was "flamboyantly African, proudly nationalistic."[19] The blackness that her mother seemed ashamed of—represented by kinky hair and dark skin—was a source of pride for the women in her father's family. Though over time she grew critical of her father's class politics, after her trip to Africa she decided it was impossible for her to suppress her black identity.

Black girls who were born in Britain internalized hair and beauty politics differently. Emma Bedford's parents migrated from Jamaica to Britain in the early 1960s. The Bedfords settled in Leamington, a town in the West Midlands, where Emma was born. Bedford was one of the youngest siblings in a family of nine children, the eldest of whom had been born in Jamaica and was fifteen years older than Emma. During her adolescence in the 1970s, she remembered, "petty racism" still existed between black and white children, largely in the form of race-based name calling. Although she claimed to have been comfortable with being black, Bedford admitted that "the thing I wish[ed] was different was my hair. I always wanted long hair." She was the only black child in her class, and she remembered her South Asian school friends asking, "Don't you wish you were white?"[20] While the motivation behind their questions was unclear to Bedford at the time, she understood that children of color were experiencing a degree of alienation that they believed could be alleviated only if they could shed the most visible markers of their black identities.[21] Bedford explained, "Hair was a big issue . . . you look different, you sound different," and "you don't want to look, in any way, that people can pull up on it." Bedford's use of the colloquial term "pull up on" referenced how children would use a noticeable difference and then make hurtful jokes based on those differences. Some differences were beyond one's control, but hair was malleable and could be transformed to efface, or at least modify, blackness. In an attempt to look less black, the caramel-complexioned Bedford endured the "horrible hot comb" that was "dragged through your hair" in order to achieve a straighter look. Despite the straightening that gave it some length, Bedford's hair was still thin and not nearly as long as her sister's. Her sister was more beautiful in Bedford's eyes because she had long hair and could wear styles that looked more similar to the ones white girls wore. Bedford had to wear black girl hairstyles. After the straightening process, her mother braided her hair into plaits that resembled "ten little islands all over my head." The tiny braids were a reminder of her West Indian heritage that even hair pressing could not erase.[22] Carol Tulloch, who was also of Jamaican descent and lived in the English Midlands, considered straightening her hair part of a public ritual to maintain a European appearance. Remembering those days, she called herself a "'coloured' girl in European guise."[23] For Tulloch, hair straightening was a performance that constituted a betrayal of her Jamaican culture.

Most young girls in the West Indies wore their hair unprocessed throughout adolescence. Caribbean anthropologist Ellen Brown, who grew up in Negril, Jamaica, during the Black Power movement years, remembered that her grandmother, who wore her hair natural her entire life, never allowed Brown to straighten her hair. Instead, her grandmother would style her hair in "tight plaits with ribbons sticking out."[24] Davis likewise recalled that in Trinidad, "I was never allowed to straighten my hair."[25] In Caribbean culture, adults believed that altering the natural state of a young girl's hair would damage it and hinder growth. It was important that a girl be presented to society as a young adult with a full head of healthy hair as a marker of her feminine beauty and potential as a wife.[26] Conversely, in the United States, getting one's hair pressed or, later, chemically relaxed was a rite of passage for young black girls that typically happened around school age.[27] For Jamaican mothers and mother figures, the plaits and ribbons that Emma Bedford deplored were a marker of good parenting and home training. They performed respectability through their immaculate styling of their daughters' hair. According to Davis, hair straightening became more common only once Afro-Caribbean women had greater contact with white people.[28] Though there may be some truth to her statement, the hair care industry in Caribbean cities burgeoned as black women began to experiment with hair straightening.

In places such as Port of Spain, Trinidad, women debated about whether or not they should have their hair straightened in commercial salons. In the 1920s and 1930s, African American beauty culturalist Madame C. J. Walker expanded her beauty and hair care empire to the Caribbean, teaching Afro-Caribbean women not only how to sell her products but also new methods to beautify themselves. In the 1940s, Trinidadian stylist Ena Au Young traveled to the United States, where she received her cosmetology license from the Wilfred Academy of Hairdressing in New York City. Upon returning to Port of Spain she opened her own beauty salon, where she hoped to provide chemical straightening treatments to her Trinidadian clientele. Young soon discovered, however, that many women were resistant to visiting her salon, considering hair treatments a private endeavor. "It is only within recent years that Trinidadian girls have got over the idea that hair straightening is a thing to be done secretly at home," beauty columnist Kitty Hannays wrote in a 1965 issue of *Flamingo* (a pan-Caribbean lifestyle magazine that was also published in Britain and West Africa).[29] Because of notions of respectability, urban women considered it distasteful to be seen in public wearing hair rollers and did not want men to see their process of beautification. For some women, this shyness was tied to the fact that they used straightening processes to boost their position on the caste hierarchy, and public styling would reveal that secret.[30] Others held strong spiritual beliefs that hair was an intimate part of one's being, and letting a stranger run their fingers through it gave that person the power to affect one's energy. Likewise, if a woman left her hair on the salon floor, someone could use it to put a curse on her.[31] A younger generation of women who wanted to participate in the emerging global black beauty culture started to break with some of these views toward hairstyling. Hannays attributed the rise in public beauty culture to "American advertisements and products."[32] The mass production of hair care products marketed toward women of African descent made them cheaper and more readily available. *Flamingo* advertised hair care products and wigs, such as "American Lifelike Nylon Wigs," which made public forms of beautification feel modern and chic.[33]

Before 1950, there were virtually no salons in Britain that catered to black hair care needs. Young Afro-Caribbean women in Britain were at a loss as to how to wear their hair. They questioned whether they should continue to uphold the private hair practices from their home countries or assimilate by attempting to straighten their hair and having their hair styled in public like their white counterparts. These were important questions because being black, in both the political and cultural senses, marked one's body as a threat to the social order. Women of African descent had to navigate the politics of their hypervisibility. They may have wanted to participate in a public beauty culture that looked similar to Englishwomen's, but there was nowhere for them to go.

By the 1970s, however, the beauty culture industry offered one of the most lucrative careers open to black women. Hair care became a booming business in London, allowing black women to gain economic autonomy while servicing members of their own community (figure 5.1).

Figure 5.1.
Afro-British hairdressing student posing for a photograph after her graduation, circa 1970. In the 1950s, there were virtually no salons that catered to black women's hair care needs in England. By the 1970s, it was one of the most financially lucrative industries for black women. Courtesy of the Lambeth Archives Department, London, England.

Black beauty culture entrepreneurs established Dyke and Dryden Ltd., Britain's first black-owned hair care line. Dame Elizabeth in Hackney; Carmen England on Oxford Street; St. Clair's in the West End, owned by Lorna and George St. Clair (who were from Jamaica and St. Vincent, respectively); and Aquarius in Finsbury Park were among the most popular black-owned hair salons. These salons were not simply places where Afro-Caribbean women went to get their hair coiffed; they became a second home for women in transplanted communities that were usually organized by nationality: Jamaican women went to a shop run by Jamaicans, and so forth. Salons were homosocial cultural spaces where women shared food dishes from home and chatted about the latest gossip.[34] As the Black Power movement gained traction in London neighborhoods such as Brixton, black women began practicing their own standards of beauty.

When Stella Dadzie, Janet Davis, and other girls who desired to celebrate their black identities came of age, they moved toward the nascent Black Power movement, finding a language of liberation in revolutionary texts. Dadzie recalled that books such as George Jackson's *Soledad Brother* "took me on a journey into the Black Panther Movement, Black Power.

A quest, really, for self-identity."[35] Dadzie was intrigued by the writings and personal experiences of Angela Davis, who, like her, had studied in Paris and fled bourgeois black society. After enduring what for Janet Davis was four years of cultural and social alienation in Wellingborough, she and Aunt Millie moved back to North London when she was sixteen; she worked at John La Rose's New Beacon Bookstore in Finsbury Park.[36] After being in an environment that was virtually devoid of any black cultural material, Davis was delighted to connect with everything she believed was beautiful about her heritage. She dove into books by a range of black authors, including Angela Davis, C. L. R. James, Kwame Nkrumah, Malcolm X, and George Jackson. These young women also discovered a set of aesthetic politics that spoke to the challenges they faced as women of African descent in Britain. As they and other residents of their neighborhoods established more cultural institutions, this black aesthetic became increasingly important.[37]

Brixton's Soul Geography

By the mid-1970s, Brixton was "Britain's Black utopia with a host of businesses that projected a powerful, black aesthetic."[38] This flourishing black community became a center for a politicized leisure culture that drew teens of various backgrounds together. Brixton had been a thriving upper-class enclave in the nineteenth century, lined with mansions and miles of green land that gave names such as Acre Lane to main thoroughfares. After the war, a sizable Afro-Caribbean population moved into Brixton, joining an elderly community of Englishmen and Englishwomen who had been artisans, white-collar workers, and theatrical performers before the war. There was also an influx of new European migrants, including Turks, Greek Cypriots, and Irish.[39]

The term "ghetto" has a different meaning in Britain than it does in the United States. In Britain, a ghetto is any neighborhood in which people of color (who may be of African and/or South Asian descent) make up 20–30 percent of its population. Brixton, Handsworth in Birmingham, Moss Side in Manchester, St. Paul's in Bristol, and Toxteth in Liverpool were considered ghettos. These neighborhoods, however, had many fewer people of African descent than so-called American ghettos such as Harlem, the South Side of Chicago, and South Central Los Angeles during the same time period.[40] Poet and Black Panther Linton Kwesi Johnson attributed the rise of soulful youth culture to the development of black cultural institutions:

You know, all of us have this dream of going back to our homeland but as time goes by and you realize the [im]possibility of changing the material conditions of your country . . . you have to accept that home is where you are, where you are at any given time. . . . The majority of blacks are here to stay in this country. And if we intend to stay it means we have to begin to think seriously about building our own cultural institutions, establishing and realizing ourselves as a force within society.[41]

This soul geography directly contested the "geography of containment," the system established to police and regulate Africana people's spatial mobility, cultural and social practices, and labor.[42] Soul was as much about establishing something that was distinctly African as it was about generating and exercising collective political power. The focus on the political aims of a collective black community that encompassed all nonwhites has overshadowed some of the specifics of how soul was used to mobilize Afro-Caribbean youth in particular.

Brixton's record stores were an integral part of Afro-Caribbean communal life for teens and young adults. Around the corner from Desmond's Hip City was Joe's Record Shack. Also located in Lambeth borough were Record Corner in Balham underground station, Beverly's in Lewisham, and Reading's in Clapham Junction.[43] In North London, two record stores run by Jewish women catered to a black clientele, one in Stamford Hill and the other in Finsbury Park. On Stroud Green Road, where New Beacon bookstore was located, was a black-owned record store call Junior's; another, Derrick's, was on Turnpike Lane, and Fat Man's was in Tottenham.[44] Record stores provided a connection to home through the exchange of music. Purchasing albums allowed Afro-Caribbean youth to possess a bit of Jamaica, Trinidad, and the United States, even though they were physically distant from these places.

Because of the scarcity of space in Brixton and restricted access to small business loans, black-owned shops often had to be multiservice entities. Many of the early black record stores were actually beauty salons that sold records on the side. For example, in addition to black hair care products and wigs, Nat's Afro Wigs shop in Brixton offered the latest records imported from Jamaica. Black women emerged wearing Afros and "elaborately styled headties" and carrying the latest Bob Marley and the Wailers records.[45] Nat's blurred the gender line between the record store, which was tacitly demarcated as a man's space, and the beauty parlor, the quintessential woman's space. Together, hair and music were among the most important aesthetic elements of Soul Power.

At the epicenter of Brixton's soul geography sat Desmond's Hip City. Looking through Desmond's pentagon-shaped storefront window at 55 Atlantic Road, one could see, suspended from the ceiling, vinyl album covers of black music imported from the Caribbean and the United States. Posters of prominent revolutionary leaders and cultural icons, including Che Guevara, Angela Davis, and Muhammad Ali, were displayed on the walls. As this decor illustrates, soul music and ephemera were not simply part of an African American expressive culture. In Britain, soul music was a sonic potpourri of U.S. soul and funk, Jamaican reggae, and Trinidadian soca. This musical heterogeneity reflected both the origins of Britain's burgeoning black community and black Britons' identification with African American music. As a space where this emerging British soul culture was created, sold, and consumed, Desmond's Hip City was a critical nodal point in the community's soul geography.

Desmond's, and black-owned record stores in general, had an interesting set of gender politics. Typically, back-alley record stores, like barbershops, were considered homosocial spaces for black men. There, away from the eyes of police officers and community elders, young men could talk about a range of male-centered issues while digging through the crates. Afro-Caribbean parents raised their daughters to avoid these shops in order to preserve their respectability, which was based on their adherence to Christian notions of purity, piety, proper grooming, and diction. However, Desmond's Hip City was on a main thoroughfare, so young women could assuage their parents' fears of the "back-alley behavior" they imagined took place in the stores off the main drag. Desmond's, like Nat's Afro Wigs, was inviting for both soul brothers and soul sisters. The mix of young women and men transformed Desmond's into a hip social space where teens could socialize with peers of the opposite sex outside of school. Brixton resident Sophia Kokkinos, who was of Greek descent, recalled that "every weekend [Desmond's] would be packed with young people."[46]

Desmond's multiracial, mixed-gender clientele incited local officials' fears of explicit sexual acts and interracial relationships. The perception that black music such as soul and reggae promoted "whining," gyrating dance moves that involved swiveling the hips in a manner that some believed led to sex, reinforced a hypersexual image of young black bodies and black expressive cultures as a whole.[47] This image underlined the fear of miscegenation among government officials, who were already struggling to determine how to police and manage the growing black and mixed-race population. Politicians used scare tactics to denigrate black youth cultures in Brixton by linking alternative lifestyles and subcultures such as soul to criminality. For example, the reactionary political leader Enoch Powell described Brixton as a "bohemian" community that had a "shifting population" and was overrun by "criminals."[48] Indeed, there was an underground economy in Brixton. Kokkinos remembered that Railton Road was "the heart of the community," with "gambling houses . . . where people would congregate."[49] Illegal gambling could also be found in many predominantly white neighborhoods in the city, but politicians used the threat of sensual soul music, Left-leaning politics, and the "radical" dress such politics was believed to inspire to create a picture of black criminality and sexual deviance in the minds of the British public and to justify racial profiling and hypersurveillance in Brixton.

Many of the young people who frequented Desmond's and other shops in Brixton's soul network were affiliated with political organizations that were central to the neighborhood's soul geography. Several radical organizations established their headquarters on Railton Road, a southern extension of Atlantic Road. Nigerian-born Black Panther Akua Rugg mapped out the Atlantic–Railton Road political landscape: "Next to the Squatters' Union, there was the Black Women's [Group] house, and across the road, there was the gay centre (run by Aunt Alice, a blonde man who always wore an Afghan coat) . . . and then there was the Peoples News Services all in one little strip."[50] Rugg recalled that the BPM also had a house just off Railton Road. The younger Panthers, most of whom had migrated to London with their parents as young children, helped to establish Desmond's Hip City as the soul music epicenter of the community. Members of the BPM Youth League would daily make the trek from the Panther House to Desmond's. Their journey down the long strip between the BPM headquarters and the cultural hub of soul music, food, and hair care is symbolic of this interrelationship between the cultural and the political elements that defined London Soul Power.

An underground soul scene was a critical aspect of this soul geography. Afro-Caribbean youths hosted events called "blues parties" that functioned as a form of politicized leisure culture where alcohol was illegally served. The parties became a means for the black teens who hosted and provided the music, food, and drinks to earn money. Activist Michael La Rose, son of John La Rose, recalls: "We had to have our parties and blues in condemned houses because that's all that was available. You couldn't hire a hall, you couldn't hire a hotel. That was how it was in those times. No one would give you the booking."[51] Afro-Caribbean youth converted abandoned spaces into a thriving nightclub scene. La Rose explained, "You would pay an entrance fee at the door" and "a sound system would be playing and all the youths would come in and go through all night."[52] Kokkinos remembered that the rooms had "a whole wall of speakers" and "the music was so loud that the floor would be shaking." "There would be dancing, drinking. You'd have somebody in the back room; they'd be cooking up curried goat."[53] The sound system played music that fused reggae, ska, soca, and U.S. soul.[54] Because there were no black radio stations at that time, with the exception of a few pirate stations that were quickly shut down, blues parties brought a taste of the music and cuisine from home to London. But the atmosphere at blues parties was not always harmonious, as teens often got into heated arguments about their island culture. Jamaicans claimed to be culturally superior to those from smaller Caribbean islands. Many Trinidadians contended that Jamaicans were socially uncouth and prone to violence, which gave all West Indians a bad reputation. Over time, though, the teens consciously and subconsciously reconstituted their Jamaican, Trinidadian, and Grenadian identities into a pan-Caribbean-inspired black British culture. Because this culture represented something "down home," or indigenous to black cultures, the language of "soul" and "blues" as a way to describe their culture resonated with Afro-Caribbean youth for reasons similar to those of African Americans.

The few English kids who attended the blues parties were considered social interlopers. Kokkinos claimed that if you went to a blues party in Brixton in the early 1970s, "the only white face you might see is me, or my brother."[55] Though she used the term "white" to describe herself, she constructs whiteness as something that is akin to but different from Englishness. She used her status as a person of Greek descent who lived in Brixton to distinguish herself from the "white English girls coming into the scene" simply because it was trendy.[56] Kokkinos was a Cypress-born Greek whose family migrated to London in 1953 and settled in Oval, a neighborhood in Lambeth that was at the top of Brixton Road. Though Kokkinos was raised by strict Orthodox parents who wanted her to remain separate from the non-Greek children in the community, she was quickly lured into the world of the mostly Jamaican girls with whom she spent her schooldays in South London. It was not long before she started spending time with these young women outside of school, learning the customs and cultures of Jamaicans. "I just found the whole Jamaican culture to be most attractive!" Kokkinos declared. She preferred dating Jamaican men and soon became pregnant by one of her friend's brothers.[57] In a largely black community such as Brixton, Kokkinos felt less white and more similar to her black friends, who became members of her self-selected family.[58]

Although some Afro-Caribbean youth may have been bothered by the nonblack presence, blues parties were more relaxed than formal political spaces. Kokkinos believed that marijuana, the "holy herb," brought diverse groups of teens together because getting high was a universal experience. In the social space of the basement party, Kokkinos felt free to "go out there and find like-minded people."[59] Janet Davis recalled that it was the music that bridged the racial divide between people of African descent and Greeks. She stated, "Greek people love black music. They used to listen to it more than the English people, I think because they were discriminated against as well. So, you find, Greeks and blacks, there was an affinity." She remembered that the Greek boys in her North London community were often her source for black music. A young Greek man who lived down the street from her used to "dress exactly like a black guy: the hat, the coat, the drainpipe trousers."[60] He would buy the latest black music, and Davis and her friends would borrow his records. Though Greeks occupied a social space that made them non-English, they still had access to soul accoutrements, which made them a valuable resource to Afro-Caribbean teens who did not have the same social and/or economic capital because they were of African descent. This tenuous cultural alliance between blacks and Greeks, however, often collapsed in the face of political issues such as police brutality.[61]

Soul Style and the Black Panther Youth League

Although the Black Power years were a precarious time for black activism in London, the Black Panther Movement was instrumental in creating a cultural-political approach that appealed to Afro-Caribbean youth. In the late 1950s and early 1960s, many of the leading pan-Africanist thinkers in Britain left to support nationalist movements in West Africa and the Caribbean, resulting in a political brain drain from London. Many of those who did stay were growing old by the mid-1960s. Claudia Jones, who was instrumental in the development of the Notting Hill Carnival and other community initiatives, passed away in 1964, leaving Afro-Caribbean youths to create their own organizations and political strategies.

The BPM was founded in 1968, just one year before the violent confrontation in front of Desmond's, by Althea Jones, Obi Egbuna, Darcus

Howe, and others, largely as a response to rampant police brutality. State violence in Britain had a different tenor than it did in the United States. London police were more widely known for the intense beatings they doled out with their truncheons rather than for the gun violence associated with police brutality in the United States. Brutality in Britain was more intimate; an officer had to get close to his or her victim in order to inflict punishment. These beatings required a physical effort that often left the officer exhausted. Corporal violence had a particularly dehumanizing effect that was deeply troubling for the young people who were most vulnerable to such attacks. The BPM created an environment in which Afro-Caribbean teens such as Olive Morris could contest social injustice while offering them a sense of community that affirmed their Caribbean blackness.[62]

As the first independent chapter of the Black Panther Party to form outside of the United States, the BPM adopted many of the U.S. party's symbols, including the panther emblem, the Black Power fist, black berets, and black leather jackets. But while the British Panthers drew upon the imagery and symbolism, rhetoric, and basic structure of the U.S. Panthers, conditions in Britain meant that their organization was significantly different. The Black Panthers in the United States called themselves a "Party for Self-Defense," while the British Panthers called themselves a "Movement." Panther Hurlington Armstrong attributed the difference in names to the fact that gun control laws in London made it difficult for the British Panthers to wage a movement based on armed self-defense. While the idea of an armed movement appealed to many of the youth connected to the Panthers, it was not a reality. When they did employ self-defense tactics, the BPM largely did so using forms of East Asian and Israeli martial arts.[63]

The BPM's style of organizing as well as their dress drew high school students because, as Panther Akua Rugg argues, the London police were "targeting the youth as the unacceptable face of blackness."[64] Panther leaders such as Althea Jones actively recruited black teens to join the Panther Youth League, where they could learn how to arm themselves intellectually and to defend themselves physically against police and white vigilante violence. A woman like Jones, who was a strong, slightly older, well-educated leader of an organization that was generally considered to be run by men, would have been a great model for younger black women like Olive Morris. Jones also inspired many of the young men in the Panther organization. Linton Kwesi Johnson remembered that Jones, rather than the male leaders, made him want to join the Panthers:

As a youth growing up in Brixton I would see these people on the streets every Saturday with their newspaper, *Black People's News*. . . . And then one of the leaders of the organisation, Althea Jones, had come to our school to take part in a debate. I can't remember what the debate was about but I was very impressed by her, and I decided to go to one of their meetings. And I eventually became a member of the Black Panther Youth League and then a member of the Black Panther Movement.[65]

Jones was a powerful force in the BPM, inspiring young black men and women to expand their knowledge base by reading major black revolutionary texts. Olive Morris was one such young person. Like many Afro-Caribbean youth, Morris left high school without receiving her diploma. During the peak years of the Black Power movement, though, she studied independently for the A-level exams required for university admission; therefore, seeing a black woman like Jones who was pursuing higher education would have been motiviating.[66] Jones and other senior Panthers encouraged young Panthers like Morris, Morris's best friend Liz Obi, Geneva DaCosta, Stella Dadzie, and Jackie Blake to read Eric Williams's *Capitalism and Slavery*, Frantz Fanon's *The Wretched of the Earth*, and W. E. B. Du Bois's *The Souls of Black Folk* and *Black Reconstruction*, as well as works by C. L. R. James, George Padmore, Angela Davis, Huey Newton, Bobby Seale, and Eldridge Cleaver. BPM leader Farrukh Dhondy, a man of South Asian descent, remembered that Morris was "very bright, very sharp" and responded well to the teachings and philosophies of the Panthers.[67] Hurlington Armstrong, who became the BPM's minister of self-defense and security, stated that young Panthers also received combat training from martial arts masters. By equipping black youth both with the texts necessary to inform their ideological beliefs on issues of race, class, and power and with the physical skills to defend themselves against the police, the BPM was endowing them with the tools of revolution (figure 5.2).[68]

Much of the BPM's early activism against police brutality consisted of public campaigns and marches. Police violence targeted at people of color was not new in the 1960s; it had existed before the arrival of the Windrush generation. But those of the younger generation decided that ending police brutality by any means necessary must be their primary focus. Rugg believed young people were targeted by police because they "were not prepared to do the shit work their parents had done."[69] Most Afro-Caribbean adults were classified as unskilled laborers and relegated to the least desirable jobs—for example, as janitors and domestics—regardless of the advanced education or vocational training they may have had in

Figure 5.2. Olive Morris (*far left*) and members of the London Black Panthers, circa 1975. Morris joined the Black Panther Youth League as a teenager and soon became one of its most outspoken members. The London Black Panther Movement was the first independent chapter of the Black Panther Party to form outside of the United States. The London Panthers adopted some of the paramilitary styling and symbols (such as the clenched fist) used by the U.S. Panthers. Courtesy of the Lambeth Archives Department, London, England.

the Caribbean. Moreover, white teachers labeled black children incompetent and unteachable, consigning them to the vocational track instead of to a course of study that would prepare them for higher education.[70] Linton Kwesi Johnson stated, "They're trying to put us back into that demoralized position my parents were in when they came here, when, if you were in a factory and the foreman said 'you black bastard' you can't do nothing about it."[71] Young Panthers like Morris, Johnson, Rugg, and others were determined to combat that feeling of powerlessness. While stringent British gun laws prevented them from taking up arms like their Panther peers in the United States and Bermuda did, they employed the mobilizing strategies of organizations such as the Student Nonviolent Coordinating Committee.[72] Armed with signs that read "HANDS OFF BLACK KIDS," "FREEDOM from POLICE BRUTALITY," and "Stop Racist Attacks by Police," Afro-coiffed black youth took to the streets in the late 1960s to protest the racist brutality of British police officers.[73]

Both the BPM and an affiliated organization called Blacks Against State Harassment (BASH) recognized that violence against black youth was cultural as well as racial. A BASH flyer read, "These attacks on the Black Communities were, of course, principally directed at the *resistance* of dignity of young Blacks and at the *cultural* practices of Black people seen to be threatening to 'public order.'"[74] In other words, it was not simply that teens like Olive Morris were black; it was that they boldly engaged in cultural practices such as buying and performing traditional black music and dance, forming their own black institutions, and exhibiting distinctive practices in a country that upheld whiteness. The BPM encouraged such forms of cultural expression. This vanguard of activists was instrumental in creating a cultural-political organizing strategy that appealed to Afro-Caribbean youth, giving the Youth League members freedom to develop political and cultural tactics that suited the social concerns of their generation while also establishing their own black cultural aesthetic in Britain. These activists created a safe environment in which Afro-Caribbean teens such as Olive Morris could contest social ills, offering a sense of community for these youth and affirming their Caribbean blackness.[75] Like SNCC, which had created a cultural-political ethos of "beloved community" in the early 1960s, the BPM was a tightly knit community in which members became each other's peer group and extended family.

Because of their race, Panther Youth League members were marginalized from many forms of social life, including club sports and afterschool programs. London youths' extracurricular activities were largely structured around social clubs or recreational centers that were unofficially but effectively designated as white spaces. Black youth had their own formal and informal social spaces, but those venues were often shut down by the police, leaving black teens to venture into the predominantly white clubs in Brixton and surrounding neighborhoods. One such place was St. Peter's Church Youth Club on Brixton Hill Road. Until the fall of 1968, the club was predominantly white, but the number of black attendees increased after a local black club was closed. Once black students started frequenting the youth center, white youths stopped coming. By 1971, the membership was almost completely black. Likewise, at the Denbigh Road Community Centre, the opening event drew a crowd that was nearly 50 percent white and 50 percent black. Yet, because Afro-Caribbean teens came wearing the "attire of Black Panthers," white youths refused to attend the dance that was scheduled for later that evening, and out of those who came, only a few stayed until the end.[76]

Women in leadership of the Panthers realized that for black youth, the main battle was one for "dignity and identity" in which their clothing was critical.[77] Their attire largely consisted of Afros and cornrows, bell-bottoms or drainpipe trousers (closely tapered pants), miniskirts, African-print head wraps, Black Power T-shirts, and tote bags with Black Power patches stitched on them.[78] Once Afro-Caribbean teens began expressing their racial pride visibly, by wearing Afros and other symbols of Black Power, school officials and police officers deemed their soul swag "confrontational."[79] Michael La Rose remembered, "We had to battle to wear our Afros. . . . At that time you weren't allowed to wear Afros in school or little badges saying black power and other slogans or little pendants with black fists on them. But we forced the school authorities to allow that and we wore our Afros and we wore our pendants and badges and so on."[80]

The Panthers offered their organization's houses as locations where youth could congregate outside of the watchful eye of authorities. Olive Morris was a ubiquitous presence in the Oval House in Brixton, where the BPM held meetings and Youth League functions, including reggae dances and poetry nights, in rooms plastered with posters of Malcolm X, Huey Newton, and Bobby Seale. The Afro-wearing teens attended BPM events in their revolutionary attire. In one photograph taken by official BPM photographer Neil Kenlock, Panther Danny DaCosta is seen wearing a black leather jacket over a Malcolm X T-shirt while his friend Patricia raises one hand in a Black Power fist while gripping a copy of Angela Davis's *If They Come in the Morning* in the other.[81]

Youth of African and South Asian descent were welcomed at the Panther house, but white youth who lived in Brixton were not. For instance,

Morris's good friend Sophia Kokkinos was denied membership in the BPM. Because of her close ties to the Afro-Caribbean community and because she was raising a black Jamaican son, Kokkinos believed she was conscious of the problems plaguing the black community in Brixton and surrounding neighborhoods in the borough. "It didn't take a lot of looking to see the struggles of black people right here in Lambeth," she recalled; "when I'm now coming into the black culture and seeing what's happening to them from their point of view, I was not happy at all with what I was seeing and it did make me feel very militant." She further remembered "going [to the Panther house] with Olive and [waiting] outside while Olive went in to see if she could get me in so I could join the Black Panthers."[82] Kokkinos was greatly disappointed when Morris returned to tell her that the Panthers would not accept her because she was not black.[83] However, the BPM had several white members and supporters, including American film editor Jane Grant, who lived in the upscale Regents Park area of London.[84] It is likely that these people were allowed to join because Panther leaders considered them a financial asset to the organization. The Youth League, though, operated on a different set of principles where the more fluid social politics of the blues parties, which tolerated some race mixing, did not hold. White youth were not welcome because they did not face the same dangers or need the same mentorship as black teens.

The tactical, cultural, and ideological focus of the BPM and the awareness that youth cultures were a form of resistance to state oppression found its clearest expression in Afro-Caribbean women's employment of Soul Power. Morris's intervention with the police's interrogation of a Nigerian diplomat in 1969 marks the rise of this woman-centered Soul Power in London.[85]

Olive Morris and Sexualized Police Brutality

The feminist politics that Olive Morris developed while a member of the Black Panther Youth League became more central to her activism in the mid-1970s. As a youth, Morris was especially visible in the BPM's police brutality campaign because of her audacious personality and androgynous style of dress. I employ the term "androgyny," largely used in fashion circles, to describe not only Olive's mixing of "masculine" and "feminine" qualities in her gender performance but also to signal her agency in incorporating these elements into her personal style. Defining androgyny as a style choice allows us to move into a conversation about why young women who were part of radical movements were opting to use the fashions of the day to defy gender norms. Morris in particular used her clothing as a sign of her militancy and to challenge notions of feminine propriety. Yet, friends and family displayed a sense of unease with Morris's gender performance. Her friends and comrades loved her; therefore, in their interviews they tried to describe Olive without using language that they deemed disparaging or reductive such as "tomboy" or "manly." But, if we use the contemporary language of "queer" (a word that members of the LGBT community have imbued with a sense of pride) to discuss Morris's gender nonconformity and behaviors performed and read as nonnormative, we can engage in a more complex reading of Morris that affirms her personal choices while helping us address why there was unease within her community around nonnormativity. To be clear, the term "queer" as I am employing it would not have been used by Morris's peers in the 1960s; however, it is still useful because it allows us to (re)examine and historicize Morris's contributions to black feminism, anti-brutality campaigns, and local expressions of soul style.

We can read soul style as already occupying a queer, or nonnormative, space when displayed by black female bodies because of the way the British government othered its nonwhite population, treating them as inherently nonnormative. But Morris added another dimension to this queering by intentionally dressing against gendered norms. Aspects of Morris's violent encounters with the police were withheld in the news coverage of the day, but Olive's own account reveals that her gender was purposely misread by the police. They used her gender nonconformity as a reason to punish her differently than her male and female peers. Though Morris's peers claim she was heterosexual (and was known to date both black and white men), officers conflated her gender performance with their perceptions of her sexual orientation and made homophobic sexual threats. Unearthing this history of sexualized violence against Morris and using the language offered by scholars invested in a queer of color critique pushes us beyond male-centered, heteronormative narratives of police brutality and Black Power and offers a new genealogy of queer expressions of Black Power in the African diaspora. Morris's visible presence in the movement helps us think about the ways in which Soul Power was also linked to forms of gender nonconformity. During one particular protest, seventeen-year-old Morris took to the streets barefoot, carrying a large sign that read "Black Sufferer Fight Police Pig Brutality." Drawing upon the phrase "black sufferer," which was common in Jamaican political language, and the term "pig," which was used by members of the U.S. Black Panthers to insult law enforcement officers, Morris positioned herself in a transnational black struggle against police brutality. Her sign boldly called for those who had been assaulted to stand up and confront their attackers. Her lit cigarette, bare feet, and androgynous clothing communicated a youthful irreverence that transgressed what many perceived as the boundaries of respectable black womanhood. In this regard, Morris was similar to the young women of SNCC who traded their dresses, cardigans, pearls, modestly heeled pumps, and neatly coiffed hairdos for denim overalls and short, natural haircuts in the early 1960s.[86] Morris's gender-nonconforming style of dress was similar to that of many women on both sides of the Atlantic who were engaged in radical activism, ranging from the feminist movement to gay rights.[87]

While the androgynous look was growing in popularity, Morris's friends and fellow activists remembered that her gender presentation set her apart from others in the BPM Youth League. Gerlin Bean recalled, "Olive was always in jeans and T-shirts. I can't think back and remember seeing Olive in a dress. . . . She's always in some trousers or something."[88] Sophia Kokkinos shared a similar memory, remarking, "Olive wore jeans and comfortable shoes."[89] Stella Dadzie described Morris as "quite dark with a short-to-medium length Afro, certainly not an Angela Davis one."[90] In making the distinction between dark-skinned Morris's short, natural hairstyle and fair-complexioned Angela Davis's large halo Afro, Dadzie was tacitly saying that Morris's style did not carry with it the sense of radical feminine chic that had become attached to the U.S. media's image of the Afro-coiffed femme fatale—or to Dadzie herself, who also fit this physical description.[91] Although Morris was not the only woman in the BPM to adopt a queer revolutionary soul sister look, there was something unique, and for some disturbing, about Morris's portrayal of the soul sister image.

Morris's violent encounter with London police officers outside of Desmond's Hip City is an example of how deeply intertwined notions of queerness, blackness, soul, and criminality were in the minds of law enforcement officers in the late 1960s. The London police flagged Desmond's Hip City as a venue frequented by supposed criminals and activists identified with Soul Power (the Mangrove restaurant in Notting Hill was another such place). Constant surveillance and periodic raids led to violence once the predominantly black crowds at these venues began to fight back.[92] On November 15, 1969, Nigerian diplomat Clement Gomwalk parked his white Mercedes outside of Desmond's, planning to join his wife and children who were shopping inside. Upon seeing Gomwalk's luxury vehicle in front of one of their targets, the officers assigned to patrol Desmond's on that Saturday afternoon physically removed Gomwalk from his car and began interrogating him. Gomwalk immediately told the officers that he was a diplomat and was in the area shopping with his family. According to witnesses, the officers began harassing Gomwalk, accusing him of stealing the vehicle and lying about being a diplomat. Witnesses also claimed that, apparently dissatisfied by his responses to their interrogation, the police beat Gomwalk. The racist British "Sus Law" (law regarding the treatment of suspects) allowed the police to question, search, and arrest Gomwalk on the mere grounds that he looked suspicious. When this law was passed as part of the Vagrancy Act of 1824, it mostly applied to whites who were using the waterfront to conduct illegal transactions. As the black population grew in the mid-twentieth century, the Sus Law permitted a form of racial profiling that allowed officers to stop and frisk black Britons without cause. Many of the young people inside Desmond's and the surrounding buildings flooded out to Atlantic Road to watch this incident of police harassment, and the officers responded by calling for reinforcements.[93]

Historically, we have treated black men as the main target of state violence and thus have centered them in stories of the anti-brutality campaigns in the 1960s, but Olive Morris's brutal beating at the hands of the London police speaks to the sexualized nature of police violence aimed at black women—queer women in particular—that has largely gone unexplored. Feminist scholars and activists have written about Morris's heroism, but their narratives present her as a lone actor and tell the story with little historical or cultural context. Morris must be situated within the cultural and political crosscurrents in Brixton's soul geography, and her actions must be interpreted within the context of the political, intellectual, and tactical training she was receiving as a member of the BPM Youth League. Morris's confrontation with the police on that brisk November afternoon is described by several black feminist scholars as the catalyst that propelled her into a lifetime of activism.[94]

Morris's own version of the story differs from accounts that place her at the center of the altercation beginning with the officers' initial contact with Gomwalk. According to journalist Ayo Martin Tajo's narrative, published ten years after the event, Morris "ran home to ask for her [coat] and had shot out to rescue the diplomat." She "broke through the crowd to the scuffle" and "tried physically to stop the police from beating the Nigerian."[95] In Morris's account of the violent event published in the *Black Peoples New Service* in May 1970 (just six months after the event), however, she stated that she "went walking in the direction of 'Desmond's Hip City' and saw a crowd around the Mercedes." This point is significant because Morris was walking toward Desmond's not to break up a fight or to rescue a diplomat but to do what she and her friends did every Saturday: hang out at Desmond's. Once she arrived at the record store, she asked her friend Steve, who was standing in the crowd, what had happened because she had seen a police wagon making its way up the road. Steve informed her that "the police had just dragged off a black man into the meat wagon." As Morris and Steve conversed, chaos erupted on Atlantic Road as people taunted the police for assaulting and arresting Gomwalk for no reason. The officers, who now had reinforcements, tore into the crowd and accosted anyone who appeared to be a threat, primarily youth of color dressed in soul attire. Morris surveyed the crowd, which she remembered was filled with "people protesting all around." She looked back in Steve's direction and "saw four policemen dragging Steve away" as he yelled, "I've done nothing. I've done nothing." Moved by seeing her friend brutalized by the police, Morris repeatedly shouted, "Leave him alone."[96] Hurlington Armstrong recalled that the police dragged Steve into Desmond's, breaking his arm in the process.[97]

It is unclear how Morris became involved in the violent scuffle, but by all accounts she was brutally beaten. Although Tajo surmises that Morris intervened to save Gomwalk, whom she did not know, Morris stated that she did not even arrive at the scene until after Gomwalk had been hauled away. It is more reasonable to conclude that she intervened in support of her friends and Panther comrades who were also on the receiving end of the officers' blows. According to Morris, a police officer then "grabbed hold of my neck and said 'you can shut up for a start.' Then another two grabbed my legs and shoved me head first into the van. The three cops who threw me into the van then climbed on top of me. . . . Then I was turned round on my back and one cop mashed my chest with his boots and bruised my breast. Each time I tried to talk or raise my head I was slapped in the face. . . . I was kicked in the chest." As blood poured down Morris's face and throat, restricting her breathing, her friend Arlene, who had also been arrested in the melee, yelled at the cops, "She's only a girl you know," alerting the police to the fact that Morris, despite her androgynous clothing, was indeed a teenage girl and that they should be ashamed for beating her up.[98]

Based on Arlene's comments and Olive's account of the ride from Desmond's to the police station, it is clear that the police were assaulting her for being a black queer radical activist. The police responded to Arlene's statement by slapping Morris and snidely remarking, "She ain't no girl." Between the beatings that the police dealt out to Morris, Steve, Arlene, and the three others in the police wagon, they yelled out racial slurs like "Bloody wogs, this is England you know."[99] "Wog" was a term that whites used to describe nonwhites of foreign birth, usually those from its former colonies. "Golliwog" referred to a blackface minstrel doll that remained popular in Britain until the 1970s. Though the doll was male, the term was applied to black women as well, which served as a way to erase their gendered identities as women.[100] In both of its forms, "wog" was a racially charged word. The combination of "wog" with the highly offensive swear word "bloody" was an emotionally damaging form of social violence. Once Morris and the officers reached the station, she remembered, they dragged her out and kicked her in the back while one officer yelled at her, "Go on you black cunt," crudely disparaging Morris's raced and gendered body. Arlene was ushered into a different section of the jail by a female officer, while Morris was left with "15 or so policemen." Arlene called out, "Why can't Olive come with me? She's a girl you know."[101] Arlene's comment about Morris's gender was even more significant in the jail. The officers were well aware that Morris was not male because they did not house her with the men, yet they did not keep her with Arlene and the other women. By housing her alone, the police were marking Morris's body as nonnormative, neither male nor female, punishing her for her queer gender performance, and setting her up to receive more physical punishment where there were no witnesses. Through their action, they were also stripping her of her right to define her gendered body on her own terms. While it is impossible to ascertain the degree to which Morris's androgynous style reflected her own perceptions of her gendered identity and/or her sexuality (because she left no record of her thoughts on these matters in her personal papers), according to those who worked alongside Morris, she made no apologies about who she was and did not feel the need to assuage others' discomforts with her gender performance.[102]

As the night wore on, the officers' sexualized threats toward Morris, who was now separated from all of her comrades, became more severe. She stated, "The policemen who stood around me teased me about my sex. Some of them said I was a girl but I looked like a man. Others said 'No that ain't no girl, that's a bloody wog.' And they all laughed." This time they deployed "wog" to erase her femaleness because, in their eyes, black women could make no claims to femininity and thus did not deserve the type of protection that white women were afforded. By defining her as both queer (in the derogatory usage of the day) and black, the officers were asserting their white supremacy and denying Morris's basic human rights. Morris continued, "They all made me take off my jumper and my bra in front of them to show I was a girl. A male cop holding a billy club said, 'Now prove you're a real woman.'"[103] He pointed the black billy club at Morris and stated, "Look it's the right colour and the right size for you. Black cunt!" His threat of rape carried with it the stereotype that black women's genitalia were larger than white women's, which allowed them to endure sexual penetration more easily than their white counterparts.[104] Another officer ordered her to "strip and get on the table and give them a little demo." The officers' demand that Morris "prove" her womanhood by performing a heteronormative sexual act played upon stereotypes of the sexually available and lascivious black woman. It was also a homophobic attack because the officers conflated Morris's gender performance through dress with their own ideas about her sexual orientation. Reading Morris as a lesbian, the one officer employed his billy club as a phallic symbol of his power and dominance while using it to threaten an act known as "corrective rape." Morris begged the female police officer, who had returned to the room, to take her away. After telling Morris to "keep her mouth shut and they won't hit you," the female officer finally relented and moved Morris to another room.[105] She had Morris take off her clothes so she could search her and examine her wounds. Although Morris in her account offered no specifics about her interaction with the female officer or the motivation behind the officer's remarks, it is clear that, while their race may have placed them on opposing sides, they probably suffered similar forms of gender oppression within the hypermasculine space of the police precinct.

After being violently attacked and sexually humiliated, Morris, along with her five comrades, was charged with assaulting a police officer, engaging in threatening behavior, and possessing "offensive weapons." She was released from the jail at 6:00 P.M. and immediately sought treatment for her wounds at King's College Hospital, where they took photographs of her swollen face and body. Her brother Basil Morris remembered that he "could hardly recognize her face, they beat her so badly."[106] Eventually Morris was found guilty of assault, fined ten pounds, and given a three-year jail sentence that was suspended and later reduced to one year.[107] After Morris's encounter with the London police, Basil claimed, "she was public enemy number one" in the eyes of the authorities and recognized as a freedom fighter among her peers (figure 5.3).[108] It took great bravery for Morris to share her story publicly in the local newspaper. Victims of physical and/or sexual assault were often shamed into silence. Most publications that described the event omitted the sexual assault she suffered in jail. Police brutality was presented as a black man's issue, which disarticulated Morris's story from her budding black feminism. But her story

Figure 5.3. Olive Morris speaking with a woman police officer outside of Morris's flat at 2 Talma Road in Brixton, circa 1978. Morris had a stormy relationship with the police because she was active in anti-brutality campaigns and was part of the squatters' movement. She had no reservations about confronting officers when she believed they were infringing upon her rights and the rights of the black community. Courtesy of the Lambeth Archives Department, London, England.

undoubtedly moved other women, including fellow Jamaican-born activist Gerlin Bean, who went on to join Morris in establishing the Brixton Black Women's Group (BBWG).

As more black women joined the BPM in the early 1970s, they realized that a feminist intervention was necessary to address the dual oppression of being black and female. Black women were hypervisible in British society, but their voices were often silenced, even within Black Power organizations.[109] Like their counterparts in the U.S. Black Panther Party, Gerlin Bean and others regularly experienced instances of sexism within the movement, a factor that contributed to the disbanding of the BPM in 1973.[110] Bean recalled that women were relegated to roles as secretaries who took minutes and brought the men tea and coffee. Although Althea Jones was a prominent leader of the BPM, even she was ridiculed by male members of the organization. Black women used their hypervisibility as an embodied political strategy. It was daring for black women to publicly flaunt their blackness and womanness in a nation that defined itself as not only white but imperial, finding its own identity through its domination of colonial subjects of color and excluding women of color from the privileges of femininity.[111]

The celebration of blackness meant that the body itself became a symbol of black women's history of colonial subjectivity and of their power to redefine themselves on their own terms. Black women intentionally made conversations about hair grooming public as a way to draw attention to their blackness. The Afro did the work of marking their bodies as naturally beautiful. Black British girls were even encouraged to love their natural hair. Social worker Vivienne Coombe produced a pamphlet titled *Afro Hair and Skin Care* (figure 5.4) designed to instruct foster parents and group home employees on how they should groom black girls' hair in order to instill cultural pride. The guide suggested hair straightening as an option for children ten and up with particularly coarse hair. Yet an asterisk pointed to a message that stated, "We are not advocating [hair straightening] as a positive measure." The guide incorporated diagrams to teach caregivers how to plait black children's hair and included a set of instructions for three-plait styles, commenting that cornrows were "more complicated but ideal for very short and fine hair" (figure 5.5).[112] By shifting the conversation around black women's and girls' bodies, Panther women like Olive Morris and Gerlin Bean were amplifying a black feminist ideology.

Olive Morris was making her own visual statements about her place as a black woman in the London movement and in the global Black Freedom movement more broadly. In a photograph taken by Neil Kenlock in 1973, Morris is pictured with activist Liz Obi. This photograph was Morris's appropriation of the famous photo of U.S. Black Panther leader Huey Newton, who, thanks in part to this iconic image, had become the symbol of desirable black masculinity. Like Newton, Morris exudes an air of confidence and power as she is seated in a high-backed rattan chair. She had let her Afro grow several inches and had her hair braided into countless tiny plaits. Dressed in the soul style fashion of the day, she is wearing a butterfly collar shirt topped with a sweater, high-waist denim jeans, and silver rings on each finger. She is flanked by her best friend, Obi, who is wearing a flower-printed caftan and also has her hair plaited. In appropriating Newton's posture, Morris was rescripting the narrative of male-centered Black Power that dominated both the U.S. and the British Panthers' ideology. Morris and Obi disrupted the image of the black woman as the political sidekick or sexual consort to the powerful black male leader that often punctuated articles on the Panthers in the mainstream media. The photo-

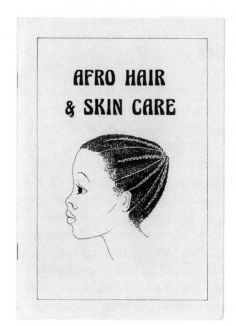

Figure 5.4. *Afro Hair and Skin Care* guide authored by social worker Vivienne Coombe for the Community Relations Commission headquartered in Covent Garden, London, in 1975. The guide was designed to educate white foster parents on how to comb their black wards' hair and cook foods that were part of the Afro-Caribbean diet. Courtesy of the Black Cultural Archives, London, England.

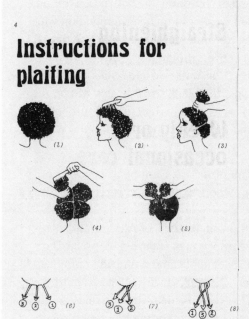

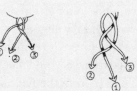

Instructions for plaiting

See diagram

Two Plaits: Part the hair down the centre forehead to nape of neck. Separate into three strands as shown in the diagram and plait tightly right to the ends. Securing with ribbons is not essential for keeping plaits in place but are decorative if tied either at the roots or at the end.

Three Plaits: Divide the hair into three sections, (aiming to have one plait at the front of the head and the other two at the back). Do the top plait first, plaiting either the left or right side of the head. Divide rest of hair into two sections with centre parting, separate into three strands and plait tightly.

Four Plaits: Divide hair as shown in diagram. Plait top two first, then include the ends of these plaits in the bottom ones. Tie ends together with ribbon or two separate ribbons.

Corn Row or Cane Row plaiting is more complicated but ideal for very short and fine hair. It is an ancient African hair-grooming technique, pretty, and a nice change from Afro. Part short hair into rows, creating the pattern as you go along. Pick up small pieces of hair and, with an underhanded motion, braid only the part near the scalp. Add the next closest pieces and interweave same until the row is completed. Tight braiding keeps the ends together. The whole look is so neat and free of upkeep that you can wear it like that for seven to ten days.

Figure 5.5. Hair braiding diagram in *Afro Hair and Skin Care* guide, 1975. Courtesy of the Black Cultural Archives, London, England.

graph not only counters the heteronormative revolutionary romance but also suggests that women could run the movement. Both in the United States and in Britain, women outnumbered men in the organization and did much of the work to coordinate its daily functions. The image is also a performance of a nonheteronormative intimacy, reflecting the emotional bonds that women within the movement forged with one another independent of men. Above all, it depicts women's political power to queer gender, which allowed a woman to "decolonize her body."[113]

Morris and several other Panther women created their own black feminist organization to address issues that affected girls and women of color. Existing organizations such as the BBWG, the Southhall Black Sisters, and Awaaz were relatively small. The Southhall Black Sisters, for example, had only about fifty members. But the number of black feminist organizations increased from the mid-1970s into the early 1980s in London and also in Manchester, Coventry, Nottingham, Birmingham, and Liverpool.[114] The BBWG met every Sunday at three o'clock at the bookstore at 121 Railton Road. Gerlin Bean, whom many consider the mother of the black feminist movement in Brixton, recalled the early days of the BBWG:

> The women from the Panthers used to come and join with us as women, from the other group . . . and then we would invite other women who weren't really aligned to anything to these meetings. . . . At the time it was the men who were in control of everything . . . so we as women decided that we would meet together . . . because we had issues as women separate from the national struggle, the black struggle as a whole. . . . As black women, we had our own issues that we had to work out before we could come together as a total group to struggle for all the wider issues.[115]

The group consisted mostly of women of Afro-Caribbean descent, but Asian women such as Anne Chang, who was Chinese, were also active members.

Morris cofounded the Organization of Women of African and Afro-Caribbean Descent (OWAAD) in February 1978 (figure 5.6). Stella Dadzie was also very active in OWAAD. Dadzie became politically mobilized after her first significant encounter with racism in college. Her initial activist efforts were with a group of Eritrean women who had immigrated to Britain to seek political asylum and were attending Warwick University.[116] OWAAD drew from various strands of political thought, including U.S. black feminism, Black Nationalism, anti-imperialism, and Marxism. This blend was necessary, perhaps even more so than in the United States,

Figure 5.6. Olive Morris leading a rally in front of the Central Library in Brixton in 1978. Morris and her comrades were protesting the police department's use of the "Special Patrol Group" to hyper-police the black community. This image has become an iconic photograph of Morris, which has been used to represent black feminism in Europe. It was also used on the Brixton pound (a local unit of currency launched in 2009 to encourage people to consume goods made by business owners in the Brixton community). Courtesy of the Lambeth Archives Department, London, England.

because the needs and experiences of women in the organization were so diverse; some had been born in Britain, while others were recent immigrants and refugees. The initial OWAAD meeting was a mix of women from the BBWG and university students, most of whom were African. OWAAD was originally envisioned as a pan-Africanist feminist organization that would link women throughout the African diaspora, particularly in Britain. But because Asian women were also victims of police brutality and labor market discrimination and of such gender-specific forms of oppression as rape, "virginity tests," and forced sterilization, OWAAD leaders decided to expand the group's focus to encompass all black women in Britain, whether Africana or not. Changing its name to the Organization of Women of Asian and African Descent, it served as a coordinating committee that worked with other women-centered organizations. Former Wailers singer Judy Mowatt's "Black Woman" (1980) became the anthem of OWAAD and other black feminist organizations.[117]

The Legacy of Black British Feminism

As the black liberation movement continued in Britain in the late 1970s and early 1980s, Olive Morris was admitted to the hospital, the pain caused by non-Hodgkin's lymphoma having become unbearable. Her movement friends Gerlin Bean, Stella Dadzie, and Liz Obi remained at her bedside. In 1979, the freedom fighter who had done so much to mobilize Afro-Caribbean youth died from cancer in her twenties like SNCC leader Ruby Doris Smith Robinson. In remembering Morris's funeral, her brother Basil Morris recalled that attendees "came from everywhere. The traffic in South London came to a standstill that day. . . . People came down from Birmingham, Manchester, and Sheffield."[118] Sophia Kokkinos remembered that those who attended Morris's funeral reflected the ways in which Morris spoke for diverse crowds in Brixton and the time in which they grew up; there were faces from the party scene, gangsters, activists, and academics. According to Stella Dadzie, Morris "represented a generation of women," but beyond that, she represented a moment of historical change in which people of African descent in Britain were defining "new ethnicities" and black identities across class lines.[119]

When we situate Olive Morris within the context of the BPM, Brixton's soul geography, and Soul Power, her story reveals a larger history about the making of black British identity and the diaspora. The quest for Soul Power, which charts the movement of Caribbean-born teens who moved to Britain during their adolescence, demonstrates how people of Afro-Caribbean descent became black British, black Britons, or Afro-British. While the term "black British" is commonly used today to describe people of African descent in Britain, it gained traction only in the mid-1980s in response to the Black Power and black feminist movements and the popularity of Afro-Caribbean cultural institutions and practices. Soul Power was central to the development of a black British identity because soul gave young Afro-Caribbean teens such as Olive Morris a language they could use to combat oppression and to create hybrid articulations of African, Caribbean, African American, and British expressive cultures. Black women in particular used the symbolism of soul culture to create a woman-centered discourse and activist strategy that spoke to their dual oppression. Black women moved throughout the diaspora, exchanging ideas about black womanhood, including attitudes about natural hairstyles and African-inspired clothing and accessories, and producing a cultural politics critical to the making of a postcolonial black identity.

Chapter 6 analyzes how the politics of dress shaped South African women's responses to black consciousness and apartheid. South African women who were seeking greater social freedoms had to combat the expectation that women would embody tradition. Soul style became a mode of dress that linked them to black British and African American women, to whom they often turned to as examples of the modern, fashion-forward woman. In South Africa, they used soul style as raw material that could be melded with Xhosa, Zulu, and Swazi fabrication techniques to produce hip, on-trend fashions. They also used their clothing as weapons of protection.

Mamphela Ramphele and Deborah Matshoba, prominent women activists in the South African Students' Organization (SASO), took to the streets in the 1970s wearing hot pants and stilettos. Their hot pants, which "hover[ed] tantalizingly around the limits of modesty," may seem like unusual attire for women on the front line of the student movement that was gaining momentum in urban spaces across South Africa.[1] For these women, however, donning this style was a deliberate choice with political, practical, and fashion-conscious motives. Young women activists used dress to challenge prevailing notions of feminine propriety and traditional womanhood, as well as patriarchy within the Black Consciousness movement and antiapartheid organizations. Women like Ramphele and Matshoba considered clothing that showed off their figures liberating, pairing their short hot pants with sky-high heels that accentuated their legs, hips, and derrieres, and wearing midriff tops or dashiki shirts in *shweshwe* prints while sporting "natty [A]fros." They resembled other fashionable women who dressed to impress. But, Matshoba remembers, they were armed: their stilettos were "dangerous weapons" that they were prepared to use to defend themselves when, as they could expect, they were assaulted by the police.[2] Matshoba's awareness of the dual function of stiletto heels speaks volumes about the politics of style for black women in apartheid-era South Africa.

Soul style, called the "Afro look" in South Africa, reflected both the gender politics of student activists and a vision of African modernity for a burgeoning class of urban women. While the two groups shared a taste for Afro hairdos, hot pants, miniskirts, and shift

6
THE SOUL WIDE WORLD

The "Afro Look" in South Africa from the 1970s to the New Millennium dresses in bold prints, they wore these garments for different reasons. Activists such as Matshoba wanted to look "real black" and used clothing to differentiate themselves from their nonactivist peers who straightened their hair or wore straight-haired wigs and used skin lightening creams and heavy makeup.[3] They espoused the transformative idea that "Black is Beautiful," which was beginning to resonate in South Africa in the 1970s, and many began using their African personal names instead of their Anglicized names.[4] Conversely, women who desired to be cosmopolitan considered the Afro look a fresh fashion trend imported from black America and black Britain. By wearing the style, they could imagine themselves as hip, modern subjects who represented the face of a new Africa. In both instances, these women were invested in projecting a woman-centered consciousness that often challenged normative constructions of femininity.

This chapter examines the cultural frictions that emerged within black and coloured communities in South Africa as young women from various walks of life began having public conversations about their dressed bodies. Because South Africa had no organizations that focused exclusively on women's issues between 1968 and 1977, *Drum* magazine became "an emancipatory space" where women engaged with the question of what it meant to be a modern African woman.[5] *Drum* had begun in the 1950s as a tabloid with a masculinist focus that glamorized gangster culture and sports, but in the era of the global Black Freedom movement it adopted a more race- and gender-conscious stance. The models, socialites, and entertainers whose images filled the pages of *Drum* became trendsetters. South African actress and model Felicia Mabuza, who was born in Sophiatown in 1950, wrote, "Although we do not have the opportunity White girls have of being trained in deportment, poise and modeling we should make the best of everything by taking tips here and there and reading magazines."[6] While men definitely played a role in this culture, fashion and shopping were gendered female, which made women central in both maintaining and destabilizing heteronormative notions of womanhood.[7] Women's ubiquitous presence in *Drum* and at the hottest nightspots represented black women's growing visibility in the public, social, and political life of apartheid-controlled South Africa. While their presence did not represent a black feminist movement, which was emerging in the United States and Britain at this time, South African women were using the opportunities offered by the black liberation struggle to fight for greater freedoms as women.[8]

Drum filtered its discourse around the Afro look through its own investment in a middle-class ethos of conspicuous consumption. The magazine defined the Afro look as a liberatory style that blended local textiles and beading and threading techniques with popular Western silhouettes. Yet it also linked these garments with a hip, jet-setter lifestyle that appealed to urban women with middle-class aspirations. Even among the nation's poorest women and men, adornment was crucial to defining liberation on their own terms.[9] The contestation over class politics became intertwined with issues of Western imperialism, as some government officials in various parts Africa contended that the Afro look was an unwelcome export from America that stripped African women of their pride and signified a rejection of local cultures and customs. Through its exploration of these imbricated race, gender, class, and imperial politics, this chapter presents a complex story of what happened to soul style as it returned to the African continent, where many of its core tenets had emerged.

The Afro Look in the Era of Protest

By the 1970s, the term "Afro" was an integral part of the black diasporic urban lexicon, the name of one of the most popular hairstyles for black women and men. But Afro meant more than a hairstyle; the word was used by blacks in the Americas and Western Europe to describe anything they believed to be of African origin. As a prefix in such compounds as Afro-American, Afro-Caribbean, and Afro-Cuban, it served to connect a racial and a national identity. This form of self-naming acknowledged that people's ancestors had been brought by force to the Americas and may have migrated to metropoles such as London, Paris, and Amsterdam after the abolition of slavery and the fall of colonial empires. "Afro" became a distinct marker of racial and cultural identity for a generation of young black people. For most Africans, in contrast, the term "Afro" specifically referenced African Americans and their culture. For example, African Americans who settled in postcolonial Ghana were collectively referred to as "the Afros."[10] Beginning in the late 1960s, the term "Afro," with all of its highly contested political and cultural meanings, circled back to the African continent, where it was adopted by some black youth in cities such as Johannesburg, Bamako, and Dar es Salaam. The soul style fashions popularized by black Americans entered the South African cultural lexicon as the "Afro look."[11]

The terms "soul" and "Afro look" were used by South Africans to perform different kinds of cultural-political work. Steve Biko and other leaders of the Black Consciousness movement were invested in a spiritually based philosophy that sought to remake the black being that had been damaged by a white value system. "Black" was an assertion of self, not merely an acceptance of the racial language employed by the apartheid government; it proclaimed the political unity of all nonwhites—blacks, South Asians, and people of mixed race who were classified as coloureds—in the struggle for liberation. What began as a set of principles developed into a large-scale movement over the course of the 1970s as black consciousness activists fought for their own social organizations and cultural institutions.[12]

For Steve Biko, soul was a cultural manifestation of the black self. In *I Write What I Like*, Biko contended that soul was "a culture of defiance, self-assertion and group pride and solidarity . . . that emanates from a situation of common experience of oppression . . . [that] now finds expression in our music and our dress."[13] Soul was firmly rooted in a grassroots political struggle that had a specific set of aesthetic politics. While the Afro look style of dress celebrated similar modes of adornment as the soul style Biko envisioned as a diasporic uniform of liberation, it was considered more commercial. By pairing "Afro" with the word "look," African tastemakers were communicating that the American-constructed notion of blackness could be packaged, sold, consumed, and performed through bodily adornment. The phrase "Afro look" had previously been used by the hairstylists who designed the first Afro wigs in the United States, giving the wigs names such as "L'Afrique," which referenced the style's supposed African origins.[14] In the United States and Britain, however, the language of soul style was still used to describe both the style of dress adopted by radical activists and the clothing that was being sold in the marketplace, though there were hotly contested discussions about cultural appropriation and commodification of blackness. The distinction in the usage of "soul" and "Afro" in the South African context is critical to understanding the class and gender politics that informed *Drum's* promotion of Afro look fashion.

In its June 8, 1973, issue, *Drum* ran an article titled "It's Afro" that defined the cultural hybridity of Afro look fashions. The piece offered a detailed description of a fashion show hosted by Johannesburg-based Topaz Creations, whose lavish "Afro Look" fashions were "catching on here fast." The photo spread featured statuesque brown-skinned women sporting halo Afro hairstyles or short-cropped coifs that represented the "natural" beauty of South African women. Topaz's "exotic Afro-look designs" included embroidered palazzo pants with matching halter tops and intricately crafted variations on the caftan. These fashions took silhouettes popular in the United States and London and embellished them with Zulu, Xhosa, Swazi, and Sotho beading techniques to create styles similar to those that were already "popular in the rest of Africa" by the early 1970s.[15] Both underground and mainstream fashion designers and college students and activists in the West had drawn much of their inspiration from their real and imagined notions of African adornment. Thus, the Afro look represented a multiply hybridized version of black style sensibilities, and this material culture symbolized the complex ways in which black culture had circulated across the African diaspora from the 1950s to the 1970s.[16]

In the early 1960s, many African women ordered their clothing from Western catalog companies because they believed that so-called traditional dress was an outdated remnant of their parents' generation. A decade later, largely motivated by the successful independence movements on the continent, African designers such as Nigerian Shade Thomas-Fahm and Swazi Zora Kumalo began drawing inspiration from local dress and adornment practices.[17] Indeed, dress was central to postcolonial articulations of African modernity.[18] Repositioning Africa in the international community was a major aim of pan-Africanism. This movement supported African fashion designers who offered new, domestically conceived interpretations of traditional styles. African designers held their own fashion shows. At "East Meets West" in Nairobi, Kenya, for example, designers from across Africa displayed their Afro look fashions made from local textiles such as East African *kanga* material, along with Nigerian placemats, beads, and jewels.[19] In 1972 *Drum* declared, "There was a time when African fashion was considered a bit of a joke in Europe. . . . But now African fashion designers are getting their own back and producing clothes every bit as good as the world's top designers."[20] Because the locus of power in the international fashion world had long resided outside Africa, African influences typically appeared as a fantasy or fetish of Western designers. This trend was especially evident in the Black Power era, when the African obsessions of European designers such as Yves Saint Laurent (who is credited for launching the first Africa Collection in 1967) and Thierry Mugler were displayed in their spectacular spring-summer lines in the late 1960s, 1970s, and 1980s. Through the Afro look, African designers, models, writers, and socialites wove together a world in which they were the purveyors of supposedly authentic—but actually distorted—African styles, constructing their own image of a luxe, modern Africa.[21]

The growing popularity of Afro look designs stirred a flurry of debate within the fashion world about the origins of the most popular 1970s silhouettes. Southern African designers and models argued that the mini-skirt and midi-skirt were African inventions. The Western fashion industry had claimed the miniskirt as a British original popularized by Bazaar

Boutique owner Mary Quant in the 1950s, even though Quant herself has stated that she was simply copying the women whom she saw outside of her shop window wearing the short skirts. Other European designers, including John Bates and André Courrèges, also laid claim to the miniskirt. But Israel-born South African designer Haya Rinoth argued that miniskirts were an East African innovation worn as a uniform with knee-high boots (similar to go-go boots) by domestic servants in the 1820s before becoming a trend among fashion-forward Tanzanian women in the late nineteenth century.[22] The history that Rinoth presents is likely not true. Domestic laborers in that time period, many of whom were enslaved, did not have standard "uniforms," like the domestic workers in South Africa wore in the 1970s. They likely would have worn whatever was common at the time, which probably would have meant draping affordable material such as *kaniki* around their waists. And they most certainly would not have been wearing boots. Rinoth's investment in linking the miniskirt to nineteenth-century domestic workers, however, warrants a conversation. By situating the ubiquitous mini's origins within East Africa's poorest class, Rinoth significantly changed the body narrative associated with the garment. Instead of symbolizing young, middle-class, white women's liberation from both the long hemlines designed to preserve their chastity and the trappings of their social class, Rinoth's African mini was directly linked to racial oppression, the marginalization of poor and working-class bodies, and the work of black women laborers in building and maintaining urban spaces under colonial rule. Like African American domestics who were forced to wear clothing chosen for them by their employers to distinguish their black subservient bodies from white authoritative bodies but quickly shed their work uniforms and adorned themselves in clothes of their own choosing when they went home, African women regarded changing their clothes as a sign of freedom, however temporary.[23] In other words, Rinoth was using the lore around the miniskirt to make the claim that African women have always been trendsetters. While there is definitely a disconnect between Rinoth's discursive mythmaking and historical reality, the story centers African women in fashion history. Rinoth's conscious representation of the domestics' miniskirt in the 1970s celebrated both black women's transgressions of markers of social difference and their position as fashion subjects.[24]

Swazi model Felicia Mabuza contended that the midi-skirt, a knee-length garment with a slit down the front, had long been part of southern African dress. The midi-skirt in the United States was also knee-length, but it had a fuller, A-line silhouette that did not feature the prominent split that Mabuza argued was a Swazi tradition. The more risqué skirt that became popular in Europe and Africa was often worn over very short hot pants. Mabuza, who was also active in the Black Consciousness movement, contended that African women "have been wearing the self-same garb for centuries now."[25] And she had a valid point. Tshidi women, who were part of the larger Tswana group, wore a similar two-piece garment that anthropologists have described as a "leather skirt and skin bodice."[26] Mabuza's claiming of the midi-skirt as Swazi in design was another example of African women centering Africa in discussions of fashion innovations. In January 1971, *Drum* ran a photo of Mabuza dressed in the Swazi garment next to another black model wearing the modern, Westernized midi. There is a strong resemblance between the two garments, although the slit in the traditional Swazi midi was more modest and did not require another garment to be worn underneath. While these images do not prove that the midi originated in Africa, they illustrate what happens when an African woman has the power to write her own fashion history. The photos also destabilize the notion that so-called folk dress and fashion were entirely distinct, supporting Rinoth's claim that African women have always had their own fashion sense.

In this sense, the African miniskirt and midi-skirt embodied the fluidity of notions of tradition. Another example of the fluidity of tradition in Tanzania (and other parts of Africa as well) was the shift from the *kaniki* to the *kanga* print. By the early twentieth century, Swahili women had abandoned the traditional *kaniki* garment associated with the "poverty and servility" of enslavement for the more colorful *kanga* print, which was linked to the abolition of slavery. Thus, it symbolized freedom, modernity, and a new social possibility for the Tanzanian body. By the late 1970s, the *kanga* print had been accepted as a form of traditional dress, while the *kaniki* was a marginalized relic of the servile past. Yet, as the myth of the domestic miniskirt suggests, a later generation may (re)claim such garments as markers of their ethnic past. This phenomenon has also occurred in the United States, as the Student Nonviolent Coordinating Committee's reclamation of denim and osnaburg suggests.[27] The Afro look's cultural-political roots lay in the murky space where high fashion met street style and discourses of oppression merged with discourses of modernity.

The children of the Sophiatown generation of the 1950s, like Mabuza, who came of age in Soweto in the 1970s not only listened to soul music but wore Afro look clothing and Afro hairstyles as a marker of modernity. In South African parlance, this in-crowd of black teens and young adults was labeled "hip," "socially conscious," "elites," "jet-setters," and "mods."[28] The word "elite" has a different meaning in the South African context than it does elsewhere. In the United States and Britain, the term is often used as a class marker. In South Africa, "elite" referred not only to those who belonged to the upper and middle classes, including indigenous royalty, doctors, teachers, and small business owners, but also to high-profile figures such as models, actors, and singers. Many of these people described themselves as living the Afro lifestyle because they had the money required to enjoy travel and luxe clothing. But, being elite was as much of a performance of an upwardly mobile state of mind as it was a label associated with one's income. Working-class people used Afro accoutrements to fantasize about a better life or to convince others that they belonged to the elite, seeking to efface the social stigma associated with living in the impoverished townships. The government made black and brown townships into ghettos by depriving their residents of equal access to education and employment. For township inhabitants, participating in and influencing the local black or coloured consumer and leisure cultures was a politicized act. Purchasing Afro look fashions and performing the lifestyle it connoted provided a chic way for ordinary people as well as social elites to transgress racial hierarchies, gendered social norms, and spatial boundaries.

Although *Drum* lauded the Afro look in haute couture, the magazine was also adamant about making the style accessible to ordinary people. This emphasis on democratizing fashion demonstrates how central issues of social consciousness and black liberation were to the politics of style. Far from being a frivolous pursuit, fashion was part of a monumental shift in the ways Africans perceived and projected themselves. In 1972, *Drum* ran an article titled "African Fashion Getting Its Own Back" that conveyed a message similar to many others the magazine had published on the Afro look between 1968 and 1972.[29] The spread included pictures of women wearing caftans, midi-skirts, gaucho-style waistcoats with matching pants, and belly tops with matching bell-bottoms made out of *kanga* cloth (figure 6.1). *Drum* writers instructed readers who could afford it to buy Afro look garments constructed from the vibrant but expensive East African cotton, encouraging readers to support African-made textiles instead of those produced by companies such Vlisco, based in the Netherlands, which had been supplying central and southern Africa with wax prints since the nineteenth century.[30] Readers who could not afford designer garments could make their own Afro look fashions: "The clothes are simple. So simple that any good dressmaker, simply by looking at these pictures, could take out her scissors and needles, and run them up quickly

Figure 6.1. African fashion spread that ran in *Drum* magazine in October 1972. *Drum* editors were encouraging black South Africans to wear clothing that celebrated local textiles and modes of dress. Courtesy of the University of California Library.

and cheaply."[31] *Drum*'s message democratized the Afro look and championed the power of women's scissors, needles, and thread in the struggle for pride, self-styling, and liberation through dress.

Fashioning the Elite Urban Woman

The many women and men who heeded *Drum*'s Afro look message helped to make the style ubiquitous among South Africa's urban elite. The Afro look was particularly important to South African women because apartheid restricted so many other areas of their lives. While many neighboring countries were gaining independence from colonial powers, the white South African government was intensifying the system of apartheid. Under these conditions, black women had even fewer legal options for exercising physical and financial power than their male counterparts. Spending money on fine clothing became a visible investment, and the public attention that the Afro look brought to dressed black bodies became a way to challenge the geography of containment created by the South African government. South African women were styling the self, or using clothing and other material goods such as skin creams, hair pomades, and jewelry, to create their own identities, which could vary from day to day.[32]

Model, actress, and socialite Nakedi Ribane remembers that most urban South African women of the 1970s were wearing "hot pants; long maxi dresses; kaftans; *dashikis*; mostly done in African prints and embroidery; big Afros; palazzos . . . platform shoes for both sexes; midis; and Donny Hathaway–styled caps worn sideways."[33] Other Soweto trendsetters such as model Thandi Kubheka and beauty pageant winners Lilian Thebe and Meisie Pilane were helping to make items like hot pants under midi-skirts and the halo Afro hairstyle fashionable.[34] Durban model Joyce Hudson and Port Elizabeth beauty queens Minnie Lucas and Shirley Nonjojo wore Afro hairstyles or stylish head wraps paired with garments in African prints.[35] Members of the burgeoning local elite donned these styles when they attended fashion shows, beauty pageants, and concerts.[36]

Analyzing *Drum*'s coverage of the Afro look in South Africa's black and coloured communities reveals the complicated gender politics surrounding the bodies of the black women who made up this urban elite. On one hand, young women were using clothing to challenge traditional notions of womanhood while celebrating the beauty of their heritage. On the other hand, government officials and older members of the black middle class were condemning these women for breaking with tradition and adopting Western forms of modernity. The gender dynamics at this particular moment of social and political unrest in South Africa illustrate how aesthetic innovation changed the cultural landscape from the grassroots level. These debates also reveal the frictions that conversations about adornment produced between and among black women and men, which led to a broader debate about black liberation in South Africa and the African diaspora. Given the political stakes of this era, terms such as "urban," "black," "Afro," "modern," and "elite," which were used to describe women wearing the Afro look, became a gendered vocabulary of transgression.

Rather than simply setting fashion trends, the young socialites who were seen as major purveyors of the Afro look and the lifestyle it promoted were challenging normative ideas about South African womanhood. Jewelry designer Nonhlanhla Ngozi from Soweto stated, "If you were a young woman, and you were urbanized, and you were *not* into fashion, you were not part of the elite."[37] Ngozi recalled that many women who looked too "rural" or "traditional" when they moved into Johannesburg quickly changed their modes of dress. For some the act of shedding a rural identity and adopting an urban identity was a liberatory act. Some urban young people were even willing to go into debt in order to dress stylishly.[38] The quest to be identified as a part of an urban elite had important implications for women.[39] Being an elite woman was at least as much a performance as a socioeconomic position. In black and coloured townships such as Soweto and Cape Flats, where most residents were impoverished, those who had access to a steady stream of income—whether through legal means or illegal means, such as sex work—or could perform the markers of wealth, such as speaking standard English, dressing in fine clothing, or partying in the finest establishments, "exercised enormous social and cultural power."[40] Women with high levels of visibility, such as models, actresses, and musicians, could build their own communities within the segregated townships. Clothing was a powerful symbol of social status that enabled urban women to efface the markers of their township identity, which some considered signs of racial inferiority. Apartheid centered not only on political disfranchisement and economic disempowerment but also on limited spatial mobility and cultural denigration. By performing a form of freedom previously extended only to white South Africans, these stylish, elite black women were able to project their bodies across the literal and figurative boundaries of apartheid. Joining the cosmopolitan black elite gave them greater visibility in the translocal public sphere.[41] Many used their cultural-social capital to promote a progressive gender politics that reflected a feminist consciousness.[42]

Drum was instrumental in highlighting the gendered politics of elite women's consumption and adornment practices. For example, in one piece the magazine followed two elite women with contrasting outlooks—Maureen Sims, a black Cape Town model, and Juanita Fleming, an African American who performed regularly in the resort city—as they shopped at local boutiques, arranged and financed by *Drum*. While browsing through clothes, Sims enthused, "I just love these new fashions. . . . They give women so much more freedom. But I think that if women are going to wear mod gear they should go whole hog." Fleming, who remarked that she never wore hot pants and miniskirts, countered, "Nonsense. . . . I think that many women think they are liberated when they wear sexy clothes but they are only fooling themselves. . . . They simply wear them to attract men. That's not liberation, that's bondage." Sims immediately acknowledged that fact but argued that women exercised agency and power in selecting clothing for themselves. "A girl cannot look pretty and attractive unless she thinks she looks pretty. I think that many girls feel pretty in see-thru tops." This shopping trip allowed the magazine's readers to be voyeurs into the world of upscale boutique culture, finding pleasure in imagining what it would be like to try on the expensive clothing. Along the way, the article explored the divergent perspectives of women who were "worlds apart in their tastes in fashion" and from different sides of the black Atlantic.[43]

This conversation has implications not only for gendered notions of tradition in South Africa but also for the differing histories of racial oppression that affected constructions of black womanhood and the politics of style in Africa and the African diaspora. The *Drum* writer framed Juanita Fleming as a "black lady," the controlling image of the morally upstanding, overachieving African American woman who is sexually repressed by the politics of respectability.[44] Performing the black lady required "aggressive shielding of the body; concealing sexuality; and foregrounding morality, intelligence, and civility as a way to counter negative stereotypes."[45] Fleming's choice to cover her body with knee-length skirts and modest tops involved a moral decision to conform to the dictates of feminine propriety in the United States.[46] She focused on deflecting the male gaze, which many contemporary feminists believed kept women virtual slaves to unrealistic beauty ideals and patriarchal control through their incessant efforts to please men. She represented a conservative sexuality that many middle-class African American women regarded as the necessary foundation of their sense of dignified womanhood. While Fleming did not represent all African American women's views of their dressed bodies, in the *Drum* article she served as a stand-in for U.S. race and gender relations.

Conversely, *Drum* framed Maureen Sims as a liberated woman who was much more modern and progressive than her American counterpart. Although sexualized stereotypes and notions of respectability also surrounded black female bodies in South Africa, they were not analogous to those in the United States because South Africa's different ethnic cultures and histories of colonialism shaped the nation's gender constructions and gender politics. Sims believed that wearing garments such as see-through shirts with bras underneath liberated the black female body. For her, women's ability to choose their own clothing was inextricably linked to their ability to define notions of beauty and sexuality on their own terms. Minis, Afros, and education were considered markers of elite Afro-look women, whereas in the United States to be elite meant to perform a respectability that veiled outward expressions of sexuality.[47] Sims's statements, then, offered a new body narrative for African women. She argued that black women should be educated, possess cultural and social capital, and break free from the trappings of middle-class propriety. Elite black women were creating their own gendered identity, constructing a new social arena and new markers of status for themselves rather than conforming to "traditional," European, or American lifestyles. By positing Sims as the face of a pro-sex, pro-body black feminism, the article decentered white feminists in the United States and the UK as the leaders of radical feminist thought.[48] This image of the "new" or "modern" African woman was important to *Drum* because the magazine was trying to appeal to its increasingly socially conscious readership while also seeking to establish itself as a cosmopolitan, cutting-edge magazine with a continental or even transatlantic audience. Moreover, *Drum* was invested in a diasporic quest for black freedom that was rooted in African nationalism.

The magazine featured advertisements and columns that reflected translocal tensions between elite women and women who adhered to traditional notions of womanhood. In various parts of Africa, elders associated women wearing short dresses or trousers and frequenting nightclubs called "shebeens" with youth and unmarried status. Once a woman reached marrying age, she was expected to abandon this lifestyle. In the early 1960s, for example, *Drum* featured a monthly column called "Girl about Town" written by socialite Marion Morel, who was the single South African woman's source for the latest news on South Africa's nightlife and fashion scene. When Morel became engaged in January 1963, she left her post, sending the message that a married woman could not be a girl about town.[49] Not only was she to give up her socialite status, but, according to custom, she was also to shed the dress of her youth and begin wearing traditional dress such as African printed housecoats and a head scarf called a *doek*.[50]

Advertisements reflect the dichotomy in the images of single and married women. Ads for grooming items such as Lux beauty soap, Karroo beauty cream, Miss Hollywood and Artra skin lighteners, and Body Mist deodorant depicted women dressed in fashionable Afro look attire in casinos and nightclubs. These ads reflected women's increasing financial independence and their disposable incomes. Companies often employed prominent models, beauty queens, and singers such as Miriam Makeba—exemplars of the Afro look lifestyle—to endorse their products in an effort to attract the socially conscious urban elite or those with such aspirations.[51] By contrast, ads for household cleaning products such as Sunlight detergent featured women wearing *doeks* and housecoats. While the Afro look's adoption of elements of local dress, including modern takes on head scarves, like the stylish West African *gele*, and Zulu, Xhosa, and Swazi prints, blurred the lines between the styles of married and single women, black South African society was still structured on an imagined distinction between these two modes of femininity.

Although for many black South Africans, traditional womanhood continued to be the barometer by which femininity was measured and defined, urban women were increasingly choosing a life of pleasure and indulgence. Nicknamed "Swinging Shirley," socialite Shirley Mashalaba, a nurse from the Port Elizabeth area of New Brighton, wore the latest fashions, had wealthy friends, and traveled to the best vacation spots. Mashalaba married a doctor but did not want to become "matronly." She told a *Drum* reporter, "I realized it was traditional for African women to remain in the background as far as their husbands were concerned, but I could not accept the role of an inferior being. . . . I made it abundantly clear that I wanted to be treated like a woman should and not in the conservative traditional ways of our people." Because Mashalaba had her own career and source of income, she had the freedom to divorce her husband and return to her active social life.[52] Although most South African women did not have this freedom, a growing number were seeking emancipation from conventional gender norms and using the Afro look to articulate a new understanding of womanhood.[53]

As urban South African women used fashion and media to project their woman-centered consciousness, they were met by a backlash. Even the pages of *Drum* were used to criticize women wearing makeup, faux furs, minis, and Afro wigs. In a 1970 article titled "Ye Gods, What Girls!," an anonymous male writer claimed that he had scoured the country's urban spaces to take stock of South African women's sense of style; in his view, this informal survey made him an expert on women's adornment. *Drum* published his scathing conclusions with a caveat that his piece did not reflect its editors' sentiments. Reacting to the growing popularity of wigs and cosmetics, the author described encountering the "unwholesome sight of a bunch of bewigged and heavily mascarad gouls" in the country's nonwhite neighborhoods. He did not attribute this "unwholesomeness" to a lower socioeconomic class of black women, commenting that even in "posh nitespot[s]" women were wearing "mock furs over sleeveless mini-frocks."[54] He believed that this contingent of urban women was ruining the social and cultural fabric of black South Africa. His comments about stylish clothes and the deterioration of traditional African customs were not new. In the 1930s, as South African "modern girls" experimented with makeup and Western clothing, the AmaRespectables—a name given to Christian conservatives by non-Christians—particularly men, used print media as a space to police women's dressed bodies and condemn them for shaming their elders and their heritage.[55]

By the 1970s, many of the so-called puritans or religious AmaRespectables linked the Afro look with crime and death. Women like Thoko "Butterfly" Ngubeni became the subjects of cautionary tales about what could happen to those who wore Afro look fashions and lived a "fast" life of pleasure and excess. Ngubeni was nicknamed "Butterfly" because of her "flashy clothes and love of nightlife." According to her sister-in-law Betty Mngweru, who helped raise Butterfly after her minister father died, "Thoko loved beautiful clothes and enjoyed listening to jazz records with her friends." Soon Butterfly became a Soweto socialite who was featured on the covers of local papers and newsletters. Many residents believed Butterfly purchased her fine clothing with money she earned by working as a prostitute and con woman who hustled black and white men out of money and fine gifts. Educated, elite women were already deemed a problem by Christian religious leaders, but urbanized women like Butterfly who were believed to gain their financial autonomy by working in the underground economy were even more problematic. On October 20, 1969, Butterfly's family learned that she had been shot to death and decapitated. Many puritans said "good riddance" when they heard the news.[56] They held Butterfly up as an example of the perils of "aggressive sexuality" and street fighting, which they considered hallmarks of gangster culture. Because of the scorn people directed at women like Butterfly who frequented nightclubs, some women would hang out in the shebeens at night in their stylish attire, but during the day they would wear clothing that was considered respectable, though gossip often revealed their double lives. Indeed, it is important to acknowledge the Afro look's connection to the criminal underworld; many township youths believed that illegal activities were a viable route to the elite lifestyle, which could liberate them from their township life.[57] So, while the condemnation of Afro look styles may have been prejudiced, underground life held great allure for young people who read *Drum*'s coverage of gangster culture.

Government officials were alarmed by the Afro look and the lifestyles it was believed to promote. Some newly independent nations banned Afro look fashions almost as soon as they became popular. While men also wore Afro look clothing, it was women who were the target of government proscriptions. In 1970 *Drum* celebrated Swazi leaders who bought Afro look styles for their wives as a show of African pride, but by 1973 the publication reported that Swaziland's King Sobhuza II and his national council had declared "no minis and slacks for women in Swaziland" because they "lower public morals." *Drum* pointed out that, ironically, traditional Swazi dress was often more revealing than a miniskirt by showing young women at a Swazi Incwala show (festival of first fruits) dressed in garments that barely covered their derrieres. But because the young women's garments were considered traditional, they were acceptable. *Drum* exposed the inconsistencies of the government's views on so-called traditional versus modern clothing. Editors warned their miniskirt-wearing readers to avoid donning such gear when they traveled to Swaziland. According to the magazine, government officials had already forced some "trendy cuties" to pay ten rand for wearing minis, while repeat "offenders" had to pay upwards of thirty rand. Comparing these fines to the price of Topaz Creations' luxe Afro look fashions, which ran between R3.99 and R22.99, makes it clear that the fines were rather steep. In other parts of Africa, women were fined and threatened with violence for wearing the Afro look. Even in Tanzania, the birthplace of the miniskirt according to Haya Rinoth, government officials and elders were saying, "The mini is just plain naughty," and warned young women that they "risked being beaten" or arrested for walking around "scantily clad."[58] These threats of violence expressed their fear of the freedom that young single women were finding by moving from rural areas to urban centers like Dar es Salaam. Yet Afro look designer Haya Rinoth told a *Drum* reporter that "if Felicia [Mabuza] had worn her [miniskirt] 150 years ago in the streets of Dar [es] Salaam, she wouldn't have raised an eyebrow of the most fashion[able] woman."[59] Clearly, Rinoth, who had lived in Dar for many years and must have been aware of its long history of "modesty" policies, was mistaken. Attacks and sanctions against miniskirt-wearing women in Tanzania continue today.

Nations like Tanzania and Swaziland can be considered part of an African bloc that envisioned pan-Africanism as a rejection of Western modernity in all forms, from fashion to feminism.[60] The Swazi government's problem with the Afro look was not simply that it was a marker of Western imperialism but that the style embodied modern gender politics. Elite women's remixing of traditional dress suggested that women could "queer" gender. This stance provoked fear because it threatened the distinction between men's and women's adornments; a number of traditional rituals were grounded in sharp differences between women and men. Many Africans viewed African women who wore trousers as imitating the androgynous style of some white European women, which they found troubling.[61] Moreover, they saw same-sex desire as a perversion imported from the West.[62] Despite and perhaps because of these fears, young urban women found it liberating to wear pants and dress "like boys." This liberated gender performance was particularly threatening in spaces like Swaziland, which was in the process of establishing a new national culture.[63] Women were admonished to represent the nation by adhering to tradition. There was a similar dynamic in Mali, where girls challenged traditional gender norms by wearing Afros, tight fitting bell-bottoms, and miniskirts, styles that transgressed notions of religious purity and public decency upheld by Islamism.[64]

As during the early years of the civil rights movement in the United States, black women carried the burden of uplifting the race by epitomizing upstanding womanhood. During the height of black consciousness in South Africa, women in particular were "called on to take pride in their God-created selves" because whites in Africa and the metropole had posited them as the antithesis of the supposedly chaste and beautiful Caucasian woman. Black women's bodies became the surfaces upon which Africans' notions of beauty, pride, health, and prosperity were projected.[65] Such patriarchal views about the sartorial performance of proper womanhood, enforced by bans on Afro look clothing, made it clear that, for government officials, racial progress did not entail sexual liberation or gender subversion.[66] *Drum* sought to counter those proscriptions, for example by running a spread that celebrated Ghanaian girls wearing miniskirts and large Afros.[67] It constructed Ghana as the vanguard of African modernity, perhaps because it was the first independent African nation and held a central position on the well-worn, multidirectional circuit between Western Europe and the Americas. In doing so, the magazine aligned South Africa with what it considered a more progressive trend on the continent, linking the Afro look with a transnational soul style aesthetic that was symbolized most visibly by the Afro hairstyle.

The Transnational Politics of the Afro Hairstyle

The cultural threads that made the Afro a popular transnational style cross and interweave in even more complex ways than at first appear. According to American journalist Stanley Meisler, the "Afro style clothes, the natural hair, [and] the soul night clubs" were a reflection of American opulence that "young, elite Africans loved."[68] Maria Obote, wife of Ugandan president Milton Obote, sported an Afro in public. So did the trendsetting flight attendants on East African airlines in Nairobi, an African fashion capital.[69] A 1969 *Drum* feature story, "Rema Doesn't Dig a Wig," presented Jamaica-born model Rema Nelson as a voice of the diaspora who could communicate what was trendy in New York and London. According to Nelson, "Practically all the good-looking girls were going for the natural look and wigs were out," which inspired her to discard her straight-haired wig and adopt an Afro.[70] Ordinary South African women, including student activists, were also trading their wigs for Afros as a way to reject notions of feminine propriety. Mamphela Ramphele's short hair was considered "boyish" by people in her community. She used to wear long, straight-haired wigs when she wanted to look respectable in public, but when she became a prominent activist she abandoned them.[71] In Africa, the Afro was both a fashionable hairdo and a political statement, much as it was in the United States and Britain. But others read the style as no more than a cultural by-product of Western imperialism and capitalism.

Some African journalists considered the Afro hairstyle an unwanted import from the West that eroded the cultural value of traditional hairstyles for women. African Americans, including the Grandassa models, contended that the Afro hairstyle was African in origin, though there were many claims to the contrary even in the United States. Wearing the style became a politicized expression of Black Power and pan-Africanism because it allowed African Americans and black Britons to reject white supremacy and Eurocentric notions of beauty. Many Africans, on the other hand, including *Tanzanian Sunday Times* writer Kadji Konde, maintained that the style was not originally African. Konde described the Afro as "a cultural invasion from imperialist and capitalist America" that "gnaw[s] at the root of the African personality."[72] His language suggests that capitalism was inherently antithetical to African people's consciousness and that those who followed such cultural impulses had been brainwashed by Western imperialism. Konde's story featured images of activist Angela Davis, presenting her and her large halo Afro as the poster woman for imperialism—a label that contradicted Davis's actual political leanings—in order to discourage Tanzanian youth from adopting the hairstyle.[73] African American expatriates like Joyce Johnson, who lived in Tanzania, complained about the newspapers' use of Angela Davis's image as a symbol of Western imperialism, arguing that "in this struggle for African world survival . . . all African hair styles can be defined as beautiful and should not be used as a tool to divide." South Africa's apartheid government employed similar divisive rhetoric to justify its ban on T-shirts with Black Power fists, a move designed to fuel debates over authenticity among student activists in hopes that infighting would weaken the movement.[74] While South African activist Steve Biko considered the Afro, and soul style more broadly, as transgressive and potentially liberating, for others it was a point of political and cultural tension.[75]

The author of the "Ye Gods" article that ran in *Drum* criticizing the Afro look claimed that the Afro hairstyle undermined traditional notions of beauty. He remarked that the elite women he saw frequenting shebeens were sporting "hairdos that remind you of the Capeflat's Port Jackson Forrest." Port Jackson, or *Acacia saligna*, a small tree with puffy yellow flowers, is a predatory imported plant that kills the local fauna in the Cape Flats area of Cape Town. By likening Afro-coiffed women to an invasive species that eliminates indigenous life forms, the writer was claiming that these women were strangling local traditions of hair care. "They are not the progeny of a beauty conscious ancestry," the article claimed.[76] In other words, women who wore Afros were not finding beauty in their natural blackness but abandoning the elaborate plaiting styles unique to their specific ethnic group and the commonly worn short-cropped natural style, which South African Miriam Makeba had made famous in the United States in the early 1960s, for the "undesirable import."[77] The author's response reflected his resentment of notions of "authentic" Africanness being defined and claimed by non-Africans, even if they were people of African descent.

The rise in popularity of the Afro wig in South Africa during the early 1970s added another layer of complexity to the discourse surrounding the Afro hairstyle. Pretoria native Lette Matthebe recalled, "Afro wigs . . . became a trend. I'm telling you. In South Africa in the seventies . . . it was the in thing."[78] As U.S.-based wig designer Walter Fontaine had predicted

in 1968, the Afro wig became very popular across the African diaspora.[79] The first ad for an Afro wig was published in *Drum* in April 1970. Columnist Vanessa King announced to her readers, "I have a wonderful surprise for you! At last the new 'Afro' wig, which has taken America and England by storm[,] has arrived in South Africa." King offered the wig to readers who could pay a two rand deposit to reserve one, since the R13.95 wigs were in limited supply (figure 6.2).[80] Soon other companies began advertising Afro wigs. A Durban-based mail order company, Selfast, advertised its "Curly Afro Wigs" for eight rand, which the company guaranteed would give customers "the glamorous look."[81] Pretoria-based company Enchantress Wigs proclaimed, "1972 is Afro year," selling the Afro wig for R7.95.[82] Though Afro wigs never reached the level of visibility in the advertising in *Drum* as they did in U.S. publications such as *Ebony* and *Essence*, there was a noticeable shift from the early 1960s to the early 1970s, when beauty products such as Lux, Ambi, Hollywood, and others started running advertisements featuring Afro-clad women. Many of these ads promoted skin-bleaching creams, which were the antithesis of the natural soul that the Afro was designed to promote, a fact that speaks to the different ways that soul style was employed in South Africa. While many women were opposed to wigs and bleaching creams, some saw these products as forms of freedom and liberation. Afro wigs allowed fashion-conscious South African women to exhibit the latest hairstyles worn by black women in Los Angeles, New York City, and London. For women like Ramphele, who were abandoning the artifice of wigs and the respectability politics that came with them and embracing their natural hair as a political statement, the Afro wig seemed problematic because these associations connected the Afro with a kind of respectability politics for hip, trendy soul sisters.

African wig sellers, however, were more often invested in showing their progressive young female customers that Afro wigs were transgressive. These ads often juxtaposed images of a housewife wearing a *doek* with hip, urban women wearing Afro wigs to symbolize their liberation. For example, Kool Look Wigs ran an ad featuring a row of three unadorned black women wearing what the ad referred to as an "old fashioned look": one had closely cropped hair, one had a passé press-and-curl, and one wore a *doek*. In the next row, the same three women were photographed sporting fashion-forward clothing and various styles of wigs, including the Afro wig, next to the tagline, "This is the NEW LOOK."[83] Advertisements sought to show that the Afro, a particular natural hairstyle imported from the West, represented a rejection of traditional South African womanhood.[84] While the imported wigs did create an air of exclusivity because they were hard to find in South Africa in the early 1970s, their popularity expressed more than a desire to have the hairstyle of black Americans. Many South African women considered the wig a sign of their power as consumers. Others believed that wigs brought out different sides of their personality, enabling them to put on and take off alternative identities as they pleased. Others, including model Felecia Buthelezi and writer Maureen Kumalo, thought that wearing a wig made them more "glamorous" and "sexier," which helped them attract men.[85]

The debates over the Afro hairstyle and wigs gave women an opportunity to have conversations about adornment politics on their own terms, which had a lasting impact on the South African beauty industry. Like the burgeoning black South African fashion industry, which women were steadily establishing even under apartheid, a black hair care industry emerged in the 1970s. The development of lucrative mail-order wig businesses and global discussions about black hair helped shift hair care in

South Africa from a private matter to a commercial enterprise. Before the 1970s, South African women were getting their hair done in their homes, and men were getting "pavement haircuts" from barbers who would cut their clients' hair on the sidewalk or in the backyard. They started to establish beauty and barber salons in the community as well as mass-produce their own hair care products after more countries imposed trade sanctions on South Africa as the global antiapartheid movement gained momentum.[86]

Legacies of the Afro Look in the Post-apartheid Era

Political turmoil, enacted both in protests and bloodshed in the streets and in conflicts over women's hairstyles and clothing choices, intensified over the course of the 1970s. The 1976 Soweto riots marked a turning point in the anti-apartheid struggle. The influence of the politics of style can be seen in the second generation of South African fashion designers and models, who came of age during the 1970s. They were inspired by *Drum* cover models; by their Afro-, dashiki-, and miniskirt-wearing parents; and by the political message of African beauty that undergirded new notions of African modernity. Their memories of the African-printed clothing, revolutionary violence, and protest songs of this era are ingrained in their bodies as much as in their minds.

In 1994, the same year that Nelson Mandela took office, black women broke barriers in the nation's beauty and fashion industries. Fifteen-year-old model Claire Mawisa of Cape Town became the first and youngest black South African woman to grace the cover of *Cosmopolitan* South Africa magazine. Her image on the magazine forever changed her life because she became instantly iconic as the face of South African democracy. She helped to integrate the beauty industry, facing racism along the way. She was the first black woman that most makeup artists and hairstylists had encountered. They did not have foundation to match her medium-brown skin or the tools to style her hair. This reality speaks to the ways that apartheid had overtaken every aspect of South African culture. Her presence on the magazine cover demonstrated that the new South Africa would have a black face. Mawisa remembered, "It was the same wave of energy that was sweeping the country [after the end of apartheid] that I was swept up in." Though Mawisa was still in high school, she had an awareness that "other African women knew I existed in the world." Her image reaffirmed the Afro look and soul culture more broadly, bringing to a mainstream audience a conversation that black South Africans had long been having within the townships. "People, still to this day, eighteen years later, still come up to me and they have their copy and they have that cover."[87]

In 2002, the internationally acclaimed South African fashion line Stoned Cherrie partnered with Bailey's African History Archive to use images such as vintage covers of *Drum* magazine and of martyred anti-apartheid leader Steve Biko on the brand's designer T-shirts. The firm's founder and lead designer, Nkhensani Nkosi, saw the T-shirts as a way to "make history a part of pop culture."[88] She wanted her clothing to reflect "the different ways in which South Africans were giving voice to resistance." For her, this meant recalling and celebrating the political leaders of the 1970s and the popular culture through which South African people established their sense of collective pride and black identity: "Over the years we have developed a design signature reminiscent of past eras: the fiery Shebeen queens, the bold intellectuals, the sparkly fifties cover girls and the urban energy that continues to sweep over the ghettos of South Africa. In an effort to rewrite our history we raised the humble crochet to the catwalk, emblazoned our heroes on T-shirts with the Biko campaign, and sought to transform the way Africans feel about themselves in twenty-first-century Africa" (figure 6.3).[89] Indeed, the shirts do more than make this history accessible to a popular audience; they exemplify the ways in which South Africa's mainstream industry in the new millennium increasingly reflects a black fashion tradition. The subversive Afro look culture that had been bubbling in the translocal black spheres of the 1970s became the inspiration for a thriving national South African fashion identity in the late 1990s and the turn of the century. Designers such as Nkhensani Nkosi became the face of South Africa's rebranded identity.

Stoned Cherrie's T-shirts demonstrate the ways in which the era of black consciousness are commemorated through adornment. When we think about how movements and movement leaders are remembered, we often think of the three *M*s: monuments, museums, and murals. We tend to treat clothing as inconsequential in the act of collective remembering. But these T-shirts, which were produced merely eight years after Nelson Mandela assumed the presidency, are at once symbols of South Africa's victorious political struggle and of the new directions and hybrid sartorial innovations that emerged in the apartheid era. Indeed, Mandela's own body is a site for all these meanings. The Desré Buirski-designed collared shirts in ethnic prints that Mandela, who was affectionately called "Madiba" by the people, wore and popularized became known as "Madiba shirts."[90] These hand-painted batik silk shirts, which Mandela

(left) Figure 6.3. "Table Mountain" dress from South African designer Nkhensani Nkosi's Stoned Cherrie fashion line, 2013 Spring/Summer Collection. The dress celebrates the beauty of the South African landscape by incorporating an image of Cape Town's Table Mountain on the garment. Courtesy of Stoned Cherrie.

(right) Figure 6.4. "Johannesburg Skyline" skirt from South African designer Nkhensani Nkosi's Stoned Cherrie fashion line, 2013 Spring/Summer Collection. The skirt, featuring a screen of the Johannesburg skyline, is one of several garments in the collection that celebrate South African culture. Courtesy of Stoned Cherrie.

wore at the dress rehearsal for the first democratic parliament in 1994, exemplify a history made tangible. Likewise, the bodies of urban teens wearing the Stoned Cherrie T-shirts became surfaces upon which this history was remembered. Youths wearing Biko T-shirts are living their history in ways that monuments, museums, and murals cannot.

The Stoned Cherrie T-shirts and the larger contemporary "Afro-chic" or "Afropolitan" genre of design they belong to connect this new generation of African designers to their design foremothers. The previous generation of designers such as Zora Kumalo, members of the urban elite, and ordinary women who innovated with the style laid the basis for an industry that celebrates local forms of dress in ways that the predominantly white mainstream industry of the apartheid era did not. Those of the second generation of South African designers, including Nkosi, Nonhlanhla Ngozi, and Palesa Mokubung, who came of age at the height of the anti-apartheid movement, have images of women of the 1970s dressed in the Afro look—oftentimes their mothers—ingrained in their memory. The body itself is a site of memory, and we are constantly "inscribing historical time on the flesh," allowing people to make meaning of their present realities.[91] Those memories have influenced their design aesthetic.

South African jewelry maker and feminist activist Nonhlanhla Ngozi says that her identity as a designer and activist was shaped by memories of her Afro look–wearing mother: "My mother never really became a traditional woman. She was more urban. She would take part in the beauty pageants." The women in the pageants "were more like rebelling. They wanted to wear pants; they wanted to wear the wigs. I'm telling you, they wanted to wear the Afro wigs. Those were popular!"[92] Pageants like Miss Soweto, founded in 1979, and Miss Black South Africa were black-sponsored and black-operated events that provided a way for locals to support and define beauty and womanhood on their own terms, while mainstream South Africa still celebrated white notions of beauty that were rooted in Western European cultures. Because of the growing black consciousness sentiment, these pageants were well supported by the black community. Ngozi's mother's experiences while winning trophies in the Miss Soweto and Miss Pirates football club pageants framed how she saw herself as a designer.[93] For Nkhensani Nkosi, who was born in Johannesburg in 1973, her mother was her primary example of how a woman should adorn herself. She recalled: "My mother is and was a very stylish woman[,] always well dressed and heeled. Her generation wore colours and prints and oversized sunglasses which I still adore. . . . Everything that I saw my mother wearing exuded confidence, sophistication and a very defined sense of self."[94] This idea of searching for and connecting to one's roots helped to propel soul style across the diaspora and into a global fashion trend. The style was rooted in notions of cultural belonging and self-discovery through studying the past as much as it was in ideologies of political solidarity. Out of this body memory, South Africans began to establish a national dress culture that upheld a vision of South Africa that was not founded in whiteness (figure 6.4).

One final thread unites the past and present. Stoned Cherrie's Biko and *Drum* T-shirts represent a cultural form through which the so-called global hip hop generation remembers the soul style era of the 1970s. The T-shirts have brought the vibrant history of apartheid-era South Africa to life, much as Angela Davis, Assata Shakur, Malcolm X, and Che Guevara T-shirts have reinscribed memories of past struggles onto the bodies of black youth in Britain and the Americas. Critics of shirts like these argue that they demonstrate the ways in which we have commodified and capitalized political activism. While the commercial element of fashion innovation is undeniable, the stories in this book demonstrate that such shirts are also part of a longer history to which the politics of style are central. These T-shirts enable the wearers, whether consciously or not, to participate in a collective remembering of the era of black freedom and black feminism across the diaspora. Retracing the history of the development and proliferation of soul style across the black world illuminates the creative ways in which entertainers, student activists, and ordinary people used their dressed bodies as sites of resistance and self-expression. With this history in mind, we can never look at a Biko, Angela Davis, Malcolm X, or Che Guevara T-shirt the same way again.

EPILOGUE

For Chelsea: Soul Style in the New Millennium

A colleague told me a story about one of his college students, a young African American woman named Chelsea, who was interested in black women's hair politics. Chelsea wanted to examine how black women her age used YouTube as a space where they could discuss natural hair care. Do-it-yourself hair care was a huge trend, and several vloggers had secured endorsement deals and corporate advertisers on their YouTube channels. Perceptively, Chelsea believed there was more at stake than simply a conversation around the commodification of black women's hair, but she was unsure about how to frame her research interests. My colleague informed her that in order to truly understand the dynamics occurring in the twenty-first century, she needed to read some of my work on the politics of style in the mid-twentieth century. He told me that he printed out some of my earlier work and gave it to her to read. My colleague's recounting of this exchange with his student solidified my reasons for writing this book. I could relate to Chelsea and her desire to know and understand her own history, culture, and the politics surrounding our adorned bodies that we as black women must negotiate daily as we move through the world. I write for the Chelseas of the world because I was once a Chelsea—a young black woman at a predominantly white university using my scholarly work to make sense of my own raced and gendered body.

This book was also born out of my attempt to make sense of my legacy as the daughter of a black feminist activist who designed and made her own clothes. In the late 1990s, I left my predominantly black community in Fort Wayne, Indiana, and headed three hours south to Indiana University in Bloomington. My mother's stories of her encounters with the Ku Klux Klan there were still vivid in my head. But I also remembered stories filled with laughter and pleasure as she shared memories of her and her black peers "stylin'" in African-printed garments, bell-bottoms, and Afro hairstyles when they attended parties sponsored by IU's black student organizations. These were moments of pride, moments in which they felt proud to be black, although they were few in number in southern Indiana. I remembered her stories of the violence and pleasure of her freshman year in 1972 as I graduated from IU exactly three decades later.

My mother and famous women like Nina Simone and Miriam Makeba, who challenged conventional notions of beauty in their own ways, helped me grapple with what black beauty meant to me once I decided to cut my chemically processed hair. After I completed my bachelor's degree at IU in May 2002, I returned to my hometown of Fort Wayne and asked my childhood hairstylist to cut my hair into a close-cropped TWA—a teeny-weeny Afro. Looking in the mirror after my big chop, I felt like I had been liberated in some inexplicable way. Yet, I did not instantly feel beautiful. I had grown accustomed to my processed hair, and without it I felt naked and exposed. It was during my transition from processed to natural hair that I discovered Nina Simone. Images of Simone and other black women activists and entertainers who wore their hair in natural hairstyles made me feel like I was part of a lineage of women who also had abandoned their processed coifs. Like my au naturel idols, I accessorized my natural hairstyle with ornate earrings and necklaces. Now, I not only felt beautiful but was also comforted by my belief that I had accomplished some *she*roic feat by cutting off my hair. I sensed closeness to my foremothers who had also endured the ridicule of many of their friends and family members and of members of the opposite sex who did not approve of their choice to go natural. Cutting my hair was a rite of passage that allowed me to travel the same road that my mother had taken when she traded her press-and-curl for a huge "Freedom 'fro" in the late 1960s. I was now a part of this collective of kinky-haired black women. I desired to learn more about the everyday black women like my mother as well as the celebrities who sported natural hairstyles as they came of age during the soul style era of the 1960s and 1970s. I believed that by learning more about my foremothers and their journey, I could more fully understand and appreciate my own identity as a black woman.

Early in my research, I considered the women who popularized the Afro in the 1960s and 1970s "authentic" soul sisters whom I could and should emulate. As I continued to grow intellectually and personally, however, I realized that I had placed my soul-styled foremothers in a narrow box. Once I gave up the need to classify all natural-haired black women as heroines in order to preserve my image of them and the role I needed them to play in *my* life, I was able to broaden my analytical framework in order to probe deeper into *their* lives. Writing *Liberated Threads* has allowed me to explore the diverse, controversial, and often contradictory reasons why women decided to join the movement and to challenge conventional standards of beauty and adornment. In doing so, I have aimed to present what I call "usable history," a story that looks beyond the "big event" history of the movement to reveal the importance of quotidian practices, such as getting dressed and styling one's hair, for the countless black women who put their bodies on the line in their pursuit of justice and equality. Bringing the story to the level of the everyday makes the people, their actions, and their tactics more relatable to a younger generation of activists who are fighting for social justice while still having to prove that black lives matter. I wanted to tell a nuanced story of the Soul Power era in which their activist foremothers' lives would inspire students like Chelsea.

One of my major goals was to provide a framework for how to think about how and why style circulates across national boundaries. The circuit of exchange that I mapped out in the 1960s and 1970s continues to flow. For example, in recent years, soul style fashions have become popular again. Garments and accessories in African prints are ubiquitous on style blogs as celebrities from Beyoncé and Michelle Obama to Gwen Stefani have rocked the styles. Today, a dynamic similar to that of the 1970s, when major ready-to-wear lines began mass-producing the styles created by African designers that were worn and copied by black college students, is occurring. Modern designers are remixing the styles and techniques of 1960s Afro look designers like Shade Thomas-Fahm, bringing them to a global, new millennium audience. South Africa's Nkhensani Nkosi of Stoned Cherrie and Palesa Mokubung of Mantsho and Nigerian designer Amaka Osakwe of Maki Oh have received praise for their innovative designs from the mainstream fashion industry. In 2013, Maki Oh launched a video campaign—featuring music by Solange Knowles—that went viral. That summer, First Lady Michelle Obama wore a Maki Oh *adire* print top with a strata panel skirt designed by Ghanaian label Osei Duro to a youth day event sponsored by MTV in Johannesburg. These designers' savvy use of social media is drawing in a larger international clientele. And with the growing number of online stores such as Zuvaa, founded by Kelechi Edozie-Anyadiegwu, women on the continent and around the world can have greater access to garments produced by African designers than they could in the 1970s.

A number of other U.S.- and European-based companies have started mass-producing imitations of African textiles and silhouettes. J. Crew, best known for its "summer in the Hamptons" wear, has even partnered with Bantu Wax, an African beach and surf lifestyle brand. Ethiopian designer Yodit Eklund launched Bantu Wax in 2008, tagging it "real swimwear from the real Africa."[1] Many U.S.- and European-based companies are moving their operations to the continent. British online fashion retailer ASOS has partnered with Kenyan production workshop SOKO to produce its ASOS Africa line. A portion of the proceeds reportedly go directly to SOKO, allowing the company to employ local workers, most of whom are women, supplying them with free lunches and on-site child care.[2]

But what this next generation of scholars and activists such as Chelsea will have to grapple with is the geopolitics of the United States' relationship with the burgeoning African fashion industry and how such politics ultimately grow America's empire. The United States has dominated other African markets—oil, copper, and diamonds—for centuries. Fashion is the new frontier.[3] Some activists are already concerned about labor exploitation now that economists are predicting that "the next Asia is Africa" as multinational companies scurry to find cheap labor. Under the guise of the African Growth and Opportunity Act (AGOA) established in 2000, the U.S. government has invested large sums of money in the African fashion market, offering trade preferences and tax breaks to designers like Yodit Eklund. Other African designers and textile producers, particularly in southern Africa, have taken advantage of the AGOA incentives. The AGOA program is so new that we are unable to assess its long-term effects, and lawmakers are still debating whether or not they want to extend the legislation and, if so, for how long.[4] It is clear, however, that without partnerships with Western investors, many African designers would not be able to launch their lines internationally due to exorbitant import tariffs. Such unequal power relationships give the United States control to shape the economic contours of Africa's fashion industry.

But this should not be a story that is told merely through the eyes of Western domination and exploitation. Fashion is part of a larger debate on the continent regarding how much African nations should depend on foreign aid. The issue was even addressed on an episode of the Ghana-based web series *An African City*, often dubbed the African version of the U.S. television series *Sex and the City*. As African nations continue to build their economies, investors are keen to control their own financial futures.

Some businesses are opting to seek funding from private, African-owned investment firms and partnerships with African-based international organizations. Keeping the economic power on the continent allows African fashion designers to counter Western paradigms of "authentic" Africanness. Fashion shows and fashion magazines such as *Abina*, *Agoo*, and *Oh Yes!* produced on the continent become spaces where African designers can (re)define what is fashionable on their own terms. Fashion and style politics is still a growing field for scholars in African American and African diaspora studies. We will need to continue to bridge different disciplines and develop new methodologies to deal with these complex issues that are unfolding in the world of fashion in the new millennium. They are the key to understanding so many other economic, political, and social issues in the diaspora. I hope this book will give the Chelseas of the world the courage to do so.

Notes

1. Lakesia Johnson began doing some of this analysis of Davis's clothing in the FBI photographs in *Iconic*, 17–18.

2. "FBI Places Angela Davis on List of Its 10 Most Wanted Fugitives," *Chicago Tribune*, August 19, 1970, 2.

3. Maurice Peterson, "Movies: Angela Davis: Portrait of a Revolutionary," *Essence*, June 1972, 22.

4. Nadelson, *Who is Angela Davis?*, 5. Black women's bodies are often hypersexualized, even when they are dressed in clothing similar to their white counterparts' clothing. This phenomenon dates back to slavery, when enslaved women were subject to sexual assault by white plantation owners. It also explains why freedwomen dressed in the prevailing Victorian style in order to claim their own sense of "respectability." They were still denigrated, however, and their bodies were marked as deviant and lascivious.

5. Craig, *Ain't I a Beauty Queen?*, 101–4.

6. Amye Glover-Ford interview.

7. Kenlock, "Photographs."

8. Stanley Meisler, "Afros: Truly African?," *Washington Post, Times Herald*, December 13, 1970, K21, 23; Ivaska, *Cultured States*, 79–81. See also Diawara, "1960s in Bamako."

9. A. Davis, "Afro Images," 24.

10. Miller, *Slaves to Fashion*, 1. For more on the appeal of soul style for young consumers, see Van Deburg, *New Day in Babylon*; and Walker, "Black Is Profitable."

11. There is a growing body of scholarship on race, gender, dress, and body politics in the United States. See Chappell, Hutchinson, and Ward, "'Dress Modestly and Neatly'"; Entwistle, *The Fashioned Body*; White and White, *Stylin'*; Baldwin, *Chicago's New Negroes*; Miller, *Slaves to Fashion*; Cheng, *Second Skin*; Carter-David, "Fashioning *Essence* Women and *Ebony* Men"; Nguyen, "Biopower of Beauty"; Pham, "Blog Ambition"; and McClendon, *Jazz and Fashion*.

12. Berger, "'We Are the Revolutionaries,'" 14. Berger's theory is also useful in unpacking the ways in which black women activists used their dressed bodies as a form of embodied activism.

13. Since the early 1990s, scholarship on the civil rights movement has linked "big events" in national history with local freedom efforts, bringing often-marginalized figures—including women and rank-and-file members—into the center. Exemplary works include Theoharis, *The Rebellious Life of Mrs. Rosa Parks*; Payne, *I've Got the Light of Freedom*; Fleming, *Soon We Will Not Cry*; Lee, *For Freedom's Sake*; Ransby, *Ella Baker*; Biondi, *To Stand and Fight*; Pierce, *Polite Protest*; Joseph, *Waitin' 'til the Midnight Hour*; Countryman, *Up South*; and Sugrue, *Sweet Land of Liberty*. We still need more studies

191

that move beyond formal organizing to examine how the struggle for civil rights was waged in everyday life. The small but growing body of literature that has taken up this issue includes Gill, *Beauty Shop Politics*; Feldstein, *How It Feels to Be Free*; and Ward, *Just My Soul Responding*.

14. Van Deburg, *New Day in Babylon*, 192–93, 194–95.

15. For various religious and cultural definitions of soul, see R. Thompson, *Flash of the Spirit*; Van Deburg, *New Day in Babylon*; Guillory and Green, *Soul*; Neal, *Soul Babies*; Baraka, "'Blues Aesthetic'"; and Ongiri, *Spectacular Blackness*.

16. For black women's expressions of "blues consciousness," see A. Davis, *Blues Legacies*.

17. Saul, *Freedom Is, Freedom Ain't*, 84.

18. Van Deburg, *New Day in Babylon*, 216–17.

19. Tulloch, "Style-Fashion-Dress," 276.

20. Camp, *Closer to Freedom*, 60–68. See also White and White's articles "Slave Clothing" and "Slave Hair."

21. Hunter, *To 'Joy My Freedom*, 168–69. Sexual and sexualized violence against black women in the workplace is a common theme in the writings of black women historians. See Hine, "Rape and the Inner Lives of Black Women," 915.

22. For more on zoot suits see White and White, *Stylin'*; Miller, *Slaves to Fashion*; Peiss, *Enigmatic Career*; and Ramirez, *Woman in the Zoot Suit*. For more on the power of working-class cultures, see Kelley, *Yo' Mama's Dysfunktional!*

23. C. Cooper, "Caribbean Fashion Week," 389.

24. Tulloch, "Style-Fashion-Dress," 276.

25. See the cover of *Essence*, August 1973. Every August thereafter through the end of the 1970s, *Essence* published a College Issue.

26. Welters, "Natural Look," 490.

27. On the global circulation of African and African-inspired fashion, see Allman, *Fashioning Africa*; Jennings, *New African Fashion*; Gott and Loughran, *Contemporary African Fashion*; Rabine, *Global Circulation of African Fashion*; Hansen, *Salaula*; Suriano, "Clothing and Changing Identities"; and Farber, "Africanized Hybridity?" African historians and fashion scholars have shaped the burgeoning field of African diaspora fashion studies. I am indebted to their frameworks.

28. Several scholars have provided useful frameworks for considering the ongoing making of the African diaspora as well as how notions of diaspora both served as points of connection and disconnections for African-descended people. See Gilroy, *Black Atlantic* and *Small Acts*; Edwards, *Practice of Diaspora*; and Patterson and Kelley, "Unfinished Migrations."

29. Black fashion theorists, including Carol Tulloch, Van Dyk Lewis, and others in the Dress and the African Diaspora Network, are invested in defining "African diasporic fashion." Tulloch posits an interesting geographical framework through which to study the evolution, proliferation, and diversity of soul style.

30. Manthia Diawara's "1960s in Bamako" and Andrew Ivaska's *Cultured States* make a compelling case for the circulation of soul style in Mali and Tanzania respectively. These fascinating studies of the tensions within the black community among natives and between natives and black American expatriates help round out my history of soul style.

31. Jaji, *Africa in Stereo*; Ngo, *Imperial Blues*; Kelley, *Africa Speaks*; Von Eschen, *Satchmo Blows Up the World*; and Gilroy, *There Ain't No Black in the Union Jack* offer useful frameworks for understanding geographies of black culture and how it circulates across national borders.

CHAPTER ONE

1. Makeba, *My Story*, 113. In response to her stance on apartheid, the South African government revoked Makeba's South African passport, and it would be decades before she would be allowed to return to her homeland.

2. For more on Miriam Makeba as a representation of Africa in America, see Sizemore-Barber, "Voice of (Which?) Africa."

3. Coplan, *In the Township Tonight!*, 170–73.

4. Makeba, *My Story*, 50.

5. Ibid., 47.

6. Ibid., 49.

7. Feldstein, "Screening Apartheid," 20. For more on the modern girl in South Africa, see Thomas, "Modern Girl."

8. Lanning, Roake, and Horning, *Life Soweto Style*, 79.

9. Jennings, *New African Fashion*, 11.

10. Suriano, "Clothing and Changing Identities," 95.

11. McGregor, "Chaos of 'Bantu' Education."

12. Goldhew, *Respectability and Resistance*, 95–99.

13. Nonhlanhla Ngozi interview.

14. Ramphele, *Across Boundaries*, 57.

15. Lette Matthebe interview.

16. See the cover of *Drum*, May 1957.

17. Thomas, "Modern Girl," 477–78.

18. Ibid., 483; Burke, *Lifebuoy Men and Lux Women*, 4, 187.

19. Makeba, *My Story*, 49.

20. Crais and McClendon, *The South African Reader*, 281.

21. Makhudu, "Introduction to Flaaitaal," 300.

22. Can Thembe writes about his personal experiences living through the destruction of Sophiatown in *Requiem for Sophiatown*.

23. Feldstein, "Screening Apartheid," 18.

24. Rogosin, dir., *Come Back, Africa*.

25. For more on the interrelationship between the African American and the black South African press, see McGee, "Negro Notes from the U.S.A."

26. Jennings, *New African Fashion*, 11.

27. Feldstein, "Screening Apartheid," 12–15.

28. See cover of *Ebony*, February 1960.

29. Quoted in Hayes and Greer, "International Dimensions of Everyday Black Political Participation," n.p.

30. "Africa's Hottest Export," *Ebony*, May 1960, 111.

31. Ibid., 111.

32. Jennings, *New African Fashion*, 11; "Fifty Years of Nigerian Fashion," http://www
.stylehousefiles.com/50-years-of-fashion-in-nigeria-the-journey-so-far/.

33. Kaurismaki, dir., *Mama Africa*.

34. Leigh Behrens, "Miriam Makeba: Before Being an Artist, I Am a Human Being,"
Chicago Tribune, March 20, 1988, http://articles.chicagotribune.com/1988-03-20/features
/8803010934_1_south-africa-miriam-makeba-harry-belafonte.

35. Makeba, *My Story*, 91.

36. Saul, *Freedom Is, Freedom Ain't*, 76.

37. Brun-Lambert, *Nina Simone*, 69.

38. Saul, *Freedom Is, Freedom Ain't*, 77.

39. Baraka, *Autobiography*, 133. See Smethurst, *Black Arts Movement*, for a rich history
of the black cultural-political community in New York City in the 1960s.

40. Makeba, *My Story*, 83. For more on Pratt, see "John Pratt Dead at 74; Designer for
the Dance," *New York Times*, March 29, 1986, 8.

41. Makeba, *Miriam Makeba*; Makeba, *The Many Voices of Miriam Makeba*.

42. Makeba, *My Story*, 83.

43. Ibid., 83.

44. "House of Beauty: Rose-Meta Salon is Biggest Negro Beauty Parlor in the World,"
Ebony, May 1946, 25; Makeba, *My Story*, 86. For more on Rose Morgan's beauty empire,
see chapter 4 of Walker, *Style and Status*.

45. Kitty Hannays, "Ena Girl with a Secret," *Flamingo*, April 1965, 54–55; Thomas,
"Modern Girl," 487; Erasmus, "Hair Politics," 391.

46. Makeba, *My Story*, 86. Belafonte was also instrumental in helping Martin and
Coretta King establish an image of "middle-class domestic responsibility." See Ward, *Just
My Soul Responding*, 315–26, for more on Belafonte's class politics.

47. *Drum*, April 1960, 27.

48. *Drum*, March 1960, 16. The Vaseline Blue Seal advertisement ran in the same issue
on page 69. These two advertisements ran in *Drum* for most of 1960.

49. "Belafonte's Protégée," *Ebony*, February 1960, 109.

50. "Makeba Tops at Village Gate," *New York Amsterdam News*, September 22, 1962, 19.

51. "Belafonte's Protégée," 109.

52. Carmichael, *Ready for a Revolution*, 99.

53. Simone, *I Put a Spell on You*, 48–49.

54. Ibid., 66–67.

55. Ibid., 98.

56. For an example of *Drum*'s coverage of Simone, see "Nina: High Priestess of Soul,"
Drum, November 1969, 35.

57. Simone, *I Put a Spell on You*, 98.

58. Ibid., 98.

59. Feldstein, "Nina Simone's Border Crossings," 290; Gaines, *American Africans in
Ghana*, 136–38.

60. Simone, *I Put a Spell on You*, 80.

61. Stroud, *Nina Simone*, 22. Simone was also photographed lying on her mother's
lawn in North Carolina in July 1961. It was common for black women to wear their hair unprocessed at home with family, but Simone's hair was shaped into a well-groomed style.

Although Simone was still performing in European wigs, she wore a natural hairstyle in her personal life. See Stroud, *Nina Simone*, 59, for a copy of the photo.

62. Simone, *I Put a Spell on You*, 98.

63. Cohen, *Rainbow Quest*, 83–84.

64. Barnett, *I Got Thunder*, 173; Ford, "Odetta."

65. Jean Godden, "Just Plain Folk," *Seattle Post Intelligencer*, March 4, 1989, C1.

66. Farber, "Africanized Hybridity?," 134.

67. Cohen, *Rainbow Quest*, 188–89, 213.

68. Baez, *And a Voice to Sing it With*, 59.

69. Quoted in Barnett, *I Got Thunder*, 178.

70. Traum, dir., *Odetta: Exploring Life, Music, and Song*.

71. Pete Seeger, "Johnny Appleseed, Jr.," *Sing Out!*, Summer 1961, 60; J. Brown, dir., *We Shall Overcome*; Cantwell, *When We Were Good*, 250–51, 272–75; Cohen, *Rainbow Quest*, 90, 204–5.

72. Carlie Collins Tartakov, "Odetta," article for International Women's Week at the University of Massachusetts, March 28, 1980, Odetta Papers, box 10, Schomburg Center for Research in Black Culture, New York, N.Y.; "Los Angeles Goes 'Natural,'" *Sepia*, January 1967, 62.

73. Angelou, *Heart of a Woman*, 169.

74. Barnett, *I Got Thunder*, 3.

75. Ibid., 2; Young, *Soul Power*, 30, 81.

76. Barnett, *I Got Thunder*, 2–3; Feldstein, "'I Don't Trust You Anymore,'" 1361–62.

77. Saul, *Freedom Is, Freedom Ain't*, 83.

78. Ibid., 84.

79. Ibid.

80. Makeba, *My Story*, 87.

81. Ibid., 97, 100.

82. Makeba, *Voice of Africa*; Makeba, *My Story*, 91–92, 112.

83. Makeba, *My Story*, 96–97.

84. Lorraine Hansberry, "This Complex of Womanhood," *Ebony*, August 1960, 40.

85. Simone, *I Put a Spell on You*, 86–87.

86. Ibid., 90.

87. Ibid., 105.

88. Ward, *Just My Soul Responding*, 301.

89. Cohodas, *Princess Noire*, 345–46.

90. Barnett, *I Got Thunder*, 179.

91. Ward, *Just My Soul Responding*, 161–65.

92. Quoted in Barnett, *I Got Thunder*, 179.

93. Kernodle, "'I Wish I Knew How It Would Feel to Be Free,'" 296.

94. Quoted in Barnett, *I Got Thunder*, 152.

95. Smith, *Dancing in the Street*, 55.

96. Simone, *I Put a Spell on You*, 70.

97. Makeba, *My Story*, 106.

98. Angelou, *Heart of a Woman*, 169.

99. Stroud, *Nina Simone*, 15, 20, 27, 52; Simone, *I Put a Spell on You*, 70.

100. Richard Cabrera, "The Miriam Makeba Story," *Sepia*, July 1968, 64.

101. Makeba, *My Story*, 128.

102. Cohen, *Rainbow Quest*, 213.

CHAPTER TWO

1. New York–based Blue Note led the industry in avant garde, politically motivated album covers long before the Black Power years. Though Blue Note issued a series of album covers with Grandassa models' images, the label was not making a company-wide statement on black beauty, and its albums did not uphold one standard of beauty. Other Blue Note records released during the same period featured both white women and black women with various hairstyles. Thus, we can surmise that artists had a certain degree of input and creative license in the design of their covers.

2. Craig, *Ain't I a Beauty Queen?*, 87–88; Walker, *Style and Status*, 182–83.

3. The growing body of literature on modernity and beauty includes Peiss, *Hope in a Jar*; Conor, *Spectacular Modern Woman*; Walker, *Style and Status*; Baldwin, *Chicago's New Negroes*; and The Modern Girl around the World Research Group, *Modern Girl*.

4. A well-established body of literature examines black women's hair in the United States. See Morrow, *400 Years without a Comb*; Mercer, "Black Hair/Style Politics"; Rooks, *Hair Raising*; Kelley, "Nap Time"; A. Davis, "Afro Images"; Banks, *Hair Matters*; Byrd and Tharps, *Hair Story*; and Craig, *Ain't I a Beauty Queen?*

5. Putnam, "Nothing Matters But Color," 109.

6. Olatunji, *Beat of My Drum*, 101. See also Lewis, *When Harlem Was in Vogue*; Stephens, *Black Empire*; Mathieu, "African American Great Migration Reconsidered"; and Edwards, *Practice of Diaspora*. Throughout the twentieth century, African Americans grappled with what Africa and African cultures could and should represent. In the 1920s, African American beauty industry entrepreneur Annie Turnbo Malone dressed her consultants in capes inspired by Ethiopian emperor Haile Selassie, relating African American fashion to East African royalty. Black cosmetic company Kashmir Chemical's Nile Queen hair and skin care lines also acknowledged African Americans' ontological connection to the continent, showing on its product labels a fair-skinned model sitting by the Nile River. In the 1935 French film *Princess Tam Tam*, American-born entertainer Josephine Baker plays a make-believe Tunisian princess whose African-inspired garments and styles of dance toed the thin line between perpetuating primitivist stereotypes of Africana women and mocking Europeans for their racist fantasies about the "dark continent" and its inhabitants. With the liberation of Ghana in 1957 and Nigeria in 1960, Maya Angelou and Lorraine Hansberry reflected on the connections between African Americans and West Africans in their writing. Maya Angelou's *All God's Children Need Traveling Shoes* chronicles her cultural-political experiences in Kwame Nkrumah's newly independent Ghana in the 1950s. In Lorraine Hansberry's 1958 award-winning play, *A Raisin in the Sun*, Beneatha Younger, a college student from a hard-working black family, develops a romantic relationship with a young Nigerian student and begins experimenting with wearing her hair unprocessed and dressing in African garments.

7. "Wig Salon Opens New Harlem Shop," *New York Amsterdam News*, August 17, 1963, 42; "Display ad 107—No Title," ibid., August 10, 1963, 28.

8. "Display ad 107—No Title."

9. Ibid. An ad that ran in the *Amsterdam News* on August 3, 1963, claimed "you made it such a success" that Wigs Parisian was giving away another five hundred wigs. This could have been a marketing ploy, since it predated the grand opening "1000 wig celebration" that Wigs Parisian began advertising on August 10, 1963.

10. "Display ad 107—No Title."

11. Banks, *Hair Matters*, 12; Mercer, "Black Hair/Style Politics," 249; Brownmiller, *Femininity*, 58.

12. For more on colorism in the modeling industry, see Haidarali, "Polishing Brown Diamonds."

13. "South African Colored Beauty Contest," *Ebony*, November 1959, 138–42; "The Beauty Queen Who Doesn't Want to Be Queen," ibid., July 1960, 110–14; "Negro Model Makes Debut in Paris," ibid., September 1960, 61. The interest in brown models was not confined to the United States; even in the Caribbean, there was a rise in popularity of black models who moved to colonial metropolises such as London and Paris to pursue their careers. These women include Althea Dean and Beryl Cunningham. See "So You Want to Be a Model," *Flamingo*, January 1965, 52–55.

14. "Cleopatra's Daughters Vie for Title of 'Miss Beaux Arts,'" *New York Amsterdam News*, August 4, 1962, 4; B. Summers, *Skin Deep*, 13. Before Max Factor created the "Light Egyptian" foundation for Lena Horne, the entertainment industry had no shade to match African American skin. The new Max Factor shade marked an important moment in makeup history, and it was used not only for fair-complexioned black actresses but also for white actresses playing mulatto roles.

15. Harris, Harris, and Harris, *Carlos Cooks*, xi–xii.

16. Martin, *Amy Ashwood Garvey*, 16.

17. Brathwaite, "Art, Artists, and Activism"; Hamlin, "Bathing Suits and Backlash," 28; White and White, *Stylin'*, 205. Pageantry was also a large industry in the Caribbean; see Rowe, "'Glorifying the Jamaican Girl.'"

18. Cooks, "Buy Black," 85.

19. Harris, Harris, and Harris, *Carlos Cooks*, xiii; M. Summers, *Manliness and Its Discontents*, 66. Cooks moved to New York City in 1929 to further his studies and to train alongside Garvey. Upon his return to Harlem in 1945, Cooks relaunched the ANPM. In its early years, the ANPM comprised mostly former members of the Universal African Nationalist Movement who followed Cooks after he was forced to leave the organization.

20. Thomasina Norford, "Wig Wearing Stirs Up a Harlem Picketing Battle," *New York Amsterdam News*, September 14, 1963, 23.

21. "Protest against Hairstyles That Weren't 'Natural' for Blacks on West 125th Street," Harlem 1963, Klytus Smith Collection, box 2, Schomburg Center for Research in Black Culture, New York, N.Y.

22. Ibid.

23. The ANPM's 1963 protest was not the first time that black Americans made the connection between themselves under a system of U.S. colonialism and the Congolese. As early as 1921, at the height of the Jazz Age and Garveyism, Arkansas activist William Pickens referred to the so-called alluvial empire of the Mississippi River valley region as the "American Congo." U.S.-based planters exploited black labor to work the soil, rich in

natural resources, and controlled every aspect of black life from church to education. Like King Leopold II, who ruled the Congo with an iron fist and chopped off the hands and heads of his colonial subjects, white planters in the Delta lynched and burned African Americans who did not conform. Both the European colonial regime and the U.S. plantation system, these activists believed, were based on brutality and notions of white supremacy. See Woodruff, *American Congo*, 1.

24. Cooks, "What Is the ANPM?," 4.

25. "Protest against Hairstyles That Weren't 'Natural'"; Wallace, "Modernism," 39–40; E. White, *Dark Continent of Our Bodies*, 124–25.

26. Mercer, "Black Hair/Style Politics," 251–52.

27. "Protest against Hairstyles That Weren't 'Natural.'"

28. Norford, "Harlem Picketing," 23; Rose Nelms, "Natural Hair Yes, Hot Irons No," *Liberator* 3, no. 7 (July 1963): 13.

29. Norford, "Harlem Picketing," 23.

30. George Simor, "Destination: Stardom," *Sepia*, March 1967, 26–27.

31. Norford, "Harlem Picketing," 23.

32. "Should Negro Women Straighten Their Hair?," *Negro Digest*, August 1963, 65–66.

33. Ibid., 67; Eleanor Mason, "Hot Irons and Black Nationalism," *Liberator* 3, no. 5 (May 1963): 21; hooks, "Straightening Our Hair," 14; Peiss, *Hope in a Jar*, 90.

34. Mason, "Hot Irons," 22.

35. Brathwaite, "Art, Artists, and Activism"; "The Natural Look Is Reborn in Brilliant New Show," *Muhammad Speaks*, February 4, 1963, 12–13; "Should Negro Women Straighten Their Hair?," 71.

36. Brathwaite, "Art, Artists, and Activism."

37. See M. Summers, *Manliness and Its Discontents*, chapter 2, for more on the shift from a producer-based to a consumer-based black American society.

38. Brathwaite, "Art, Artists, and Activism."

39. Ibid.

40. White and White, *Stylin'*.

41. Ibid., 87–88, 207; Rooks, *Ladies' Pages*, 28–32. Rooks describes *Ringwood's Afro-American Journal of Fashion* as a mix between *Essence* and *Vogue* magazines. Its use of "Afro-American" in the title, instead of "colored" or "Negro," was progressive for the time. See Miller, *Slaves to Fashion*.

42. White and White, *Stylin'*, 207, 211–12; B. Summers, *Skin Deep*, 29.

43. "African Fashions for the Holidays," *Sepia*, February 1968, 40–45; "New Look by New Breed," ibid., September 1968, 36–41; Niessen, "Re-orienting Fashion Theory," 105, 107, 109. See also Rabine, *Global Circulation of African Fashion*.

44. Brathwaite, "Art, Artists, and Activism."

45. "Grandassa Models Pose for 'Naturally '63,'" Kwame Brathwaite Collection, Schomburg Center for Research in Black Culture, New York, N.Y.

46. White and White, *Stylin'*, 213; B. Summers, *Skin Deep*, 29.

47. Rooks, *Ladies' Pages*, 49.

48. Ibid.

49. Ibid.; Mercer, "Black Hair/Style Politics," 252.

50. Nelms, "Natural Hair Yes," 12–13. Nina W. Gwatkin argues that the "Afro Natural"

was not African in origin, claiming that the Afro was an African American–invented style, but women such as South African singer Miriam Makeba were wearing the style long before it became popular in the United States. Though the origins of the cropped natural are unclear, it is important to note that the Grandassa models wore the hairstyle, believing that it was a traditional African style. See Gwatkin, *Yoruba Hairstyles*, 41.

51. Craig, *Ain't I a Beauty Queen?*, 87–88; Walker, *Style and Status*, 182–83; Brathwaite, "Art, Artists, and Activism"; Nelms, "Natural Hair Yes," 12–13.

52. Brathwaite, "Arts, Artists, and Activism."

53. "Should Negro Women Straighten Their Hair?," 70.

54. Tolliver, "Chapter 16: The Grandassa Models."

55. Cara Buckley, "Toasting 40 Years of Breaking News and Happy Talk," *New York Times*, November 9, 2008, http://www.nytimes.com/2008/11/10/nyregion/10legends.html ?_r=0 (accessed March 8, 2015).

56. Bailey, *Black America*, 36; Holloway, *Codes of Conduct*, 61; Kinloch, "Rhetoric of Black Bodies," 96–97.

57. Brathwaite, "Art, Artists, and Activism."

58. Powe-Temperley, *Mods and Hippies*, 10–11. Even in the early twentieth century, fashion trends were largely decided upon and then marketed by a complex fashion machine that involved design houses, strategically placed models, celebrity endorsements, and the media, which inconspicuously suggested to people around the globe what they should wear. The rise in popularity of ethnic fashion in the early 1960s marked an exceptional moment in which the movement to ethnic fashions came from the bottom up. See Lang and Lang, "Power of Fashion," 83; and Ash, "Business of Couture." Though I am highlighting boutiques on the East Coast of the United States, the Midwest and the South had bohemian districts as well: Chicago's North Side, the Little Five Points area of Atlanta, and even Fort Wayne, Indiana, had bohemian fashion scenes. For more on the significance of thrift stores for ethnic and vintage fashions, see McRobbie, "Second-Hand Dresses."

59. Makeba, *My Story*, 156–57. Her plans were thwarted once the Bahamian government received intelligence from the United States that Makeba's soon-to-be husband, Stokely Carmichael, was a radical activist.

60. Jeanette, "Thru Women's Eyes," *Liberator* 3, no. 10 (October 1963): 15. The implications for this informal fashion network were vast, especially in the United States, where youths' decisions to shop in thrift stores and privately owned boutiques also meant that they were not shopping in department stores that upheld de facto segregation. Thus, the rise in the underground fashion network was a form of indirect boycotting of chain stores like Woolworth's that, both in the South and in the North, participated in discriminatory hiring practices and unfair treatment of black consumers.

61. Marsh and Callingham, *Cover Art*, 9–10, 12, 79–78.

62. Ibid., 80.

63. Cooks, "Ethiopia, Haiti, Liberia, Kenya," 104.

64. For a history on the significance of album cover art, see the introduction to Benedict and Barton, *Phonographics*. For more on album cover art by black artists and its significance in the African diaspora, see Gilroy, *Small Acts*; and Huss, "'Zinc-Fence Thing.'"

65. Nelms, "Natural Hair Yes," 13.

66. Brathwaite, "Art, Artists, and Activism."

67. Brathwaite, "Art, Artists, and Activism"; "Natural Look Is Reborn in Brilliant New Show," 12.

68. "Should Negro Women Straighten Their Hair?," 70; Robert S. Browne, "Separation," *Ebony*, August 1970, 48.

CHAPTER THREE

1. Moody, *Coming of Age*, 11, 20, 288. Although narratives of black women activists who earned their soul stripes through "trials by fire" dominated the black and mainstream presses during the Black Power era, at this time they were less common.

2. Gosse, *Rethinking the New Left*, 1–8. While scholars of SNCC have convincingly argued that its political strategies appealed to northern white student activists and provided the basis for the Students for a Democratic Society (SDS), less attention has been paid to SNCC women's interactions with the bohemian factions of the New Left, particularly outside the South. Gosse defines the New Left as a "movement of movements" that included the Black Freedom movement, feminist movement, gay rights movement, and free speech movement, opening the door for the inclusion of the folk music revival, black arts movement, and hippie movement. See also Hogan, *Many Minds*. The relationship between SNCC and white student activists in the North involved SNCC members traveling north, as well as white students traveling south.

3. Debbie Amis Bell interview; Ransby, *Ella Baker*, 240; Zinn, *SNCC*, 16, 18, 23.

4. Chappell, Hutchinson, and Ward, "'Dress Modestly and Neatly," 96. This advice was given to Vivian Malone and James Hood before they registered for classes at the recently integrated University of Alabama in 1963 (ibid., n. 1). Stokely Carmichael recalled that dressing neatly and behaving politely were among the rules he was taught as a member of the Nonviolent Action Group (the others were have a clear strategy, research your opponent, be focused and uncompromising but also creative, and maintain a sense of humor); Carmichael, *Ready for a Revolution*, 148.

5. Higginbotham, *Righteous Discontent*, 14–15; Lowe, *Looking Good*, 41; Wolcott, *Remaking Respectability*, 6–9. See also Foster, *Troping the Body*; and D. White, *Too Heavy a Load*.

6. Lowe, *Looking Good*, 57–61; Fleming, *Soon We Will Not Cry*, 39–40; Tice, "Queens of Academe," 252; Stephanie Evans, *Black Women in the Ivory Tower*, 44–47. Stephanie Camp analyzes how enslaved women used clothing as a form of resistance, expressing what she calls their "third body," used for pleasure and leisure. See Camp, *Closer to Freedom*, 60–68. For more on black activism and respectability, see Gaines, *Uplifting the Race*.

7. B. Summers, *Skin Deep*, 26–27; "Prison Charm School," *Ebony*, January 1960, 75–77. See also McAndrew, "Selling Black Beauty."

8. McGuire, *At the Dark End of the Street*, 76–77, 88; Chappell, Hutchinson, and Ward, "'Dress Modestly and Neatly,'" 76–77, 92–93; Robnett, *How Long?*, 42–44.

9. There is a well-established body of work on black women and controlling images. These texts include Collins, *Black Feminist Thought*; L. Thompson, *Beyond the Black Lady*; K. Brown, *Writing the Black Revolutionary Diva*; L. Johnson, *Iconic*; and Harris-Perry, *Sister Citizen*.

10. Fleming, *Soon We Will Not Cry*, 113.

11. For more on the history of activism between black and white women, see Breines, *Trouble between Us*, 19–20. See also Greene, *Our Separate Ways*; and Curry et al., *Deep in Our Hearts*.

12. Moody, *Coming of Age*, 266; see also Zinn, *SNCC*, 56. Anne Moody's outfit was common attire for students during the early sit-ins. The mob at Woolworth's was predominantly male, but it was common for white women to join in the violence. Ruby Doris Smith Robinson's sister, Mary Ann Smith, recalled a sit-in protest at Davidson's department store in downtown Atlanta in October 1960 where a waitress threw a Coke bottle at Ruby Doris's head. Fleming, *Soon We Will Not Cry*, 57.

13. Collins, *Black Feminist Thought*, 89. Collins notes that little black girls sang chants that reflected their perceptions of color:

Now, if you're white, you're all right
If you're brown, stick around
But if you're black, Git back! Git back! Git back!

14. Moody, *Coming of Age*, 267–68. See also O'Brien, *We Shall Not Be Moved*.

15. Ibid. See also Gill, *Beauty Shop Politics*, 98–99, 117; Gill, "'I Had My Own Business'"; and Bose, "From Humanitarian Intervention to the Beautifying Mission."

16. Quoted in Fleming, *Soon We Will Not Cry*, 77.

17. Wade-Gayles, *Pushed Back to Strength*, 143; Craig, *Ain't I a Beauty Queen?*, 86–87.

18. Moody, *Coming of Age*, 279–80.

19. Ibid.; Fleming, *Soon We Will Not Cry*, 66. The day after the rape of her bunkmate, Norma June Davis demanded to speak to the warden and threatened to expose the conditions of the jail. The warden promptly replaced the male guards with female guards. See also McGuire, *At the Dark End of the Street*; and Lee, *For Freedom's Sake*, chapter 3.

20. Bell interview.

21. Carson, *In Struggle*, 50.

22. Bell interview.

23. Carson, *In Struggle*, 51.

24. Entwistle, "Dressed Body," 93–94.

25. Bell interview; Martha Prescod Norman Noonan interview; Fleming, *Soon We Will Not Cry*, 113. For more on sharecroppers and grassroots organizing, see Kelley, *Hammer and Hoe*; and Payne, *I've Got the Light of Freedom*.

26. Sullivan, *Jeans*, 5, 41, 112; Franklin and Moss, *From Slavery to Freedom*, 148.

27. Judy Richardson interview.

28. On the multiple meanings of denim, see de Marley, *Working Dress*, 144, 162; Scheuring, "Heavy Duty Denim," 227; and Fraser, *Fashionable Mind*, 91–95.

29. Quoted in Fleming, *Soon We Will Not Cry*, 31.

30. Moody, *Coming of Age*, 263.

31. Bell interview.

32. Ibid.

33. Joyce Ladner interview.

34. Wade-Gayles, *Pushed Back to Strength*, 155–57; Moody, *Coming of Age*, 272–73.

35. Wade-Gayles, *Pushed Back to Strength*, 157.

36. Richardson interview.

37. Moody, *Coming of Age*, 239; Fleming, *Soon We Will Not Cry*, 174–75. According to Mary King, Jean Wheeler Smith was a student at Howard when the dean of women, Patricia Roberts Harris, asked her to straighten her hair, a request that Smith ardently refused. Later, Smith and Harris became close friends and enjoyed a mentor/mentee relationship built on mutual respect; see King, *Freedom Song*, 463. Fleming tells of a similar story concerning Gwen Robinson, who was told by a Spelman College dean that natural hair was a "disgrace"; Fleming, *Soon We Will Not Cry*, 174–75. Conversely, Stokely Carmichael remembers a Howard University dean coming to the defense of his girlfriend when she was told to straighten her natural hair; Carmichael, *Ready for a Revolution*, 119. While there was a general distaste for natural hair on the ground that it was not respectable, there was no uniform university policy regarding natural hair within a given institution or throughout the historically black colleges and universities system.

38. Richardson interview.

39. Ibid; Ladner interview.

40. Carson, *In Struggle*, 144.

41. Richardson interview.

42. For more on the class politics of Dexter Avenue Baptist Church, see Branch, *Parting the Waters*, especially chapter 1.

43. Chappell, Hutchinson, and Ward, "'Dress Modestly and Neatly,'" 90–91.

44. Payne, *I've Got the Light of Freedom*, 241.

45. Fleming, *Soon We Will Not Cry*, 113–14.

46. Makeba, *My Story*, 154–55.

47. White and White, *Stylin'*, 173; Sullivan, *Jeans*, 112.

48. Bell interview.

49. Saunders, *The Day They Marched*, 9, 39, 50–52, 60, 66.

50. Moody, *Coming of Age*, 307.

51. Hayden, "In the Attics of My Mind," 381–88, 386.

52. Although this is an emerging field of inquiry, most of the scholarship on clothing and queerness centers on white dressed bodies. See Skerski, "Tomboy Chic"; and Hillman, "'Clothes I Wear.'"

53. White and White, *Stylin'*, 190.

54. Bell interview.

55. Richardson interview.

56. Quoted in Richardson, "SNCC: My Enduring 'Circle of Trust,'" 355.

57. Richardson interview.

58. Quoted in Simmons, "Little Memphis Girl," 29.

59. Fleming, *Soon We Will Not Cry*, 47.

60. Quoted in Simmons, "From Little Memphis Girl to Mississippi Amazon," 15.

61. Quoted in Ransby, "Ella Baker," 59; Fleming, *Soon We Will Not Cry*, 113.

62. Quoted in Greenburg, *Circle of Trust*, 27.

63. Clemente, *Dress Casual*, 62–63.

64. Bell interview.

65. Ladner interview; Greenburg, *Circle of Trust*, 28.

66. King, *Freedom Song*, 464.

67. Moody, *Coming of Age*, 239; Fleming, *Soon We Will Not Cry*, 174–75.

68. Bell interview.

69. Ladner interview.

70. Fleming, *Soon We Will Not Cry*.

71. Ibid., 166–67, 114, 121.

72. Martinez, *Letters from Mississippi*, 18.

73. William J. Raspberry, "Whites Urged to Stay North," *Washington Post, Times Herald*, December 2, 1963, A12.

74. Fleming, *Soon We Will Not Cry*, 113.

75. Ibid., 2.

76. Quoted in ibid., 3. See also Toure and Hamilton, *Black Power*.

77. Cleaver, "Women, Power, and Revolution," 123.

78. Giddings, *When and Where I Enter*, 277.

CHAPTER FOUR

1. Alan Ebert, "Inside Cecily," *Essence*, February 1973, 40.

2. "Campus Living," ibid., August 1973, 61.

3. James E. Lyons and Clarence G. Williams, "Black Coed, White Campus," ibid., 37.

4. For more on the black feminist movement and its overlaps with Black Power, see E. Brown, *Taste of Power*, 65; Baxandall, "Re-visioning the Women's Liberation Movement's Narrative," 230; Sara Evans, *Personal Politics*; and Gaines, "From Center to Margin."

5. For more on how radical U.S. activists employed the tactics of third world activists, see Young, *Soul Power*.

6. A well-established body of work situates the roots of Black Power ideologies and activist strategies in the period preceding 1965. See Tyson, *Radio Free Dixie*; and Joseph, *Waitin' 'til the Midnight Hour*.

7. For more on the history of the transformation from dressy to casual on campus, see Clemente, *Dress Casual*.

8. "What We Want, What We Believe," *Black Panther*, August 9, 1969, 26; Hayes and Kiene, "All Power to the People," 159–60; Franklynn Peterson, "The Black Panthers: The Group Was Organized to Make the World Safe for All People," *Sepia*, December 1968, 12, 14–17.

9. Kochiyama, Huggins, and Kao, "'Stirrin' Waters' 'n Buildin' Bridges," 152.

10. Toure and Hamilton's *Black Power* offers a sense of SNCC's early Black Power philosophy that influenced the Black Panther Party. See Nelson, *Body and Soul*, for a compelling take on the Black Panthers' health care initiatives.

11. Giddings, *When and Where I Enter*, 271.

12. Widener, *Black Arts West*, 199.

13. E. Brown, *Taste of Power*, 156.

14. Widener, *Black Arts West*, 199; Angelo, "Black Panthers in London," 18; Cleaver, "Women, Power, and Revolution," 124.

15. Federal Bureau of Investigation, Student Nonviolent Coordinating Committee File, Report number AT 100-6488, p. 3, March 20, 1964.

16. Clemente, *Dress Casual*, 62–63. For more on the black student movement in the

late 1960s, see Biondi, *Black Revolution on Campus*; Rogers, *Black Campus Movement*; Rojas, *From Black Power to Black Studies*; and Murch, *Living for the City*.

17. "Group Members Not Qualified: Black Students," *Indianapolis Recorder*, April 6, 1968, 1.

18. Welters, "Natural Look," 499–500. For more on the mainstream student movement and the counterculture, see Gosse, *Rethinking the New Left*; Hogan *Many Minds, One Heart*; Gitlin, *Whole World Is Watching*; Beard and Berlowitz, *Greenwich Village*; Lipsitz, "Who Will Stop the Rain?," 216–17; Geary, "'Becoming International Again,'" 711–12; and Barber, *Hard Rain Fell*.

19. Widener, *Black Arts West*, 188, 203–5. For more on the cultural politics of Black Power, see Baldwin, "'Culture Is a Weapon'"; Jones, "Need for a Cultural Base to Civil Rights and Black Power Movements"; and S. Brown, *Fighting for US*.

20. "Washington's Wonderful World of Women," *Sepia*, June 1968, 43.

21. Ibid.

22. Ibid., 44.

23. Ibid.

24. Feldstein, *How It Feels to Be Free*, 103.

25. Simone, *I Put a Spell on You*, 108. The Congress of Racial Equality declared "To Be Young, Gifted, and Black" the "National Anthem of Black America" in 1969.

26. Stroud, *Nina Simone*, 55.

27. Quoted in Garland, *Sound of Soul*, 183.

28. "Los Angeles Goes 'Natural,'" *Sepia*, January 1967, 58–63.

29. Byrd and Tharps, *Hair Story*, 57.

30. Rooks, *Hair Raising*, 6.

31. "Washington's Wonderful World of Women," 44. For more of Mehlinger's commentary on issues of black women and beauty, see *Jet*, March 19, 1964, 24, and April 25, 1974, 40. There is a picture of Mehlinger in *Ebony*, November 1975, 191–92. Mehlinger also wrote black-centered fiction. In 1973 he published *Coal Black and the Seven Dudes*, a black version of *Snow White and the Seven Dwarfs*.

32. "Washington's Wonderful World of Women," 44. While Mehlinger discussed black women's growing sense of pride exemplified through their natural hairstyles, he also used the term "Negro," which some African Americans regarded as passé. The term "black," however, was used mainly by activists, college students, and some celebrities. "Black," like "soul sister," was considered hip and politically charged, while the black bourgeoisie preferred the term "Negro" and considered any verbal allusion to their skin color offensive. By linking the Afro with the term "Negro," Mehlinger suggested that even those who did not define themselves as "black" had legitimate access to the Afro hairstyle and the social and cultural consciousness it represented.

33. *Caldron*, 1970, 113. Here I am analyzing the yearbook from Glover's junior year in high school (1970–71).

34. Ibid; Glover-Ford interview.

35. Lynch, dir., *Free Angela and All Political Prisoners*.

36. For more on the Angela Davis trial, see "Kate Millett on Angela Davis," *Ms.*, August and September 1972; and Aptheker, *Morning Breaks*. For Davis's own account of the trial, see A. Davis, *Angela Davis*.

37. Nadelson, *Who Is Angela Davis?*, 7.

38. "The Angela Davis Case," *Newsweek*, October 26, 1970, 20.

39. Ibid., 18. *Ebony* magazine ran a feature story on Angela Davis that explored her childhood and her entry into radical politics. Unlike the *Newsweek* story, however, the *Ebony* magazine article does not depict Davis as a glamorous diva. Instead, the author describes her as a highly intelligent yet warm family member. "The Radicalization of Angela Davis," *Ebony*, July 1971, 114, 120.

40. "Angela Davis Case," 20.

41. Kochiyama, Huggins, and Kao, "'Stirrin' Waters' 'n Buildin' Bridges," 155.

42. A. Davis, "Afro Images," 27.

43. Nadelson, *Who Is Angela Davis?*, 13. See Gitlin, *Whole World Is Watching*, for more on the ways in which the media was complicit in constructing images of leftist activists, making them celebrities while also creating and/or exacerbating tensions within New Left organizations.

44. Nadelson, *Who Is Angela Davis?*, 13.

45. A. Davis, "Afro Images," 28.

46. Quoted in Banks, *Hair Matters*, 15–16.

47. A. Davis, "Afro Images," 28.

48. Julie Byrne, "Natural Afro Losing Its Frizz as Relaxed Hair Comes Back," *Los Angeles Times*, October 27, 1972, 7. Various periodicals ran articles that discussed Angela Davis, the popularity of the Afro, and the hairstyle's ties to black politics: "Los Angeles Goes Natural," *Sepia*, January 1967, 58–63; Marjorie Driscoll, "Pros, Cons of Looking Natural with Afro," *Los Angeles Times*, March 26, 1970, H1; Stanley Meisler, "Afro Hairstyle: A U.S. Original, Africans Say," *Los Angeles Times*, September 22, 1970, 9; Renee Minus White, "Focus on Fashion: Black Beauty," *New York Amsterdam News*, August 7, 1976, B5.

49. Glover-Ford interview.

50. *Arbutus*, 1972, 325.

51. See *Essence*, August 1974 College Issue.

52. "*Essence* Explores the Ten Most Popular Soul Cities," ibid., March 1973, 35.

53. "On Campus at Hampton: 13 Lucky Separates," ibid., August 1975, 52.

54. "Campus '73: Casually Coordinated," ibid., August 1973, 43.

55. Ibid., 50.

56. "Fall in Fly," ibid., August 1974, 44.

57. Ibid., 44–53; "Designer of the Month: Karlotta Nelson," ibid., April 1974, 60; "Essence Designer of the Month: Ollie and Pat," ibid., November 1973, 58.

58. Van Deburg, *New Day in Babylon*, 198.

59. "New Look by New Breed," *Sepia*, September 1968, 36–41; Franklin, *Amazing Grace*. The album's liner notes state that the ornate caftan and matching headpiece Franklin wears on the cover were designed by New Breed. Van Deburg, *New Day in Babylon*, 198.

60. Glover-Ford interview.

61. "Campus '73," 45.

62. Ibid., 42–51.

63. Lyons and Williams, "Black Coed, White Campus," 37.

64. Renee Ferguson, "Blacks: The Ebony Tower of IU," *Arbutus*, 1970, 32.

65. Ibid.

66. Ibid.

67. Ibid., 31.

68. Stephanie Madison, "Black Coed, White Campus," *Essence*, August 1973, 36.

69. Ibid., 68.

70. Lyons and Williams, "Black Coed, White Campus," 37.

71. Glover-Ford interview.

72. Quoted in Jones et al., "Ebony Minds," 182.

73. Gilmour, *The 70s*, 19.

74. Welters, "Natural Look," 490, 500–501; Rabine, *Global Circulation of African Fashion*, 107–9.

75. "Afro Wigs," *Sepia*, November 1968, 48, 49, 50, 52.

76. Angela Davis, "Rhetoric vs. Reality: Angela Davis Tells Why Black People Should Not Be Deceived by Words," *Ebony*, July 1971, 115–20; Angela Davis, "Angela Davis on Black Women," *Ms.*, August 1972, 55, 57, 59, 116. For analysis of the ways in which black women activists used their autobiographies to construct their own revolutionary identities, see Young, *Soul Power*, chapter 5; and Perkins, *Autobiography as Activism*.

77. Lott, *Love and Theft*, 26.

78. Cook, "Black Pride?," 149, 150.

79. Pat Evans, "The Name of the Game Is . . . ," *Essence*, January 1972, 14.

80. "Black Is Busting Out All Over," *Life*, October 17, 1969, 36.

81. P. Evans, "Name of the Game Is . . . ," 14.

82. Quoted in B. Summers, *Skin Deep*, 109.

83. Ward, "Jazz and Soul," 185–86.

CHAPTER FIVE

1. Ibrahiim, "Calling All Afro and 'Fro Wearing Brothers and Sistahs."

2. Hurlington Armstrong interview, date not given.

3. For more on race and cultural politics in Britain and the African diaspora, see Centre for Contemporary Cultural Studies, *Empire Strikes Back*; and Hall, "What Is This 'Black' in Black Popular Culture?"

4. Gilroy, *There Ain't No Black in the Union Jack*, 202. For more on the formation of cultural ties among Africana people in diaspora, see Yelvington's introduction to his edited collection, *Afro-Atlantic Dialogues*.

5. Hanchard, *Orpheus and Power*, 111.

6. Gilroy, *There Ain't No Black in the Union Jack*, 203, 205.

7. Ramdin, *Black Working Class*, 4.

8. Ibid., 9.

9. Patterson, *Dark Strangers*, 36–38; Angelo, "Black Panthers in London," 21; John Solomos, *Race and Racism in Britain*, 61–64. See also Guild, "You Can't Go Home Again"; Thomas-Hope, *Freedom and Constraint*; and Chamberlain, *Caribbean Migration*.

10. See Basil Morris interview and Jennifer Lewis interview.

11. Patterson, *Dark Strangers*, 50. See also Commonwealth Immigrants Act, 1–3.

12. Morris interview.

13. Janet Davis interview (alias used at interviewee's request).

14. Debbie Weekes, "Shades of Blackness," 118. See also Rowe, "'Glorifying the Jamaican Girl.'"

15. Davis interview.

16. Ifekwunigwe, "Diaspora's Daughters," 130–31; Weekes, "Shades of Blackness," 113–26. See also Ifekwunigwe, *Scattered Belongings*; and Bhattacharyya, *Tales of Dark-Skinned Women*.

17. Stella Dadzie interview.

18. For more on the dynamics of interracial families, see Twine, *White Side of Black Britain*.

19. Dadzie interview.

20. Emma Bedford interview.

21. Ibid.; Weekes, "Shades of Blackness," 114.

22. Bedford interview.

23. Tulloch, "That Little Magic Touch," 216.

24. Ellen Brown interview (alias used at interviewee's request).

25. Davis interview.

26. Natanya Duncan interview.

27. hooks, "Straightening Our Hair," 14.

28. Davis interview.

29. Kitty Hannays, "Ena Girl with a Secret," *Flamingo*, April 1965, 54–55.

30. Candelario, *Black behind the Ears*, 234–41.

31. Duncan interview.

32. Hannays, "Ena Girl with a Secret," 55.

33. Sydney Rose of London wig advertisement, *Flamingo*, January 1965, 23.

34. Duncan interview; Wade, *Black Enterprise in Britain*, 101, 102; Hannah, *Growing Out*, 49.

35. Dadzie interview.

36. Davis interview.

37. Dadzie interview; Davis interview.

38. Tulloch, "That Little Magic Touch," 216.

39. Patterson, *Dark Strangers*, 51. Susan Benson's *Ambiguous Ethnicities* offers a rich description of Brixton and Lambeth borough.

40. Small, "Introduction," xxx.

41. Quoted in Chris May, "Poet Laureate," *Black Music and Jazz Review*, October 1978, 29.

42. Camp, "Pleasures of Resistance," 535. Camp borrows the phrase "geography of containment" from a talk Houston Baker gave at the University of Pennsylvania on March 27, 1997, titled "Temporality, Transnationalism, and Afro-Modernity."

43. Bradley, *This Is Reggae Music*, 135–36.

44. La Rose, "Michael La Rose," 129. Junior, the owner of Junior's Record Store, also owned an indie record label and became an organizer for the Sunsplash festival in Jamaica. Thus, there was a direct, cross-Atlantic connection between the Afro-British music scene and the reggae scene in Jamaica.

45. Tulloch, "That Little Magic Touch," 216.

46. Sophia Kokkinos interview.

47. Miller-Young, "Hip Hop Honeys," 265.

48. Patterson, *Dark Strangers*, 51. See also Benson, *Ambiguous Ethnicities*.

49. Kokkinos interview.

50. Akua Rugg interview.

51. La Rose, "Michael La Rose," 126.

52. Ibid., 124. Paul Gilroy traces the origins of U.S. hip hop to the sound system culture that originated in Jamaica. See Gilroy, *There Ain't No Black in the Union Jack*, 258–62. See also Weheliye, *Phonographies*.

53. Kokkinos interview.

54. Gilroy, *There Ain't No Black in the Union Jack*, 216–17, 252–55, 261–65; Lipsitz, *Dangerous Crossroads*, 95–116.

55. Kokkinos interview.

56. Ibid.; Gilroy, *There Ain't No Black in the Union Jack*, 128, 279.

57. Kokkinos interview.

58. Mama, *Beyond the Masks*, 112.

59. Kokkinos interview.

60. Davis interview.

61. For more on the interracial politics of the underground British music and dance scene, see Bakare-Yusuf, "Raregrooves and Raregroovers."

62. Ramdin, *Black Working Class*, 370–71. See also Davies, *Left of Karl Marx*; Adi and Sherwood, *Pan-African History*; Sherwood, *Claudia Jones*; and B. Johnson, *"I Think of My Mother."*

63. Armstrong interview.

64. Rugg interview. For more on black youth's perceived criminality and their responses to it, see P. Evans, *Attitudes of Young Immigrants*.

65. L. K. Johnson, "Linton Kwesi Johnson," 54–55; Farrukh Dhondy interview; Armstrong interview.

66. In 1975, Morris enrolled in Manchester University. She became active in Manchester's Moss Side neighborhood, which was populated by Afro-Caribbean migrants. She joined the Black Women's Co-Op, Abasindi, and was involved in the antiapartheid and anticolonialism movements. See Keleman, "Olive in Manchester"; and Ruiz, "Diane Watt Interview."

67. Dhondy interview.

68. Armstrong interview.

69. Rugg interview.

70. Bryan, Dadzie, and Scafe, *Heart of the Race*, 63–67.

71. Quoted in May, "Poet Laureate," 29.

72. For similarities in tactics used by British activists and SNCC, see Tuck, "From Greensboro to Notting Hill."

73. Black Power Movement Photograph Collection, George Padmore Institute, London, England.

74. BASH flyer, Olive Morris Papers (hereafter OMP), iv/279/7/74/5, Lambeth Archives, London, England; Ramdin, *Black Working Class*, 452. BASH was formed from a collective of black- and Asian-centered organizations, including the Black Socialist Alliance, Bradford Asian Youth, MUKHTI, the Black Peoples Information Centre, the Black

Liberator, the "Sus" Campaign, Brixton Ad-hoc Committee against Police Repression, and the Brixton Black Women's Group.

75. Ramdin, *Black Working Class*, 370-71.

76. Benson, *Ambiguous Ethnicities*, 47.

77. La Rose, "Michael La Rose," 125.

78. Patterson, *Dark Strangers*, 21; Solomos, *Race and Racism in Britain*, 61-64.

79. Patterson, *Dark Strangers*, 48, 54.

80. La Rose, "Michael La Rose," 125.

81. Kenlock, "Photographs," 23.

82. Kokkinos interview.

83. Akua Rugg remembered similar sentiments within the Black Parents movement, which was formed by John La Rose and others in North London in the early 1970s. Though Rugg recalled that they were "a tight knit coalition," there was division among the group on whether nonblack parents with biracial children should be able to join the group. The Black Nationalists within the Black Parents movement won out, and nonblack parents were barred from joining. Rugg interview.

84. Angelo, "Black Panthers in London," 29; Dhondy interview; Kokkinos interview. Unlike many black organizations in London, the BPM refused to accept funding from the government, considering it an inherent conflict of interest. Therefore, it relied heavily upon fund-raising and on the income of its more wealthy members to pay for the organization's houses—on Portabello Road in Notting Hill, Barnsbury Road in Islington, and Shakespeare Road in Brixton—and its bookshop on Railton Road in Brixton. Farrukh Dhondy claimed that he and other gainfully employed Panthers had to use their own line of credit to purchase the houses. See Dhondy interview.

85. Dhondy interview; Angelo, "Black Panthers in London," 22; Kenlock, "Photographs," 23; Springer, "Stepping into the Struggle," 9.

86. De La Torre, "Finding Olive." The image described in the text of Morris at the protest was taken in 1969 by Neil Kenlock, the official BPM photographer, which suggests that she was a member of the BPM at this time.

87. On feminism, queerness, and dress, see Hillman, "'Clothes I Wear Help'"; Skerski, "Tomboy Chic"; Groeneveld, "'Be a Feminist or Just Dress Like One'"; and Scott, *Fresh Lipstick*. Most of this work centers on white women.

88. Gerlin Bean interview.

89. Kokkinos interview.

90. Dadzie interview.

91. Kochiyama, Huggins, and Kao, "'Stirrin' Waters' 'n Buildin' Bridges," 155.

92. Gutzmore, "Carnival," 332-33.

93. Springer, "Stepping into the Struggle"; "Callaghan Rebukes Diplomat," *Times* (London), November 18, 1969.

94. Springer, "Stepping into the Struggle"; Bryan, Dadzie, and Scafe, *Heart of the Race*, 152.

95. Ayo Martin Tajo, "In Remembrance of Olive Morris," OMP, iv/279/1/20/1.

96. "Transcription of Olive Morris's account of her encounter with the London Police in front of Desmond's Hip City" (hereafter "Olive Morris's Account") originally published in the *Black Peoples News Service*, May 1970, OMP, iv/279/1/23/29-31.

97. Ibid.; Hurlington Armstrong interview; Morris interview; Springer, "Stepping into the Struggle."

98. "Olive Morris's Account."

99. Ibid.

100. For images of the golliwog, see the digital archive of the Jim Crow Museum of Racist Memorabilia, http://www.ferris.edu/JIMCROW/golliwog/ (accessed August 19, 2014).

101. "Olive Morris's Account."

102. Bean interview; Armstrong interview.

103. "Olive Morris's Account."

104. Mireille Miller-Young discusses how these notions have played out historically in the sex industry in *Taste for Brown Sugar: Black Women in Pornography.*

105. "Olive Morris's Account."

106. Morris interview.

107. "Olive Morris's Account"; Springer, "Stepping into the Struggle."

108. Morris interview.

109. In their interviews, Akua Rugg, Gerlin Bean, and Stella Dadzie discuss what Rugg refers to as black men's "dreadful misogyny" within Black Power organizations in Britain. As a result, women formed their own formal and informal groups and organizations to address black women's dual oppression, birthing the black feminist movement in the mid-1970s. See also Bryan, Dadzie, and Scafe, *Heart of the Race*; Sudbury, *"Other Kinds of Dreams"*; Carby, "White Woman Listen!"; Amos and Parmar, "Challenging Imperial Feminism"; and Patel, "Third Wave Feminism."

110. For more on sexism within the U.S. Black Panther Party, see Matthews, "No One Ever Asks."

111. Mama, *Beyond the Masks*, 114.

112. Coombe, *Afro Hair and Skin Care.*

113. Clarke, "Lesbianism," 242.

114. Sudbury, *"Other Kinds of Dreams,"* 10.

115. Bean interview.

116. Bryan, Dadzie, and Scafe, *Heart of the Race*, 165.

117. Dadzie interview; Sudsbury, *"Other Kinds of Dreams,"* 10-11; Amos and Parmar, "Challenging Imperial Feminism," 56; Bean interview.

118. Morris interview.

119. Dadzie interview.

CHAPTER SIX

1. Ramphele, *Across Boundaries*, 58.

2. Alexander and Mngxitama, "Interview with Deborah Matshoba," 275, 280.

3. Ibid., 275.

4. Ramphele, *Across Boundaries*, 57-58. For more on "Black is Beautiful" in South Africa, see *Drum*, April 1970 issue.

5. Odhiambo, "Black Female Body," 76.

6. "Hot Pants Give Felicia a Big Pain," *Drum*, February 8, 1972, 45.

7. Suriano, "Clothing and Changing Identities," 95, 96.

8. Magaziner, "Pieces of a (Wo)man," 49.

9. Lanning, Roake, and Horning, *Life Soweto Style*, 79; Ribane, *Beauty*, 97.

10. The rich body of literature on cultural identity politics and self-naming among African diasporic subjects includes Gilroy, *Black Atlantic*; Angelou, *All God's Children Need Traveling Shoes*; Hartman, *Lose Your Mother*; Hanchard, *Orpheus and Power*; and Campt, "Afro-German Cultural Identity."

11. For more on soul culture, American blackness, and its contestations in Africa, see Plageman, *Highlife Saturday Night*; Ivaska, *Cultured States*; and Diawara, "1960s in Bamako."

12. Magaziner, "Pieces of a (Wo)man," 47–49.

13. Biko, *I Write What I Like*, 46.

14. "Afro Wigs," *Sepia*, November 1968, 48.

15. "It's Afro," *Drum*, June 8, 1973, 37.

16. Farber, "Africanized Hybridity?," 129, 131. For more on the history of the intersection of African and Western fashion, see Suriano, "Clothing and Changing Identities," 95–101; and Ribane, *Beauty*, 10.

17. Jennings, *New African Fashion*, 11.

18. Allman, *Fashioning Africa*, 5.

19. "When East Meets West It's Lovely," *Drum*, May 22, 1972, 38.

20. "African Fashion Getting Its Own Back," ibid., October 8, 1972, 63.

21. On Africans' responses to the Western fashion industry, see Allman, *Fashioning Africa*, 2–3; Draper, dir., *Versailles '73*, Nuttall, *Beautiful/Ugly*, 8; Jennings, *New African Fashion*, 12–13; Niessen, "Re-orienting Fashion Theory"; Gott and Loughran, *Contemporary African Fashion*, 1–8; and Mbembe, "Writing the World from an African Metropolis."

22. "150 Years Old . . . It's the Latest Look," *Drum*, June 22, 1972, n.p.; Gross, *Model*, 166. Gross argues that the miniskirt emerged from British street culture in the 1950s and that Quant's trendy Bazaar Boutique was merely the launching point that helped to popularize the silhouette. Even so, Gross's narrative of the history of the miniskirt renders it a Western innovation. See Prestholdt, *Domesticating the World*, for more on Tanzanian fashion in the global marketplace.

23. See Fair, *Pastimes and Politics*, for more on dress and culture in nineteenth- and early twentieth-century Tanzania; Lanning, Rourke, and Horning, *Life Soweto Style*, 79.

24. This mode of repurposing laborers' uniforms became an even more prominent aspect of South African haute couture postapartheid as lines such as the popular Loxion Kulća (slang for local culture) made fashionable the jacket-pants combo called the *mdantsane* (named after South Africa's second largest township), worn by migrant workers and miners, producing it in bright colors. See Nuttall, "Stylizing the Self," 437.

25. ". . . And They Call It Fashion . . . ," *Drum*, January 1971, 37.

26. Camaroff, *Body of Power*, 115–16.

27. Allman, *Fashioning Africa*, 3; Suriano, "Clothing and Changing Identities," 107. See also Hansen, *Salaula*.

28. Stanley Meisler, "Afros: Truly African?," *Washington Post, Times Herald*, December 13, 1970, K23. In 1969, *Drum* ran two consecutive articles on the elite jet set in South Africa that described a life a leisure filled with alcohol, fine clothing, nice homes and cars, and

beautiful people. We seldom associate such opulence with blacks in apartheid-era South Africa. But this lifestyle helped set a tone of resistance that crept into the expanding coverage of the Afro look and black consciousness as a whole. Paddy Tobin, "Welcome Loves Them All," *Drum*, December 1969, 26–27; Lionel Cupido, "It's One, Long Swinging Affair, ibid., December 1969, 28–29.

29. "African Fashion Getting Its Own Back," 62.

30. Suriano, "Clothing and Changing Identities," 107; Farber, "Africanising Hybridity?," 138, 142; Leon von Solms interview; Nonhlanhla Ngozi interview.

31. "African Fashion Getting Its Own Back," 62.

32. Nuttall, "Stylizing the Self," 432.

33. Ribane, *Beauty*, 74. Throughout the early 1970s, *Drum* ran advertisements for Kangol's "Big Apple cap," which Ribane calls the "Donny Hathaway cap" because the African American R&B crooner popularized the hat. See *Drum*, September 1971, 41, for an example.

34. "Everybody's Getting Steamed-up about Hot Pants," *Drum*, April 1971, 61; "The Beauty Queen," ibid., December 1971, 30; Starfield and Gardiner, *Citizenship and Modernity in Soweto*, 61, 70.

35. *Drum*, February 1971, 8.

36. "Let the Midi Go to Your Head," ibid., February 1971, 61; Sid Matlhaku, "Their Answer to Woodstock?," ibid., December 1970, 52.

37. Ngozi interview.

38. Suriano, "Clothing and Changing Identities," 99; Salo, "Negotiating Gender," 181, 185–86; Mager, *Gender*, 146.

39. Salo, "Negotiating Gender," 186; Thomas, "Modern Girl," 463. For more on urban dynamics and translocal politics, see Lohnert and Steinbrink, "Rural and Urban Livelihoods"; and Mbembe, "Aesthetics of Superfluity."

40. Salo, "Negotiating Gender," 174; Welsh, *Rise and Fall of Apartheid*, 93. For more on racial developments after apartheid, see MacDonald, *Why Race Matters in South Africa*; and Mbembe, "Aesthetics of Superfluity," 375–80.

41. Suriano, "Clothing and Changing Identities," 95; Mager, *Gender*, 146.

42. By feminist consciousness, I mean that there is evidence of feminist thinking. I am not trying to frame their politics within a Western model of the feminist movement. For more on African feminisms and challenging Western frameworks of feminism in Africa and Asia, see Spurlin, "Resisting Heteronormativity"; Mohanty, "Under Western Eyes" and *Feminism Without Borders*; Mekgwe, "Post Africa(n) Feminism?"; M. Cooper, "Preventing the Gendered Reproduction of Citizenship"; and Daymond, *South African Feminisms*.

43. "Colourama," *Drum*, June 1971, 41.

44. Lubiano, "Black Ladies," 335.

45. L. Thompson, *Beyond the Black Lady*, 2. See also Tamale, *African Sexualities*.

46. Glick, "Sex Positive," 20.

47. Sanger, "Imagining Possibilities," 64.

48. Ciclitira, "Pornography, Women, and Feminism," 281.

49. Marion Morel, "Girl about Town," *Drum*, January 1963, 17.

50. Suriano, "Clothing and Changing Identities," 106; Salo, "Negotiating Gender," 180.

51. Burke, *Lifebuoy Men and Lux Women*, 4, 187; Ribane, *Beauty*, 82.

52. "Why Swinging Shirley Ditched Her Doc Hubby," *Drum*, January 1970, 44.

53. Mekgwe, "Post Africa(n) Feminism?," 193; Mager, *Gender*, 161; Salo, "Negotiating Gender," 179; Spurlin, "Resisting Heteronormativity," 15, 18.

54. "Ye Gods, What Girls!," *Drum*, March 1970, 32.

55. Thomas, "Modern Girl," 466.

56. "Butterfly," *Drum*, January 1970, 41–42.

57. Mager, *Gender*, 161; Salo, "Negotiating Gender," 179–80, 185–86. See also Mager, *Beer, Sociability, and Masculinity in South Africa*.

58. "You Have Been Warned," *Drum*, July 7, 1973, 41.

59. "150 Years," n.p.

60. Meisler, "Afros," K23; Ivaska, *Cultured States*, 79–81.

61. Suriano, "Clothing and Changing Identities," 107; "Oh Boy!," *Drum*, August 8, 1972, 47.

62. Spurlin, "Resisting Heteronormativity," 15.

63. For more on the role of culture in nation building during the struggle for independence and in postcolonial Africa, see Askew, *Performing the Nation*; and Moorman, *Intonations*. Together, these works help us think critically about how culture is both used by the state as a nation-building project and by "the people" as a form of resistance.

64. Diawara, "1960s in Bamako."

65. Magaziner, *Law and the Prophets*, 111.

66. Mudaly, "Shattering and Reassembling Hypersexual Moments," 228.

67. "Oh Those 'Immoral' Minis," *Drum*, February 1969, 39. See also Ivaska, "'Anti-mini Militants Meet Modern Misses.'"

68. Meisler, "Afros," K21.

69. "When East Meets West It's Lovely," 38; Meisler, "Afros," K21.

70. "Rema Doesn't Dig a Wig," *Drum*, June 1969, 44.

71. Ramphele, *Across Boundaries*, 57.

72. Quoted in Meisler, "Afros," K21.

73. Ibid.

74. Magaziner, *Law and the Prophets*, 47. *Drum*'s coverage of the student protests related to black consciousness focused on young men; images of male youth with raised clenched fists dominated the coverage. For examples, see "Trouble at the Tribal Varsities," *Drum*, July 8, 1972, 23–26; "SASO: A New Dawn or a Final Sunset," *Drum*, August 8, 1972, 7–10; and "Student Power Stirs at Orlando," *Drum*, October 22, 1972, 46–48.

75. Biko, *I Write What I Like*, 46. See also "Rema Doesn't Dig a Wig," 44.

76. "Ye Gods, What Girls!," 32.

77. Meisler, "Afros," K21.

78. Lette Matthebe interview.

79. "Afro Wigs," 50.

80. Vanessa King, "It's Here at Last!," *Drum*, April 1970, 7. In my examination of three decades of *Drum* magazine, this is the earliest advertisement I have seen for an Afro wig, which confirms King's claim. In the early 1970s, most of the *Drum* cover girls wore Afros, Afro wigs, or other tightly curled styles that mimicked the Afro. On the significance of magazine cover models, see Odhiambo, "Black Female Body."

81. Selfast wig advertisement, *Drum*, October 1970, 21.

82. Enchantress Wigs advertisement, ibid., September 8, 1972, 55.

83. Kool Look Wigs advertisement, ibid., June 22, 1972, 3.

84. Meisler, "Afros," K21.

85. Maureen Kumalo, "If You Want a Man Get a Wig," *Drum*, September 1971, 43.

86. Ribane, *Beauty*, 76–77; Erasmus, "Hair Politics," 389–92.

87. Claire Mawisa interview.

88. Farber, "Africanized Hybridity?," 150.

89. Nkhensani Nkosi interview.

90. Philani Nombembe, "Madiba Shirts All the Rage," *Times Live*, June 27, 2013, http://www.timeslive.co.za/thetimes/2013/06/27/madiba-shirts-all-the-rage (accessed December 15, 2013).

91. Fassin, *When Bodies Remember*, xv.

92. Ngozi interview.

93. Barnard, "Contesting Beauty," 352; Ribane, *Beauty*, 93.

94. Nkosi interview.

EPILOGUE

1. Adam Klapholtz, "Buy a Swimsuit, Save Africa," *Vanity Fair*, September 16, 2008, http://www.vanityfair.com/online/daily/2008/09/buy-a-swimsuit-save-africa (accessed November 23, 2014).

2. Olivia Bergin, "ASOS Africa Goes from Stitch to Strength," *Telegraph*, October 21, 2013, http://fashion.telegraph.co.uk/article/TMG10393884/ASOS-Africa-goes-from -stitch-to-strength.html (accessed November 23, 2014).

3. Liz Alderman, "Fashion Weighs a Deeper Investment in Africa," *New York Times*, November 15, 2012, http://www.nytimes.com/2012/11/16/business/global/fashion-houses -take-notice-of-africas-rise.html?_r=1& (accessed June 12, 2014); Howard W. French, "The Next Asia Is Africa: Inside the Continent's Rapid Economic Growth," *Atlantic*, May 21, 2012, http://www.theatlantic.com/international/archive/2012/05/the-next-asia-is -africa-inside-the-continents-rapid-economic-growth/257441/ (accessed September 20, 2014).

4. Simon Mevel et al., "The African Growth and Opportunity Act: An Empirical Analysis of the Possibilities Post-2015," *Brookings*, July 2013, http://www.brookings.edu /research/reports/2013/07/african-growth-and-opportunity-act (accessed December 1, 2014).

Bibliography

MANUSCRIPT AND SPECIAL COLLECTIONS

Berkeley, Calif.
    University of California Periodical Collection
        Drum (microfilm)
Bloomington, Ind.
    Indiana University Archives
        Black Student Life/Activism Papers
Chicago, Ill.
    Center for Black Music Research, Columbia College
        Album Collection
        Sue Cassidy Clark Collection
London, England
    Black Cultural Archives
        Black Culture Ephemera Collection
        Olive Morris Collection
    George Padmore Institute
        Black Power Movement Photograph Collection
        Race Today Collection
    Lambeth Archives
        Do You Remember Olive Morris Oral History Project (DYROM)
        Olive Morris Papers
Madison, Wisc.
    Wisconsin Historical Society
        CORE Papers
New York, N.Y.
    Schomburg Center for Research in Black Culture
        Kwame Brathwaite Collection
        Klytus Smith Collection
        Miriam Makeba Portrait Collection
        Odetta Papers
        Odetta Photograph Collection
        Odetta Portrait Collection

INTERVIEWS

Armstrong, Hurlington. Interviewed by DYROM. Date not given.
Bean, Gerlin. Interviewed by DYROM. September 9, 2009.
Bedford, Emma. Interviewed by author. London, England. November 26, 2009.

Bell, Debbie Amis. Interviewed by author via telephone. June 14, 2011.

Brown, Ellen (alias). Interviewed by author. London, England. December 14, 2009.

Dadzie, Stella. Interviewed by DYROM. May 29, 2009.

Davis, Janet (alias). Interviewed by author. London, England. October 13, 2009.

De La Torre, Ana Laura Lopez. Interviewed by author. London, England. December 16, 2009.

Dhondy, Farrukh. Interviewed by DYROM. Date not given.

Duncan, Natanya. Interviewed by author via telephone. July 25, 2014.

Glover-Ford, Amye. Interviewed by author via telephone. November 17, 2010.

Kokkinos, Sophia. Interviewed by DYROM. July 22, 2009.

Ladner, Joyce. Interviewed by author via e-mail. June 13, 2014.

Lewis, Jennifer. Interviewed by DYROM. October 14, 2009.

Matthebe, Lette. Interviewed by author. Johannesburg, South Africa. March 3, 2012.

Mawisa, Claire. Interviewed by author. Johannesburg, South Africa. April 2, 2012.

Morris, Basil. Interviewed by DYROM. October 9, 2009.

Ngozi, Nonhlanhla. Interviewed by author. Johannesburg, South Africa. April 2, 2012.

Nkosi, Nkhensani. Interviewed by author via e-mail. June 10, 2013.

Noonan, Martha Prescod Norman. Interviewed by author via telephone. February 2, 2013.

Richardson, Judy. Interviewed by author via telephone. July 13, 2011.

Rugg, Akua. Interviewed by author. London, England. December 13, 2009.

Singh, Rashna. Interviewed by author via telephone. December 18, 2008.

Solms, Leon von. Interviewed by author. Johannesburg, South Africa. April 5, 2012.

GOVERNMENT PAMPHLETS AND DOCUMENTS

Coombe, Vivienne. *Afro Hair and Skin Care*. Community Relations Commission, December 1975. Black Culture Ephemera Collection, Black Cultural Archives, London, England.

Federal Bureau of Investigation. Student Nonviolent Coordinating Committee File. Indiana University Bloomington (microfilm).

Parliament of the United Kingdom. Commonwealth Immigrants Act. April 18, 1962. https://www.gov.uk/government/uploads/system/uploads/attachment_data/file/268009/immigrationacts.pdf (accessed February 21, 2011).

MAGAZINES AND SERIALS

Atlantic	*Flamingo*
Black Music and Jazz Review	*Indianapolis Recorder*
Black Panther	*Liberator*
Chicago Tribune	*Life*
Drum	*Los Angeles Times*
Ebony	*Ms.*
Essence	*Muhammad Speaks*

Negro Digest	*Sepia*
Newsweek	*Sing Out!*
New York Amsterdam News	*Soul Illustrated*
New York Times	*Style House Files*
Pittsburgh Courier	*Telegraph*
Playboy	*The Times* (London)
Race Today	*Times Live*
Roctober Magazine	*Vanity Fair*
San Diego Union Tribune	*Washington Post, Times Herald*
Seattle Post Intelligencer	

ALBUMS

Brown, James. *It's a Man's Man's Man's World*. King Records, 1966.

Donaldson, Lou. *Good Gracious*. Blue Note, 1963.

———. *The Natural Soul*. Blue Note, 1962.

Franklin, Aretha. *Amazing Grace*. Atlantic, 1972.

Makeba, Miriam. *The Many Voices of Miriam Makeba*. Kapp Records, 1962.

———. *Miriam Makeba*. RCA Record, 1960.

———. *The Voice of Africa*. RCA, 1964.

Odetta. *Odetta Sings Ballads and Blues*. Tradition, 1956.

———. *Odetta Sings Folk Songs*. RCA Victor, 1963.

———. *The Tin Angel*. Vanguard, 1954.

Patton, Big John. *Oh Baby!* Blue Note, 1965.

Roach, Freddie. *Brown Sugar*. Blue Note, 1964.

Roach, Max. *We Insist!: Max Roach's Freedom Now Suite*. Candid Records, 1960.

Simone, Nina. *Black Gold*. RCA Victor, 1969.

———. *High Priestess of Soul*. Phillips, 1967.

FILMS

Come Back, Africa. Directed by Lionel Rogosin. Milestone Films, 1959.

Free Angela and All Political Prisoners. Directed by Shola Lynch. LionsGate, 2013.

Mama Africa. Directed by Mika Kaurismaki. Starhaus Filmproduktion, 2011.

Odetta: Exploring Life, Music, and Song. Directed by Happy Traum. Homespun Entertainment, 1999.

Versailles '73: American Runway Revolution. Directed by Deborah Riley Draper. Coffee Bluff Pictures, 2012.

We Shall Overcome. Directed by Jim Brown. California Newsreel, 1989.

YEARBOOKS

Arbutus. Indiana University, Bloomington, Indiana.

Caldron. Central High School, Fort Wayne, Indiana.

ARTICLES AND BOOK CHAPTERS

Alexander, Amanda, and Andile Mngxitama. "Interview with Deborah Matshoba."
    In *Biko Lives!: Contesting the Legacies of Steve Biko*, edited by Amanda Alexander,
    Nigel C. Gibson, and Andile Mngxitama, 275–84. New York: Palgrave, 2008.
Amos, Valerie, and Pratibha Parmar. "Challenging Imperial Feminism." In *Black British
    Feminism: A Reader*, edited by Heidi Safia Mirza, 54–58. New York: Routledge, 1997.
Angelo, Anne-Marie. "The Black Panthers in London, 1967–1972: A Diasporic Struggle
    Navigates the Black Atlantic." *Radical History Review*, no. 103 (Winter 2009): 17–35.
Ash, Juliet. "The Business of Couture." In *Zoot Suits and Second-Hand Dresses: An
    Anthology of Fashion and Music*, edited by Angela McRobbie, 208–14. Boston: Unwin
    Hyman, 1988.
Bakare-Yusuf, Bibi. "Raregrooves and Raregroovers: A Matter of Taste, Difference, and
    Identity." In *Black British Feminism: A Reader*, edited by Heidi Safia Mirza, 81–96.
    New York: Routledge, 1997.
Baldwin, Davarian. "'Culture Is a Weapon in Our Struggle for Liberation': The Black
    Panther Party and the Cultural Politics of Decolonization." In *In Search of the Black
    Panther Party: New Perspectives on a Revolutionary Movement*, edited by Jama
    Lazerow and Yohuru Williams, 289–305. Durham: Duke University Press, 2006.
Baraka, Amiri. "The 'Blues Aesthetic' and the 'Black Aesthetic': Aesthetics as the
    Continuing Political History of a Culture." *Black Music Research Journal* 11, no. 2
    (Autumn 1991): 101–9.
Barnard, Rita. "Contesting Beauty." In *Senses of Culture: South African Cultural Studies*,
    edited by Sarah Nuttall and Cheryl-Ann Michael, 344–62. New York: Oxford
    University Press, 2000.
Baxandall, Rosalyn. "Re-visioning the Women's Liberation Movement's Narrative: Early
    Second Wave African American Feminists." *Feminist Studies* 27, no. 1 (Spring 2001):
    225–45.
Bose, Purnima. "From Humanitarian Intervention to the Beautifying Mission: Afghan
    Women and Beauty without Borders." *Genders* 51 (2010). http://www.genders.org/g51
    /q51bose.html (accessed August 2010).
Brathwaite, Kwame (Ronnie). "Art, Artists, and Activism: The Black Arts Movement
    Revisited." Posted on the *National Conference of Artists of New York* website,
    ncanewyork.com/2006_flies/revisted.htm (accessed May 5, 2009).
Camp, Stephanie. "The Pleasures of Resistance: Enslaved Women and Body Politics in
    the Plantation South, 1830–1961." *Journal of Southern History* 68, no. 3 (August 2002):
    533–72.
Campt, Tina. "Afro-German Cultural Identity and the Politics of Positionality: Contests
    and Contexts in the Formation of a German Ethnic Identity." *New German Critique*
    58 (Winter 1993): 109–27.
Carby, Hazel. "White Woman Listen!: Black Feminism and the Boundaries of
    Sisterhood." In *The Empire Strikes Back: Race and Racism in 70s Britain*, edited by
    Centre for Contemporary Cultural Studies, 183–211. London: Hutchinson, 1982.
Chappell, Marissa, Jenny Hutchinson, and Brian Ward. "'Dress Modestly and Neatly
    . . . as if You Were Going to Church': Respectability, Class, and Gender in the

Montgomery Bus Boycott and the Early Civil Rights Movement." In *Gender and the Civil Rights Movement*, edited by Peter J. Ling and Sharon Monteith, 69–100. New Brunswick, N.J.: Rutgers University Press, 2004.

Ciclitira, Karen. "Pornography, Women, and Feminism: Between Pleasure and Politics." *Sexualities* 7, no. 3 (2004): 281–301.

Clarke, Cheryl. "Lesbianism: An Act of Resistance." In *Words of Fire: An Anthology of African-American Feminist Thought*, edited by Beverly Guy-Sheftall, 242–52. New York: New Press, 1995.

Cleaver, Kathleen Neal. "Women, Power, and Revolution." In *Liberation, Imagination, and the Black Panther Party: A New Look at the Panthers and Their Legacy*, edited by Kathleen Cleaver and George Katsiaficas, 123–27. New York: Routledge, 2001.

Clemons, Michael L., and Charles E. Jones. "Global Solidarity: The Black Panther Party in the International Arena." In *Liberation, Imagination, and the Black Panther Party: A New Look at the Panthers and Their Legacy*, edited by Kathleen Cleaver and George Katsiaficas, 20–39. New York: Routledge, 2001.

Cook, Ann. "Black Pride? Some Contradictions." In *The Black Woman: An Anthology*, edited by Toni Cade, 149–61. New York: Penguin, 1970.

Cooks, Carlos. "Buy Black." In *Modern Black Nationalism: From Marcus Garvey to Louis Farrakhan*, edited by William Van Deburg, 85–92. New York: New York University Press, 1997.

———. "Ethiopia, Haiti, Liberia, Kenya: The Black Woman." In *Carlos Cooks and Black Nationalism from Garvey to Malcolm X*, edited by Robert Harris, Nyota Harris, and Grandassa Harris, 89–106. Dover, Mass.: Majority Press, 1992.

———. "What Is the ANPM?" *Carlos Cooks and Black Nationalism from Garvey to Malcolm X*, edited by Robert Harris, Nyota Harris, and Grandassa Harris, 3–4. Dover, Mass.: Majority Press, 1992.

Cooper, Carolyn. "Caribbean Fashion Week: Remodeling Beauty in 'Out of Many One' Jamaica." *Fashion Theory* 14, no. 2 (September 2010): 387–404.

Cooper, Meghan. "Preventing the Gendered Reproduction of Citizenship: The Role of Social Movements in South Africa." *Gender and Development* 3, no. 19 (November 2011): 357–70.

Craig, Maxine. "The Decline and Fall of the Conk; or, How to Read a Process." *Fashion Theory* 1, no. 4 (December 1997): 399–420.

Davis, Angela. "Afro Images: Politics, Fashion, and Nostalgia." In *Soul: Black Power, Politics, and Pleasure*, edited by Monique Guillory and Richard C. Green, 23–31. New York: New York University Press, 1998.

De La Torre, Ana Laura Lopez. "Finding Olive." In *Do You Remember Olive Morris?*, edited by Anna Collin, Tanisha Ford, Ana Laura Lopez De La Torre, and Kimberly Springer, 63. London: Gasworks and Remembering Olive Collective, 2009.

Diawara, Manthia. "The 1960s in Bamako: Malick Sidibè and James Brown." In *Black Cultural Traffic: Crossroads in Global Performance and Popular Culture*, edited by Harry J. Elam Jr. and Kennell Jackson, 242–65. Ann Arbor: University of Michigan Press, 2005.

Entwistle, Joanne. "The Dressed Body." In *The Fashion Reader*, edited by Linda Welters and Abby Lillethun, 93–104. New York: Berg, 2007.

Erasmus, Zimitri. "Hair Politics." In *Senses of Culture: South African Cultural Studies*, edited by Sarah Nuttall and Cheryl-Ann Michael, 380–92. New York: Oxford University Press, 2000.

Farber, Leora. "Africanized Hybridity? Toward an Afropolitan Aesthetic in Contemporary South African Fashion Design." *Critical Arts* 24, no. 1 (2010): 128–67.

Feldstein, Ruth. "'I Don't Trust You Anymore': Nina Simone, Culture, and Black Activism in the 1960s." *Journal of American History* 91, no. 4 (March 2005): 1349–79.

———. "Nina Simone's Border Crossings: Black Cultural Nationalism and Gender on a Global Stage." In *Race, Nation, and Empire in American History*, edited by James T. Campbell, Matthew Pratt Guterl, and Robert G. Lee, 277–306. Chapel Hill: University of North Carolina Press, 2007.

———. "Screening Apartheid: Miriam Makeba, 'Come Back, Africa,' and the Transnational Circulation of Black Culture and Politics." *Feminist Studies* 39, no. 1 (March 2013): 12–39.

Ford, Tanisha C. "Odetta." In *African American National Biography*, edited by Henry Louis Gates Jr. and Evelyn Brooks Higginbotham, 178–79. New York: University of Oxford Press, 2007.

Gaines, Kevin. "From Center to Margin: Internationalism and the Origins of Black Feminism." In *Materializing Democracy: Toward a Revitalized Cultural Politics*, edited by Russ Castronovo and Dana Nelson, 294–313. Durham: Duke University Press, 2002.

Geary, Daniel. "'Becoming International Again': C. Wright Mills and the Emergence of a Global New Left, 1956–1962." *Journal of American History* 93, no. 3 (December 2008): 710–36.

Gill, Tiffany M. "'I Had My Own Business . . . So I Didn't Have to Worry': Beauty Salons, Beauty Culturalists, and the Politics of African American Female Entrepreneurship." In *Beauty and Business: Commerce, Gender, and Culture in Modern America*, edited by Phillip Scranton, 169–94. New York: Routledge, 2001.

Glick, Elisa. "Sex Positive: Feminism, Queer Theory, and the Politics of Transgression." *Feminist Review* 64 (Spring 2000): 19–45, 20.

Groeneveld, Elizabeth. "'Be a Feminist or Just Dress Like One': *Bust*, Fashion and Feminism." *Journal of Gender Studies* 18, no. 2 (June 2009): 179–90.

Gutzmore, Cecil. "Carnival, the State, and the Black Masses in the United Kingdom." In *Black British Culture and Society*, edited by Kwesi Owusu, 332–46. New York: Routledge, 2000.

Haidarali, Laila. "Polishing Brown Diamonds: African American Women, Popular Magazines, and the Advent of Modeling in Early Post-war America." *Journal of Women's History*, no. 17 (2005): 10–37.

Hall, Stuart. "What Is This 'Black' in Black Popular Culture?" In *Black Popular Culture*, edited by Gina Dent, 21–36. New York: New Press, 1998.

Hamlin, Kimberly A. "Bathing Suits and Backlash: The First Miss America Pageants, 1921–1927." In *There She Is, Miss America: The Politics of Sex, Beauty, and Race in America's Most Famous Pageant*, edited by Elwood Watson and Darcy Martin, 27–52. New York: Palgrave, 2004.

Hayden, Casey. "In the Attics of My Mind." In *Hands on the Freedom Plow: Personal*

Accounts from Women in SNCC, edited by Faith S. Holsaert et al., 381–88. Urbana-Champaign: University of Illinois Press, 2012.

Hayes, Floyd W., and Francis A. Kiene. "All Power to the People: The Political Thoughts of Huey P. Newton and the Black Panther Party." In *The Black Panther Party Reconsidered*, edited by Charles E. Jones, 157–76. Baltimore: Black Classic Press, 1998.

Hayes, Robin J., and Christina M. Greer. "The International Dimensions of Everyday Black Political Participation." *Journal of African American Studies*, December 19, 2013, n.p.

Hillman, Betty Luther. "'The Clothes I Wear Help Me to Know My Own Power': The Power of Gender Presentation in the Era of Women's Liberation." *Frontiers* 34, no. 2 (June 2013): 155–85.

Hine, Darlene Clark. "Rape and the Inner Lives of Black Women in the Middle West: Preliminary Thoughts on the Culture of Dissemblance." *Signs: Journal of Women in Culture and Society* 14, no. 4 (Summer 1989): 912–20.

hooks, bell. "Straightening Our Hair." *Z Magazine*, Summer 1998, 14–18.

Huss, Hasse. "The 'Zinc-Fence Thing': When Will Reggae Album Covers Be Allowed Out of the Ghetto?" *Black Music Research Journal* 20, no. 2 (Autumn 2000): 181–94.

Ibrahiim, Khadijah. "Calling All Afro and 'Fro Wearing Brothers and Sistahs." In *Do You Remember Olive Morris?*, edited by Anna Collin, Tanisha Ford, Ana Laura Lopez De La Torre, and Kimberly Springer, 35. London: Gasworks and Remembering Olive Collective, 2009.

Ifekwunigwe, Jayne O. "Diaspora's Daughters, Africa's Orphans: On Lineage, Authenticity, and 'Mixed' Race Identity." In *Black British Feminism: A Reader*, edited by Heidi Safia Mirza, 127–52. New York: Routledge, 1997.

Ivaska, Andrew. "'Anti-mini Militants Meet Modern Misses': Urban Style, Gender, and the Politics of 'National Culture' in 1960s Dar es Salaam, Tanzania." *Gender and History* 14, no. 3 (November 2002): 584–607.

Johnson, Linton Kwesi. "Linton Kwesi Johnson: In Conversation with John La Rose." In *Changing Britannia: Life Experience with Britain*, edited by Roxy Harris and Sarah White, 51–79. London: New Beacon Books for the George Padmore Institute, 1999.

Jones, Adele, et al. "Ebony Minds, Black Voices." In *The Black Woman: An Anthology*, edited by Toni Cade, 180–88. New York: Penguin, 1970.

Jones, Leroi. "The Need for a Cultural Base to Civil Rights and Black Power Movements." In *The Black Power Revolt*, edited by Floyd B. Barbour, 119–26. Boston: Extended Horizons, 1968.

Keleman, Paul. "Olive in Manchester." In *Do You Remember Olive Morris?*, edited by Anna Collin, Tanisha Ford, Ana Laura Lopez De La Torre, and Kimberly Springer, 40–41. London: Gasworks and Remembering Olive Collective, 2009.

Kelley, Robin D. G. "Nap Time: Historicizing the Afro." *Fashion Theory* 1, no. 4 (1997): 339–51.

Kenlock, Neil. "Photographs." In *Do You Remember Olive Morris?*, edited by Anna Collin, Tanisha Ford, Ana Laura Lopez De La Torre, and Kimberly Springer, 20–24. London: Gasworks and Remembering Olive Collective, 2009.

Kernodle, Tammy L. "'I Wish I Knew How It Would Feel to Be Free': Nina Simone and the Redefining of the Freedom Song of the 1960s." *Journal of the Society for American Music* 2, no. 3 (2008): 295-317.

Kinloch, Valerie Felita. "The Rhetoric of Black Bodies: Race, Beauty, and Representation." In *There She Is, Miss America: The Politics of Sex, Beauty, and Race in America's Most Famous Pageant*, edited by Elwood Watson and Darcy Martin, 93-110. New York: Palgrave, 2004.

Kochiyama, Yuri, Ericka Huggins, and Mary Uyematsu Kao. "'Stirrin' Waters' 'n Buildin' Bridges: A Conversation with Ericka Huggins and Yuri Kochiyama." *Amerasian Journal* 35, no. 1 (2009): 140-67.

Lang, Kurt, and Gladys Engel Lang. "The Power of Fashion." In *The Fashion Reader*, edited by Linda Welters and Abby Lillethun, 83-86. New York: Berg, 2007.

La Rose, Michael. "Michael La Rose." In *Changing Britannia: Life Experience with Britain*, edited by Roxy Harris and Sarah White, 121-48. London: New Beacon Books for the George Padmore Institute, 1999.

Lipsitz, George. "Who Will Stop the Rain? Youth Culture, Rock n' Roll, and Social Crisis." In *The 60s: From Memory to History*, edited by David Farber, 206-34. Chapel Hill: University of North Carolina Press, 1994.

Lohnert, B., and M. Steinbrink. "Rural and Urban Livelihoods: A Translocal Perspective in a South African Context." *South Africa Geographical Journal* 87, no. 2 (2005): 95-103.

Lubiano, Wahneema. "Black Ladies, Welfare Queens, and State Minstrels: Ideological War by Narrative Means." In *Race-ing Justice, En-gendering Power: Essays on Anita Hill, Clarence Thomas, and the Construction of Social Reality*, edited by Toni Morrison, 323-63. New York: Pantheon, 1992.

Magaziner, Daniel R. "Pieces of a (Wo)man: Feminism, Gender, and Adulthood in Black Consciousness, 1968-1977." *Journal of Southern African Studies* 37, no. 1 (March 2011): 45-61.

Makhudu, K. D. P. "An Introduction to Flaaitaal." In *Language and Social History: Studies in South African Sociolinguistics*, edited by Rajend Mesthrie, 298-305. Cape Town: David Phillip Publishers, 1995.

Mathieu, Sarah-Jane. "The African American Great Migration Reconsidered." *OAH Magazine of History* 23 (October 2009): 19-23.

Matthews, Tracye. "No One Ever Asks What a Man's Role in the Revolution Is: Gender and the Politics of the Black Panther Party, 1966-1971." In *The Black Panther Party Reconsidered*, edited by Charles E. Jones, 267-304. Baltimore: Black Classic Press, 1998.

Mbembe, Achille. "The Aesthetics of Superfluity." *Public Culture* 16, no. 3 (Fall 2004): 373-405.

Mbembe, Achille, and Sarah Nuttall. "Writing the World from an African Metropolis." *Public Culture* 16, no. 3 (Fall 2004): 347-71.

McAndrew, Malia. "Selling Black Beauty: African American Modeling Agencies and Charm Schools in Postwar America." *OAH Magazine of History* 24, no. 1 (January 2010): 29-32.

McGee, Holly Y. "Negro Notes from the U.S.A.: Social Perception and Interpretations of Race and Gender in the United States and South Africa, 1945-1965." *Journal of Pan African Studies* 3, no. 1 (September 2009): 54-74.

McGregor, Murray. "The Chaos of 'Bantu' Education." https://murraymcgregor
.wordpress.com/chapter-15-the-chaos-of-"bantu"-education/ (accessed July 23,
2013).

McMichael, Robert K. "'We Insist—Freedom Now!': Black Moral Authority, Jazz, and
the Changeable Shape of Whiteness." *American Music* 16, no. 4 (Winter 1998): 375–
416.

McRobbie, Angela. "Second-Hand Dresses and the Ragmarket." In *Zoot Suits and
Second-Hand Dresses: An Anthology of Fashion and Music*, edited by Angela
McRobbie, 25–49. Boston: Unwin Hyman, 1988.

Mekgwe, Pinkie. "Post Africa(n) Feminism?" *Third Text* 24, no. 2 (March 2010): 189–94.

Mercer, Kobena. "Black Hair/Style Politics." In *Out There: Marginalization and
Contemporary Cultures*, edited by Russell Ferguson et al., 247–64. Cambridge, Mass.:
MIT Press, 1990.

Miller-Young, Mireille. "Hip Hop Honeys and Da Hustlaz: Black Sexualities in the New
Hip Hop Pornography." *Meridians: Feminism, Race, and Transnationalism* 8, no. 1
(2008): 261–92.

Mohanty, Chandra. "Under Western Eyes: Feminist Scholarship and Colonial
Discourses." *Feminist Review* 30 (1988): 61–88.

Monson, Ingrid. "The Problem with White Hipness: Race, Gender, and Cultural
Conceptions in Jazz Historical Discourse." *Journal of American Musicology Society*
48, no. 3 (Autumn 1995): 396–422.

Mudaly, Ronika. "Shattering and Reassembling Hypersexual Moments: Girls Indulging
in the Pursuit of Pleasure." *Sexualities* 15, no. 2 (March 2012): 225–42.

Nguyen, Mimi Thi. "The Biopower of Beauty: Humanitarian Imperialisms and Global
Feminisms in the War on Terror." *Signs: Journal of Women in Culture and Society* 26,
no. 2 (2011): 359–83.

Niessen, Sandra. "Re-orienting Fashion Theory." In *The Fashion Reader*, edited by Linda
Welters and Abby Lillethun, 105–10. New York: Berg, 2007.

Nuttall, Sarah. "Stylizing the Self: The Y Generation in Rosebank, Johannesburg." *Public
Culture* 16, no. 3 (Fall 2004): 430–52.

Odhiambo, Tom. "The Black Female Body as a 'Consumer and a Consumable' in
Current *Drum* and *True Love* Magazines in South Africa." *African Studies* 67, no. 1
(April 2008): 71–80.

Patel, Pragna. "Third Wave Feminism and Black Women's Activism." In *Black British
Feminism: A Reader*, edited by Heidi Safia Mirza, 255–68. New York: Routledge, 1997.

Patterson, Tiffany Ruby, and Robin D. G. Kelley. "Unfinished Migrations: Reflections on
the African Diaspora and the Making of the Modern World." *African Studies Review*
43, no. 1 (April 2000): 11–45.

Pham, Minh-Ha T. "Blog Ambition: Fashion, Feelings, and the Political Economy of the
Digital Raced Body." *Camera Obscura: Feminism, Culture, and Media Studies* 26,
no. 1 (April 2011): 1–37.

Powell, Azizi. "African Women's Attire at CFUN." Posted on www.cocojams.com
/clothing.htm, January 7, 2006 (accessed May 7, 2009).

———. "Why I Started Wearing African Dresses." Posted on www.cocojams.com
/clothing.htm, January 8, 2006 (accessed May 7, 2009).

Putnam, Lara. "Nothing Matters but Color: Transnational Circuits, the Interwar Caribbean, and the Black International." In *From Toussaint to Tupac: The Black International since the Age of Revolution*, edited by Michael O. West, William G. Martin, and Fanon Che Wilkins, 107–29. Chapel Hill: University of North Carolina Press, 2009.

Richardson, Judy. "SNCC: My Enduring 'Circle of Trust.'" In *Hands on the Freedom Plow: Personal Accounts from Women in SNCC*, edited by Faith S. Holsaert et al., 348–65. Urbana-Champaign: University of Illinois Press, 2012.

Rowe, Rochelle. "'Glorifying the Jamaican Girl': The 'Ten Types—One People' Beauty Contest, Racialized Femininities, and Jamaican Nationalism." *Radical History Review*, no. 103 (Winter 2009): 36–58.

Ruiz, Sheila. "Diane Watt Interview." In *Do You Remember Olive Morris?*, edited by Anna Collin, Tanisha Ford, Ana Laura Lopez De La Torre, and Kimberly Springer, 42–47. London: Gasworks and Remembering Olive Collective, 2009.

Salo, Elaine. "Negotiating Gender and Personhood in the New South Africa: Adolescent Women and Gangsters in Manenberg Township on the Cape Flats." In *Limits to Liberation after Apartheid: Citizenship, Governance, and Culture*, edited by Steven L. Robins, 173–89. Athens: Ohio University Press, 2005.

Sanger, Nadia. "Imagining Possibilities: Feminist Cultural Production, Non-violent Identities, and Embracing the Other in Post-colonial South Africa." *African Identities* 11, no. 1 (2013): 61–78.

Scheuring, Dirk. "Heavy Duty Denim: 'Quality Never Dates.'" In *Zoot Suits and Second-Hand Dresses: An Anthology of Fashion and Music*, edited by Angela McRobbie, 225–36. Boston: Unwin Hyman, 1988.

Shor, Francis. "Utopian Aspirations in the Black Freedom Movement: SNCC and the Struggle for Civil Rights, 1960–1965." *Utopian Studies* 15, no. 2 (Winter 2004): 173–89.

Simmons, Gwendolyn Zoharah (Gwendolyn Robinson). "From Little Memphis Girl to Mississippi Amazon." In *Hands on the Freedom Plow: Personal Accounts from Women in SNCC*, edited by Faith S. Holsaert et al., 9–32. Urbana-Champaign: University of Illinois Press, 2012.

Sizemore-Barber, April. "The Voice of (Which?) Africa: Miriam Makeba in America." *Safundi: The Journal of South African Studies* 13, nos. 3–4 (July–October 2012): 251–76.

Skerski, Jamie. "Tomboy Chic: Re-fashioning Gender Rebellion." *Journal of Lesbian Studies* 15 (October 2011): 466–79.

Small, Stephen. "Introduction: The Empire Strikes Back." In *Black Europe and the African Diaspora*, edited by Darlene Clark Hine, Trica Danielle Keaton, and Stephen Small, xxiii–xxxviii. Urbana-Champaign: University of Illinois Press, 2009.

Smitherman, Geneva. "Soul 'n Style" *English Journal* 63, no. 4 (April 1974): 16–17.

Springer, Kimberly. "Stepping into the Struggle." In *Do You Remember Olive Morris?*, edited by Anna Collin, Tanisha Ford, Ana Laura Lopez De La Torre, and Kimberly Springer, 9. London: Gasworks and Remembering Olive Collective, 2009.

Spurlin, William J. "Resisting Heteronormativity/Resisting Colonization: Affective Bonds between Indigenous Women in Southern Africa and the Differences of Postcolonial Feminist History." *Feminist Review* 95 (2010): 10–26.

"Statement, Third World Women's Alliance." In *Dear Sisters: Dispatches from the Women's Liberation Movement*, edited by Rosalyn Baxandall and Linda Gordon, 65. New York: Basic Books, 2000.

Suriano, Maria. "Clothing and Changing Identities of Tanganyikan Urban Youths, 1920s–1950s." *Journal of African Cultural Studies* 20, no. 1 (June 2008): 95–115.

Thomas, Lynn M. "The Modern Girl and Racial Respectability in 1930s South Africa." *Journal of African History* 47, no. 3 (2006): 461–90.

Tice, Karen W. "Queens of Academe: Campus Pageantry and Student Life." *Feminist Studies* 31, no. 2 (Summer 2005): 250–83.

Tolliver, Melba. "Chapter 16: The Grandassa Models." *The Caldwell Journals*. Posted on http://www.mije.org/historyproject/caldwell_journals/chapter16 (accessed July 5, 2009).

Tuck, Stephen. "From Greensboro to Notting Hill: The Sit-Ins in England." In *From Sit-Ins to SNCC: The Student Civil Rights Movement in the 1960s*, edited by Iwan Morgan and Philip Davis, 153–70. Gainesville: University Press of Florida, 2012.

Tulloch, Carol. "Style-Fashion-Dress: From Black to Post-Black." *Fashion Theory* 14, no. 3 (September 2010): 273–304.

———. "That Little Magic Touch: The Headtie." In *Black British Culture and Society*, edited by Kwesi Owusu, 207–19. New York: Routledge, 2000.

Walker, Susannah. "Black Is Profitable: The Commodification of the Afro, 1960–1975." In *Beauty and Business: Commerce, Gender, and Culture in Modern America*, edited by Phillip Scranton, 254–77. New York: Routledge, 2001.

Wallace, Michelle. "Modernism, Postmodernism and the Problem of the Visual in Afro-American Culture." In *Out There: Marginalization and Contemporary Cultures*, edited by Russell Ferguson et al., 39–50. Cambridge, Mass.: MIT Press, 1990.

Ward, Brian. "Jazz and Soul, Race and Class, Cultural Nationalists and the Black Panthers: A Black Power Debate Revisited." In *Media, Culture, and the Modern African American Freedom Struggle*, edited by Brian Ward, 161–96. Gainesville: University Press of Florida, 2001.

Weekes, Debbie. "Shades of Blackness: Young Black Female Constructions of Beauty." In *Black British Feminism: A Reader*, edited by Heidi Safia Mirza, 113–26. New York: Routledge, 1997.

Welters, Linda. "The Natural Look: American Style in the 1970s." *Fashion Theory* 12, no. 4 (2008): 489–510.

White, Shane, and Graham White. "Slave Clothing and African-American Culture in the Eighteenth and Nineteenth Centuries." *Past and Present* 148 (August 1995): 149–86.

———. "Slave Hair and African American Culture in the Eighteenth and Nineteenth Centuries." *Journal of Southern History* 61, no. 1 (February 1995): 45–76.

Wilkins, Che Fanon. "The Making of Black Internationalists: SNCC and Africa before the Launching of Black Power, 1960–1965." *Journal of African American History* 92, no. 4 (Fall 2007): 468–91.

Woodard, Jennifer Bailey, and Teresa Mastin. "Black Womanhood: *Essence* and Its Treatment of Stereotypical Images of Black Women." *Journal of Black Studies* 36, no. 2 (November 2005): 264–81.

BOOKS AND DISSERTATIONS

Adi, Hakim, and Marika Sherwood. *Pan-African History: Political Figures from Africa and the Diaspora since 1787*. New York: Routledge, 2003.

Allman, Jean, ed. *Fashioning Africa: Power and the Politics of Dress*. Bloomington: Indiana University Press, 2004.

Angelou, Maya. *All God's Children Need Traveling Shoes*. New York: Vintage, 1986.

———. *The Heart of a Woman*. New York. Random House, 1981.

Aptheker, Bettina. *The Morning Breaks: The Trial of Angela Davis*. New York: International, 1975.

Askew, Kelly M. *Performing the Nation: Swahili Music and Cultural Production in Tanzania*. Chicago: University of Chicago Press, 2002.

Baez, Joan. *And a Voice to Sing It With*. New York: Summit Books, 1987.

Bailey, Eric J. *Black America, Body Beautiful: How the African American Image Is Changing Fashion, Fitness, and Other Industries*. Westport, Conn.: Praeger, 2008.

Baldwin, Davarian L. *Chicago's New Negroes: Modernity, the Great Migration, and Black Urban Life*. Chapel Hill: University of North Carolina Press, 2007.

Banks, Ingrid. *Hair Matters: Beauty, Power, and Black Women's Consciousness*. New York: New York University Press, 2000.

Baraka, Amiri. *The Autobiography of LeRoi Jones/Amiri Baraka*. New York: Freundlich, 1984.

Barber, David. *A Hard Rain Fell: SDS and Why It Failed*. Oxford: University Press of Mississippi, 2008.

Barnett, LaShonda, ed. *I Got Thunder: Black Women Songwriters on Their Craft*. New York: Thunder Mouth Press, 2007.

Beard, Rick, and Leslie Cohen Berlowitz, eds. *Greenwich Village: Culture and Counterculture*. New Brunswick, N.J.: Rutgers University Press, 1993.

Benedict, Brad, and Linda Barton. *Phonographics: Contemporary Album Cover Art and Graphics*. New York: Collier Books, 1977.

Benson, Susan. *Ambiguous Ethnicities: Interracial Families in London*. New York: Cambridge University Press, 1981.

Berger, Dan. "'We Are the Revolutionaries': Visibility, Protest, and Racial Formation in Prison Radicalism." Ph.D. diss., University of Pennsylvania, 2010.

Bhattacharyya, Gargi. *Tales of Dark-Skinned Women: Race, Gender, and Global Culture*. London: University College London Press, 1998.

Biko, Steve. *I Write What I Like: A Selection of His Readings*. Oxford: Heinemann, 1978.

Biondi, Martha. *The Black Revolution on Campus*. Berkeley: University of California Press, 2012.

———. *To Stand and Fight: The Struggle for Civil Rights in Postwar New York City*. Cambridge, Mass.: Harvard University Press, 2003.

Bradley, Lloyd. *This Is Reggae Music: The Story of Jamaica's Music*. New York: Grove Press, 2000.

Branch, Taylor. *Parting the Waters: America in the King Years, 1954–1963*. New York: Simon and Schuster, 1988.

Breines, Winifred. *The Trouble between Us: An Uneasy History of White and Black Women*. New York: Oxford University Press, 2006.

Bricknell, Katherine, and Ayona Datta, eds. *Translocal Geographies: Spaces, Places, and Connections*. Burlington, Vt.: Ashgate, 2011.

Brown, Elaine. *A Taste of Power: A Black Woman's Story*. New York: Anchor Books, 1992.

Brown, Jacqueline Nassy. *Dropping Anchor, Setting Sail: Geographies of Race in Black Liverpool*. Princeton: Princeton University Press, 2005.

Brown, Kimberly Nichele. *Writing the Black Revolutionary Diva: Women's Subjectivity and the Decolonizing Text*. Bloomington: Indiana University Press, 2010.

Brown, Scot. *Fighting for US: Maulana Karenga, the US Organization, and Black Cultural Nationalism*. New York: New York University Press, 2003.

Brownmiller, Susan. *Femininity*. New York: Linden Press/Simon and Schuster, 1984.

Brun-Lambert, David. *Nina Simone: The Biography*. London: Aurum, 2009.

Bryan, Beverley, Stella Dadzie, and Suzanne Scafe. *The Heart of the Race: Black Women's Lives in Britain*. London: Virago, 1985.

Bukhari, Safiya. *The War Before: The True Life Story of Becoming a Panther, Keeping the Faith in Prison, and Fighting for Those Left Behind*. New York: Feminist Press, 2010.

Burke, Timothy. *Lifebuoy Men and Lux Women: Commodification, Consumption, and Cleanliness in Modern Zimbabwe*. Durham: Duke University Press, 1996.

Byrd, Ayana D., and Lori L. Tharps. *Hair Story: Untangling the Roots of Black Hair in America*. New York: St. Martin's Press, 2001.

Camaroff, Jean. *Body of Power, Spirit of Resistance: The Culture and History of a South African People*. Chicago: University of Chicago Press, 1985.

Camp, Stephanie. *Closer to Freedom: Enslaved Women and Everyday Resistance in the Plantation South*. Chapel Hill: University of North Carolina Press, 2004.

Candelario, Ginetta E. B. *Black behind the Ears: Dominican Racial Identity from Museums to Beauty Shops*. Durham: Duke University Press, 2007.

Cantwell, Robert. *When We Were Good: The Folk Revival*. Cambridge, Mass.: Harvard University Press, 1996.

Carmichael, Stokely. *Ready for a Revolution: The Life and Struggles of Stokely Carmichael*. New York: Scribner, 2003.

Carson, Clayborne. *In Struggle: SNCC and the Black Awakening of the 1960s*. Cambridge, Mass.: Harvard University Press, 1981.

Carter-David, Siobhan. "Fashioning *Essence* Women and *Ebony* Men: Sartorial Instruction and the New Politics of Racial Uplift in Print, 1970–1993." Ph.D. diss., Indiana University, Bloomington, 2011.

Centre for Contemporary Cultural Studies. *The Empire Strikes Back: Race and Racism in 70s Britain*. London: Hutchinson, 1982.

Chamberlain, Mary. *Caribbean Migration: Globalised Identities*. New York: Routledge, 1998.

Cheng, Anne Anlin. *Second Skin: Josephine Baker and the Modern Surface*. New York: Oxford University Press, 2011.

Clemente, Dierdre. *Dress Casual: How College Students Redefined American Style*. Chapel Hill: University of North Carolina Press, 2014.

Cohen, Ronald. *Rainbow Quest: The Folk Music Revival and American Society, 1940–1970*. Amherst: University of Massachusetts Press, 2000.

Cohodas, Nadine. *Princess Noire: The Tumultuous Reign of Nina Simone*. New York: Pantheon, 2010.

Collins, Patricia Hill. *Black Feminist Thought: Knowledge, Consciousness, and the Politics of Empowerment*. New York: Routledge, 2000.

Conor, Liz. *The Spectacular Modern Woman: Feminine Visibility in the 1920s*. Bloomington: Indiana University Press, 2004.

Coplan, David B. *In the Township Tonight! South Africa's Black City Music and Theatre*. 2nd ed. Chicago: University of Chicago Press, 2008.

Countryman, Matthew J. *Up South: Civil Rights and Black Power in Philadelphia*. Philadelphia: University of Pennsylvania Press, 2007.

Craig, Maxine Leeds. *Ain't I a Beauty Queen? Black Women, Beauty, and the Politics of Race*. New York: Oxford University Press, 2002.

Crais, Clifton, and Thomas V. McClendon, eds. *The South African Reader: History, Culture, and Politics*. Durham: Duke University Press, 2014.

Curry, Constance, et al. *Deep in Our Hearts: Nine White Women in the Freedom Movement*. Athens: University of Georgia Press, 2000.

Davies, Carole Boyce. *Left of Karl Marx: The Political Life of Black Communist Claudia Jones*. Durham: Duke University Press, 2007.

Davis, Angela Y. *Angela Davis: An Autobiography*. New York: International, 1988.

———. *Blues Legacies and Black Feminism: Gertrude "Ma" Rainey, Bessie Smith, and Billie Holiday*. New York: Pantheon, 1998.

Davis, Michael. *Street Gang: The Complete History of Sesame Street*. New York: Viking, 2008.

Daymond, M. J., ed. *South African Feminisms: Writing, Theory, and Criticism, 1990–1994*. New York: Garland, 1996.

De Marley, Diana. *Working Dress: A History of Occupational Clothing*. London: Holmes and Meier, 1987.

D'Emilio, John. *Lost Prophet: The Life and Times of Bayard Rustin*. New York: Free Press, 2003.

Edwards, Brent Hayes. *The Practice of Diaspora: Literature, Translation, and the Rise of Black Internationalism*. Cambridge, Mass.: Harvard University Press, 2003.

Egbuna, Obi. *Destroy This Temple: The Voice of Black Power in Britain*. London: MacGibbon and Kee, 1971.

Entwistle, Joanne. *The Fashioned Body: Fashion, Dress, and Modern Social Theory*. Cambridge, United Kingdom: Polity, 2000.

Evans, Peter. *The Attitudes of Young Immigrants*. London: Runnymede Trust, 1971.

Evans, Sara. *Personal Politics: The Roots of Women's Liberation in the Civil Rights Movement and the New Left*. New York: Knopf, 1979.

Evans, Stephanie. *Black Women in the Ivory Tower, 1850–1954: An Intellectual History*. Gainesville: University Press of Florida, 2007.

Fair, Laura. *Pastimes and Politics: Culture, Community, and Identity in Post-abolition Urban Zanzibar, 1890–1945*. Athens: Ohio University Press, 2001.

Fassin, Didier. *When Bodies Remember: Experiences and Politics of AIDS in South Africa.* Berkeley: University of California Press, 2007.

Feldstein, Ruth. *How It Feels to Be Free: Black Women Entertainers and the Civil Rights Movement.* New York: Oxford University Press, 2013.

Fleming, Cynthia Griggs. *Soon We Will Not Cry: The Liberation of Ruby Doris Smith Robinson.* Lanham, Md.: Rowman and Littlefield, 1998.

Foster, Gwendolyn Audrey. *Troping the Body: Gender, Etiquette, and Performance.* Carbondale: Southern Illinois University Press, 2000.

Franklin, John Hope, and Alfred A. Moss Jr. *From Slavery to Freedom: A History of African Americans.* New York: Knopf, 2000.

Fraser, Kennedy. *The Fashionable Mind: Reflections on Fashion, 1970–1981.* New York: Knopf, 1981.

Gaines, Kevin. *American Africans in Ghana: Black Expatriates and the Civil Rights Era.* Chapel Hill: University of North Carolina Press, 2007.

———. *Uplifting the Race: Black Leadership, Politics, and Culture in the Twentieth Century.* Chapel Hill: University of North Carolina Press, 1996.

Garland, Phyl. *The Sound of Soul.* Chicago: Henry Regnery, 1969.

George, Nelson. *Buppies, B-Boys, Baps and Bohos: Notes on Post-Soul Black Culture.* New York: HarperCollins, 1992.

Giddings, Paula. *When and Where I Enter: The Impact of Black Women on Race and Sex in America.* New York: William Morrow, 1984.

Gill, Tiffany M. *Beauty Shop Politics: African American Women's Activism in the Beauty Industry.* Urbana-Champaign: University of Illinois Press, 2010.

Gilmour, Sarah. *The 70s: Punks, Glam Rockers, and New Romantics.* Milwaukee: Gareth Stevens, 2000.

Gilroy, Paul. *The Black Atlantic: Modernity and Double-Consciousness.* Cambridge, Mass.: Harvard University Press, 1993.

———. *Small Acts: Thoughts on the Politics of Black Cultures.* New York: Serpent's Tail, 1993.

———. *There Ain't No Black in the Union Jack.* New York: Routledge Classics, 2002.

Gitlin, Todd. *The Whole World Is Watching: Mass Media in the Making and Unmaking of the New Left.* Berkeley: University of California Press, 1980.

Goldhew, David. *Respectability and Resistance: A History of Sophiatown.* Westpoint, Conn.: Praeger, 2004.

Gordon, Lorraine. *Alive at the Village Vanguard: My Life in and out of Jazz Time.* New York: Hal Leonard, 2006.

Gosse, Van. *Rethinking the New Left: An Interpretive History.* New York: Palgrave, 2005.

Gott, Suzanne, and Kristyne Loughran, eds. *Contemporary African Fashion.* Bloomington: Indiana University Press, 2010.

Greenburg, Cheryl Lynn. *A Circle of Trust: Remembering SNCC.* New Brunswick, N.J.: Rutgers University Press, 1998.

Greene, Christina. *Our Separate Ways: Women and the Black Freedom Movement in Durham, North Carolina.* Chapel Hill: University of North Carolina Press, 2005.

Grier, William H., and Price M. Cobbs. *Black Rage.* New York: Bantam, 1968.

Gross, Michael. *Model: The Ugly Business of Beautiful Women*. New York: It Books, 2011.

Guild, Joshua. "You Can't Go Home Again: Migration, Citizenship, and Black Community in New York and London, World War II–1980." Ph.D. diss., Yale University, 2007.

Guillory, Monique, and Richard C. Green, eds. *Soul: Black Power, Politics, and Pleasure*. New York: New York University Press, 1998.

Guralnick, Peter. *Sweet Soul Music: Rhythm and Blues and the Southern Dream of Freedom*. New York: Back Bay, 1986.

Gwatkin, Nina W. *Yoruba Hairstyles: A Selection of Hairstyles in Southern Nigeria*. Lagos, Nigeria: Craft Centre, National Museum Compound, 1971.

Hajdu, David. *Positively Fourth Street: The Lives and Times of Joan Baez, Bob Dylan, Mimi Baez Fariña, and Richard Fariña*. New York: Farrar, Straus and Giroux, 2001.

Halisi, Clyde, ed. *The Quotable Karenga*. Los Angeles: US Organization, 1967.

Hanchard, Michael. *Orpheus and Power: The Movimiento Negro of Rio de Janeiro and Sao Paulo, Brazil, 1945–1988*. Princeton: Princeton University Press, 1998.

Hannah, Barbara Blake. *Growing Out: Black Hair and Black Pride in the Swinging Sixties*. London: Hansib, 2010.

Hansen, Karen Tranberg. *Salaula: The World of Secondhand Clothing and Zambia*. Chicago: University of Chicago Press, 2000.

Harris, Robert, Nyota Harris, and Grandassa Harris, eds. *Carlos Cooks and Black Nationalism from Garvey to Malcolm X*. Dover, Mass.: Majority Press, 1992.

Harris-Perry, Melissa. *Sister Citizen: Shame, Stereotypes, and Black Women in America*. New Haven: Yale University Press, 2013.

Hartman, Saidiya. *Lose Your Mother: A Journey along the Atlantic Slave Route*. New York: Farrar, Straus and Giroux, 2007.

Heap, Chad. *Slumming: Sexual and Racial Encounters in American Nightlife, 1885–1940*. Chicago: University of Chicago Press, 2009.

Higginbotham, Evelyn Brooks. *Righteous Discontent: The Women's Movement in the Black Baptist Church, 1880–1920*. Cambridge, Mass.: Harvard University Press, 1993.

Hiro, Dilip. *Black British, White British: A History of Race Relations in Britain*. London: Grafton, 1991.

Hogan, Wesley C. *Many Minds, One Heart: SNCC's Dream for a New America*. Chapel Hill: University of North Carolina Press, 2007.

Holloway, Karla. *Codes of Conduct: Race, Ethics, and the Color of Our Character*. New Brunswick, N.J.: Rutgers University Press, 1995.

hooks, bell. *Black Looks: Race and Representation*. Boston: South End Press, 1992.

Howell, Georgina. *In Vogue: 75 Years of Style*. New York: Random House, 1992.

Hunter, Tera W. *To 'Joy My Freedom: Southern Black Women's Lives and Labors after the Civil War*. Cambridge, Mass.: Harvard University Press, 1997.

Ifekwunigwe, Jayne O. *Scattered Belongings: Cultural Paradoxes of "Race," Nation, and Gender*. New York: Routledge, 1999.

Ivaska, Andrew. *Cultured States: Youth, Gender, and Modern Style in 1960s Dar es Salaam*. Durham: Duke University Press, 2011.

Jaji, Tsitsi. *Africa in Stereo: Modernism, Music, and Pan-African Solidarity*. New York: Oxford University Press, 2014.

Jennings, Helen. *New African Fashion*. New York: Prestel, 2011.

Johnson, Buzz. *"I Think of My Mother": Notes on the Life and Times of Claudia Jones*. London: Karia Press, 1985.

Johnson, Lakesia. *Iconic: Decoding Images of Revolutionary Black Women*. Waco, Tex.: Baylor University Press, 2012.

Joseph, Peniel. *Waitin' 'til the Midnight Hour: A Narrative History of Black Power in America*. New York: Holt, 2006.

Josephson, Barney, with Terry Trilling-Josephson. *Café Society: The Wrong Place for the Right People*. Urbana-Champaign: University of Illinois Press, 2009.

Kelley, Robin D. G. *Africa Speaks, America Answers: Modern Jazz in Revolutionary Times*. Cambridge, Mass.: Harvard University Press, 2012.

———. *Hammer and Hoe: Alabama Communists during the Great Depression*. Chapel Hill: University of North Carolina Press, 1990.

———. *Yo' Mama's Dysfunktional! Fighting the Culture Wars in Urban America*. New York: Beacon, 1998.

King, Mary Elizabeth. *Freedom Song: A Personal Story of the 1960s Civil Rights Movement*. New York: William Morrow, 1987.

Lanning, Mark, Neil Roake, and Glynis Horning. *Life Soweto Style*. Cape Town: Struik, 2003.

Lee, Chana Kai. *For Freedom's Sake: The Life of Fannie Lou Hamer*. Urbana-Champaign: University of Illinois Press, 1999.

Lewis, David Levering. *When Harlem Was in Vogue*. New York: Knopf, 1981.

Lipsitz, George. *Dangerous Crossroads: Popular Music, Postmodernism and the Poetics of Place*. New York: Verso, 1997.

Lott, Eric. *Love and Theft: Blackface Minstrelsy and the American Working Class*. New York: Oxford, 1993.

Lowe, Margaret A. *Looking Good: College Women and Body Image, 1875–1930*. Baltimore: Johns Hopkins University Press, 2005.

MacDonald, Michael. *Why Race Matters in South Africa*. Cambridge, Mass.: Harvard University Press, 2006.

Magaziner, Daniel R. *The Law and the Prophets: Black Consciousness in South Africa, 1968–1977*. Athens: Ohio University Press, 2010.

Mager, Anne Kelk. *Beer, Sociability, and Masculinity in South Africa*. Bloomington: Indiana University Press, 2010.

———. *Gender and the Making of a South African Bantustan: A Social History of the Ciskei, 1945–1959*. Portsmouth, N.H.: Heinemann, 1999.

Makeba, Miriam. *Makeba: My Story*. New York: New American Library, 1987.

Malik, Michael Abdul. *From Michael de Freitas to Michael X*. London: Andre Deutsch, 1968.

Mama, Amina. *Beyond the Masks: Race, Gender, and Subjectivity*. New York: Routledge, 1995.

Marsh, Graham, and Glyn Callingham. *The Cover Art of Blue Note Records: The Collection*. London: Collins and Brown, 2010.

Martin, Tony. *Amy Ashwood Garvey: Pan-Africanist, Feminist and Mrs. Marcus Garvey No. 1; or, A Tale of Two Amies*. Dover, Mass.: Majority Press, 2007.

Martinez, Elizabeth. *Letters from Mississippi: Reports from Civil Rights Volunteers and Freedom School Poetry of the 1964 Freedom Summer*. Brookline, Mass.: Zephyr, 2007.

McClendon, Alphonso. *Jazz and Fashion: Dress, Identity, and Subcultural Improvisation*. New York: Bloomsbury, 2015.

McGuire, Danielle L. *At the Dark End of the Street: Black Women, Rape, and Resistance—A New History of the Civil Rights Movement from Rosa Parks to Black Power*. New York: Knopf, 2010.

Miller, Monica L. *Slaves to Fashion: Black Dandyism and the Styling of Black Diasporic Identity*. Durham: Duke University Press, 2009.

Miller-Young, Mireille. *A Taste for Brown Sugar: Black Women in Pornography*. Durham: Duke University Press, 2014.

The Modern Girl around the World Research Group. *The Modern Girl around the World: Consumption, Modernity, and Globalization*. Durham: Duke University Press, 2008.

Mohanty, Chandra. *Feminism without Borders: Decolonizing Theory, Practicing Solidarity*. Durham: Duke University Press, 2003.

Moody, Anne. *Coming of Age in Mississippi: An Autobiography*. New York: Laurel, 1976.

Moorman, Marissa J. *Intonations: A Social History of Music and Nation in Luanda, Angola, from 1945 to Recent Times*. Athens: Ohio University Press, 2008.

Morrow, Willie. *400 Years without a Comb*. San Diego: Black Publishers of San Diego, 1973.

Muhammad, Khalil Gibran. *The Condemnation of Blackness: Race, Crime, and the Making of Modern Urban America*. Cambridge, Mass.: Harvard University Press, 2010.

Murch, Donna. *Living for the City: Migration, Education, and the Rise of the Black Panther Party in Oakland, California*. Chapel Hill: University of North Carolina Press, 2010.

Nadelson, Regina. *Who Is Angela Davis? The Biography of a Revolutionary*. New York: Peter H. Wyden, 1972.

Neal, Mark Anthony. *Soul Babies: Black Popular Culture and the Post-Soul Aesthetic*. New York: Routledge, 2002.

Nelson, Alondra. *Body and Soul: The Black Panther Party and the Fight against Medical Discrimination*. Minneapolis: University of Minnesota Press, 2013.

Ngo, Fiona I. B. *Imperial Blues: Geographies of Race and Sex in the Jazz Age*. New York. Durham: Duke University Press, 2014.

Nuttall, Sarah, ed. *Beautiful/Ugly: African and Diaspora Aesthetics*. Durham: Duke University Press, 2007.

O'Brien, M. J. *We Shall Not Be Moved: The Jackson Woolworth's Sit-In and the Movement It Inspired*. Jackson: University Press of Mississippi, 2013.

Olatunji, Babatunde. *The Beat of My Drum: An Autobiography*. Philadelphia: Temple University Press, 2005.

Ongiri, Amy. *Spectacular Blackness: The Cultural Politics of the Black Power Movement and the Search for a Black Aesthetic*. Charlottesville: University of Virginia Press, 2009.

Patterson, Sheila. *Dark Strangers: A Sociological Study of the Absorption of a Recent West*

Indian Migrant Group in Brixton, South London. Bloomington: Indiana University Press, 1964.

Payne, Charles M. *I've Got the Light of Freedom: The Organizing Tradition and the Mississippi Freedom Struggle.* Berkeley: University of California Press, 1995.

Peiss, Kathy. *The Enigmatic Career of an Extreme Style.* Philadelphia: University of Pennsylvania Press, 2011.

———. *Hope in a Jar: The Making of America's Beauty Culture.* New York: Holt, 1998.

Perkins, Margo V. *Autobiography as Activism: Three Black Women of the 60s.* Jackson: University Press of Mississippi, 2000.

Pierce, Richard. *Polite Protest: The Political Economy of Race in Indianapolis, 1920–1970.* Bloomington: Indiana University Press, 2005.

Plageman, Nathan. *Highlife Saturday Night: Popular Music and Social Change in Urban Ghana.* Bloomington: Indiana University Press, 2013.

Powe-Temperley, Kitty. *The 60s: Mods and Hippies.* Milwaukee, Wisc.: Gareth Stevens, 2000.

Prestholdt, Jeremy. *Domesticating the World: African Consumerism and the Genealogies of Globalization.* Berkeley: University of California Press, 2008.

Rabine, Leslie W. *The Global Circulation of African Fashion.* New York: Berg, 2002.

Ramdin, Ron. *The Making of the Black Working Class in Britain.* Brookfield, Vt.: Gower, 1987.

———. *Reimaging Britain: Five Hundred Years of Black and Asian History.* Sterling, Va.: Pluto, 1999.

Ramirez, Catherine S. *The Woman in the Zoot Suit: Gender, Nationalism, and the Cultural Politics of Memory.* Durham: Duke University Press, 2009.

Ramphele, Mamphela. *Across Boundaries: The Journey of a South African Woman Leader.* New York: Feminist Press, 1995.

Randall, Herbert, and Bobs M. Tusa. *Faces of Freedom Summer.* Tuscaloosa: University of Alabama Press, 2001.

Ransby, Barbara. *Ella Baker and the Black Freedom Movement: A Radical Democratic Vision.* Chapel Hill: University of North Carolina Press, 2003.

Ribane, Nakedi. *Beauty: A Black Perspective.* Scottsville, South Africa: University of KwaZulu–Natal Press, 2006.

Rivero, Yeidy. *Tuning Out Blackness: Race and Nation in the History of Puerto Rican Television.* Durham: Duke University Press, 2005.

Robnett, Belinda. *How Long? How Long? African American Women in the Struggle for Civil Rights.* New York: Oxford University Press, 1997.

Rogers, Ibram H. *The Black Campus Movement: Black Students and the Racial Reconstitution of Higher Education, 1965–1972.* New York: Palgrave, 2012.

Rojas, Fabio. *From Black Power to Black Studies: How a Radical Social Movement Became an Academic Discipline.* Baltimore: Johns Hopkins University Press, 2010.

Rooks, Noliwe. *Hair Raising: Beauty, Culture, and African American Women.* New Brunswick, N.J.: Rutgers University Press, 1996.

———. *Ladies' Pages: African American Women's Magazines and the Culture That Made Them.* New Brunswick, N.J.: Rutgers University Press, 2004.

Rowley, Hazel. *Richard Wright: The Life and Times*. Chicago: University of Chicago Press, 2008.

Saul, Scott. *Freedom Is, Freedom Ain't: Jazz and the Making of the Sixties*. Cambridge, Mass.: Harvard University Press, 2003.

Saunders, Doris E., ed. *The Day They Marched*. Chicago: Johnson Publishing Company, 1963.

Scott, Linda. *Fresh Lipstick: Redressing Fashion and Feminism*. New York: Palgrave, 2005.

Sherwood, Marika. *Claudia Jones: A Life in Exile*. London: Lawrence and Wishart, 1999.

Simone, Nina. *I Put a Spell on You*. Cambridge, Mass.: Da Capo, 1991.

Smethurst, James Edward. *The Black Arts Movement: Literary Nationalism in the 1960s and 1970s*. Chapel Hill: University of North Carolina Press, 2005.

Smith, Suzanne E. *Dancing in the Street: Motown and the Cultural Politics of Detroit*. Cambridge, Mass.: Harvard University Press, 2001.

Solomos, John. *Race and Racism in Britain*. 2nd ed. New York: St. Martin's Press, 1993.

Starfield, Jane, and Michael Gardiner. *Citizenship and Modernity in Soweto*. New York: Oxford University Press, 2000.

Stephens, Michelle Ann. *Black Empire: The Masculine Global Imaginary of Caribbean Intellectuals in the United States, 1914–1962*. Durham: Duke University Press, 2005.

Stroud, Andrew. *Nina Simone: Black is the Color*. New York: Xlibris, 2005.

Sudbury, Julia. *"Other Kinds of Dreams": Black Women's Organisations and the Politics of Transformation*. New York: Routledge, 1998.

Sugrue, Thomas J. *Sweet Land of Liberty: The Forgotten Struggle for Civil Rights in the North*. New York: Random House, 2009.

Sullivan, James. *Jeans: A Cultural History of an American Icon*. New York: Gotham Books, 2007.

Summers, Barbara. *Skin Deep: Inside the World of Black Fashion Models*. New York: Amistad Press, 1998.

Summers, Martin. *Manliness and Its Discontents: The Black Middle Class and the Transformation of Masculinity, 1900–1930*. Chapel Hill: University of North Carolina Press, 2004.

Swan, Quito. *Black Power in Bermuda: The Struggle for Decolonization*. New York: Palgrave Macmillan, 2009.

Tamale, Sylvia, ed. *African Sexualities: A Reader*. Cape Town: Pambazuka, 2011.

Theado, Matt, ed. *The Beats: A Literary Reference*. New York: Carroll and Graf, 2001.

Thembe, Can. *Requiem for Sophiatown*. New York: Penguin, 2006.

Theoharis, Jeanne. *The Rebellious Life of Mrs. Rosa Parks*. New York: Beacon, 2014.

Thomas-Hope, Elizabeth, ed. *Freedom and Constraint in Caribbean Migration and Diaspora*. Miami: Ian Randle, 2008.

Thompson, Lisa. *Beyond the Black Lady: Sexuality and the New African American Middle Class*. Urbana-Champaign: University of Illinois Press, 2012.

Thompson, Robert Farris. *Flash of the Spirit: African and Afro-American Art and Philosophy*. New York: Vintage, 1984.

Toure, Kwame, and Charles Hamilton. *Black Power: The Politics of Liberation*. New York: Vintage, 1992.

Twine, France Winddance. *A White Side of Black Britain: Interracial Intimacy and Racial Literacy*. Durham: Duke University Press, 2011.

Tyson, Timothy. *Radio Free Dixie: Robert F. Williams and the Roots of Black Power*. Chapel Hill: University of North Carolina Press, 1999.

Van Deburg, William. *New Day in Babylon: The Black Power Movement and American Culture, 1965–1975*. Chicago: University of Chicago Press, 1992.

Von Eschen, Penny M. *Satchmo Blows Up the World: Jazz Ambassadors Play the Cold War*. Cambridge, Mass.: Harvard University Press, 2006.

Wade, Tony. *Black Enterprise in Britain*. London: Wiseworks, 2003.

Wade-Gayles, Gloria. *Pushed Back to Strength: A Black Woman's Journey Home*. Boston: Beacon Press, 1993.

Walker, Susannah. *Style and Status: Selling Beauty to African American Women, 1920–1975*. Lexington: University Press of Kentucky, 2007.

Ward, Brian. *Just My Soul Responding: Rhythm and Blues, Black Consciousness, and Race Relations*. Berkeley: University of California Press, 1998.

Watson, Steven. *The Birth of the Beat Generation*. New York: Pantheon, 1995.

Weheliye, Alexander G. *Phonographies: Grooves in Sonic Afro-Modernity*. Durham: Duke University Press, 2005.

Welsh, David. *The Rise and Fall of Apartheid*. Charlottesville: University of Virginia Press, 2009.

Werner, Craig. *A Change Is Gonna Come: Music, Race, and the Soul of America*. Ann Arbor: University of Michigan Press, 1996.

White, Deborah Gray. *Too Heavy a Load: Black Women in Defense of Themselves, 1894–1994*. New York: W. W. Norton, 1999.

White, E. Frances. *Dark Continent of Our Bodies: Black Feminism and the Politics of Respectability*. Philadelphia: Temple University Press, 2001.

White, Shane, and Graham White. *Stylin': African American Expressive Culture from Its Beginnings to the Zoot Suit*. Ithaca: Cornell University Press, 1998.

Widener, Daniel. *Black Arts West: Culture and Struggle in Postwar Los Angeles*. Durham: Duke University Press, 2010.

'Wii Muk'willixw (Art Wilson). *A First Nations Artist Records Injustice and Resistance*. East Haven, Conn.: New Society, 1996.

Williams, John. *Michael X: A Life in Black and White*. London: Century, 2008.

Wilson, Andrew. *Northern Soul: Music, Drugs, and Subcultural Identity*. Portland, Oreg.: Willan, 2007.

Wolcott, Victoria. *Remaking Respectability: African American Women in Interwar Detroit*. Chapel Hill: University of North Carolina Press, 2001.

Woodruff, Nan Elizabeth. *American Congo: The African American Freedom Struggle in the Delta*. Cambridge, Mass.: Harvard University Press, 2003.

Yelvington, Kevin A., ed. *Afro-Atlantic Dialogues: Anthropology in the Diaspora*. Sante Fe: School of American Research Press, 2006.

Young, Cynthia A. *Soul Power: Culture, Radicalism, and the Making of a U.S. Third World Left*. Durham: Duke University Press, 2006.

Zinn, Howard. *SNCC: The New Abolitionists*. Cambridge, Mass.: South End Press, 1964.

Index

Abasindi, 208 (n. 66)

Abina, 189

Abu, Jimmy, 52, 53

Accra, Ghana, 53

Adderley, "Cannonball," 34

Adu, Frank, 53

Advertisements: in *Drum* magazine, 18, 26, 171, 172, 178–79, 194 (n. 48), 213 (n. 80); of Wigs Parisian, 44, 197 (n. 9)

African American college women: political ideologies of, 2, 92; and dorm room decorations, 2, 95, 115–16; and soul style, 7–8, 95, 96, 97, 102, 104, 110–17, 120–21; as fashion designers, 7–8, 96, 113, 115; and *Essence* magazine, 8, 95, 110–17, 192 (n. 25); language of soul, 10, 66, 97; and black-owned boutiques, 59, 112–13; as soul sisters, 67, 95, 97, 98, 102, 104, 106, 107, 110–15, 117, 118, 120–21, 204 (n. 32); and Student Nonviolent Coordinating Committee, 67, 69, 73–74, 78–79, 84, 86–87, 98; and casual clothing, 68, 76, 81, 83–84, 87, 88, 89, 98, 111; redefining women's roles, 68, 87; at turn of twentieth century, 70; and respectability, 70–72, 105; and natural hairstyles, 78–79, 87, 102, 114, 202 (n. 37); and denim clothing, 86, 88–89, 95; college dress codes challenged by, 87, 88, 96, 101; and Afro hairstyle, 108–9, 114, 115; and interracial interactions, 114–17

African Americans: cultural solidarity with Afro-Britons, 2, 135; conceptions of African culture, 16, 20–22, 27, 43, 57, 196 (n. 6); and African models of style, 20–28, 65; beauty and fashion ideals of, 24, 28; and African diaspora, 30, 31; as consumers, 44, 53–54, 55, 65, 199 (n. 60); and economic autonomy, 46, 47, 52; and

ideal body type, 53; history of fashion shows, 54–55; term "Afro" in reference to, 161, 162; as domestics, 164

Africana women: and fashion design, 3, 8; and soul style, 7, 18; self-definition of, 11; Cooks on beauty of, 61; primitivist stereotypes of, 196 (n. 6)

African City, An (web series), 188

African culture: language of soul reflecting, 5; and African diaspora, 8, 14, 20, 21, 32; African Americans' conceptions of, 16, 20–22, 27, 43, 57, 196 (n. 6); and black press, 20, 21–22; and African fashion industry, 21–22, 29, 32, 53; and modernity, 22, 163, 165, 175–76; traditional African dress, 22, 163, 172, 174, 175; Odetta on, 31; and Grandassa models, 39; and conceptions of beauty, 45–46; hairstyles of, 50. *See also* African-inspired accessories; African-inspired clothing; Swazi culture; Xhosa culture; Zulu culture

African diaspora: and Angela Davis's soul style image, 2; contention over soul style of black women, 3, 5; Black is Beautiful as rallying cry, 4, 160; and circulation of soul style, 5, 8, 9, 59, 60, 121, 162, 163, 184, 192 (n. 30); defining blackness, 6; and African culture, 8, 14, 20, 21, 32; as points of connection and disconnection, 9, 192 (n. 28); language of soul marketed and exported to, 10; and style politics, 13, 170; and African Americans, 30, 31; and Black Freedom movement, 33, 121; and Grandassa models, 39, 42, 63; and Harlem, 43; debates on wigs and skin lighteners, 44–45; and African fashion industry, 53, 59; and black women as fashion designers, 55; and African Jazz-Art Society, 59; and album covers, 62; international fashions in, 68; and black feminism, 155; and Afro look, 163; debates on black liberation, 169; and Afro wigs, 178; and fashion studies, 192 (n. 27)

African fashion industry: and *Drum* magazine, 8, 11, 160, 162–63, 165–66, 168–76, 181, 183; and antiapartheid activism, 11, 17, 159–60; and African culture, 21–22, 29, 32, 53; and African diaspora, 53, 59; and soul style, 59, 184, 187; growth of, 179; and style politics, 180; and Western imperialism, 188–89

African Growth and Opportunity Act (AGOA), 188

African independence movements, 13, 31

African-inspired accessories: and beads, 4, 22, 60, 95, 103, 112, 116, 161, 162–63; and earrings, 89, 95, 102, 112, 186; and postcolonial black identity, 156; and necklaces, 186

African-inspired clothing: and Black Power movement, 3, 7, 163; and soul style, 4, 42, 64, 121, 163, 186; on album covers, 6; and Grandassa models, 56, 58; and fashion industry, 65, 119, 163, 183, 187; and Student Nonviolent Coordinating Committee, 89; and African American college women, 97; and postcolonial black identity, 156; and Afro look, 161, 162–65, 166. *See also* African prints

African Jazz-Art Society (AJAS): and Grandassa models, 41, 52–53, 55–58, 59; and soul style, 42, 59, 64–65; fashion shows of, 53, 55–58, 59

African Jazz-Art Society and Studios (AJASS), 59, 60–64

African leaders, 21–22

African Nationalist Pioneer Movement (ANPM): and soul style, 42; protest against Wigs Parisian, 43, 47–50, 51, 197 (n. 23); and Cooks, 46, 47, 197 (n. 19); beauty pageant of, 46–47, 51, 53; and respectability, 58; and black press, 59; political momentum of, 65

Africanness: debates on, 20; Western imperialism in tension with, 26; natural hairstyles associated with, 32, 56–57, 58, 89, 162, 198–99 (n. 50)

African personal names, replacing Anglicized names, 160

African Pride magazine, 63

African prints: as element of soul style, 4, 16, 97, 98, 113, 143, 187; and African culture, 21, 22, 30, 97, 180, 181; and fashion industry, 118–19, 188

Afro-Britons: cultural solidarity with African Americans, 2, 135. *See also* Black British identity; Black British women

Afro-Caribbeans: migration to Britain, 125–26, 127, 128, 129–30, 131, 137, 156; British citizenship status of, 126–27; lack of desirable jobs for, 140, 142. *See also* Black British women; Brixton neighborhood, London

Afro-chic design, 183

Afro hairstyle: of Angela Davis, 1–2, 3, 105, 106, 107–8, 146, 177; Afro wigs, 18, 118, 134, 162, 172, 173, 176, 177–78, 179, 183; short-cropped Afros, 25, 26, 31–32, 41, 56, 103, 104, 162, 177, 186, 199 (n. 50); origin of, 92, 104, 176, 198–99 (n. 50); and Black Power movement, 96, 176; popularity of, 104, 108, 118; and African American college women, 108–9, 114, 115; and *Essence* magazine, 110; in Brixton neighborhood, London, 134–35; and Black Panther Youth League, 143; of Olive Morris, 146, 148, 152; and black British women, 152; and black South African women, 159, 165, 168; transnational politics of, 176–80. *See also* Natural hairstyles

Afro look: and soul style, 97, 159; Afro hairstyle as, 118; and *Drum* magazine, 160–61, 162, 163, 166, 168, 172, 176, 177, 212 (n. 28); and African-inspired clothing, 161, 162–65, 166; and gender politics, 168–69; as resistance, 168; criminality associated with, 173, 174; and respectability, 173–74; legacies in post-apartheid era, 180–84; African designers of, 187

Afropolitan design, 183

Afro Sheen, 18, 65

Black arts movement, 200 (n. 2)

Black as term, 204 (n. 32)

Black Atlantic world, 29

Black bodies: scars of corporeal punishment, 7; political and aesthetic value created for, 87; hypersexual image of, 135–36. *See also* Black women's bodies

Black British identity, and Afro-Caribbean migration to Britain, 125–26, 137, 156

Black British women: head scarves of, 4; establishment of black cultural institutions, 8; and beauty politics, 129–33; and politics of hypervisibility, 131, 151–52; respectability of, 135; as soul sisters, 135, 146; use of Soul Power, 144; and Afro hairstyle, 152; and feminism, 156–57

Black community: and Soul Power, 9, 102; colorism within, 45, 58, 65, 114; tensions within, 192 (n. 30)

Black consciousness: expression through dress, 7; and Miss Natural Standard of Beauty contest, 47; of Grandassa models, 63; Afro hairstyle as symbol of, 104, 109; black South African women's responses to, 156–57

Black Consciousness movement, in South Africa, 159, 161–62, 165, 175, 181, 183

Black cultural renaissance, 43

Blackface minstrelsy, 119, 149

Black folk music traditions, 34

Black Freedom movement: dress and style as aspect of, 3–4, 5, 69; soul style expressing tensions in, 10; Africana women redefining themselves within, 11; and African-derived style, 20, 21, 56; and natural hairstyles, 28, 41, 52; and African diaspora, 33, 121; Makeba as icon of global movement, 35; Odetta's visibility in, 37; and Grandassa models, 62, 63; and Jim Crow segregation, 65–66, 67, 69; celebrities joining, 89; soul sisters of, 92; and urban areas, 98, 116; *Essence* magazine on, 110; in Britain, 125; and Olive Morris, 152; and *Drum* magazine, 160; and New Left, 200 (n. 2)

Black is Beautiful: Angela Davis as embodiment of, 2; and elements of soul style, 4; and Grandassa models, 41, 98, 102; and African Jazz-Art Society, 55; and African American college women, 102; in South Africa, 160

Black liberation: and style politics, 3, 166, 168, 169; and re-aestheticizing of black body, 7, 35

Black Liberator, 208–9 (n. 74)

Black men: and Afro hairstyle, 4, 105, 108; masculinity and language of soul, 34; attitudes toward Grandassa models, 57; and longer hairstyles, 84

Black middle class: and respectability, 1, 25, 27, 67, 68, 71–72, 75, 88, 109, 194 (n. 46); and natural hairstyles, 49; and fashion shows, 54; and civil rights movement, 71, 98; and black working class, 80–81; and college students, 99–100; in South Africa, 160–61, 168; and Negro as term, 204 (n. 32)

Black Nationalism: and Grandassa models, 39, 41, 52–53, 55, 57, 90; and soul style, 42–43, 52, 59, 65; and Wigs Parisian's advertisements, 44; and natural hairstyles, 50–51, 52; and Black Panther Party, 99, 101; and Organization of Women of African and Afro-Caribbean Descent, 154; in Britain, 209 (n. 83)

Blackness: African diaspora defining, 6; re-aestheticization of, 7, 29; and concept of soul, 9–10, 34, 91, 102; soul style as expression of, 14–15, 162; debates on, 20, 95, 97, 102, 152; purity of African body, 43; and racial purity, 46–47, 53; ideological frameworks for representation of, 49, 50–51; pan-African concept of, 60; commodification of, 93, 117, 162; and African American college women, 95, 97, 114; police's association of criminality with, 97, 107, 136, 146, 174; performance of, 102; and fashion industry, 119, 120, 121; in Brixton neighborhood, London, 124; immigrant as euphemism for black in Britain, 126; and mixed-race British women, 128–29; and London police's targeting of Afro-Caribbean youth, 139; in South Africa, 161–62

Black-owned boutiques: and black fashion network, 9, 112–13, 199 (n. 58); and African American college women, 59, 112–13; and Makeba, 59, 199 (n. 59); in Harlem, 59–60; and consumer market, 65

Black-owned record stores in London: violent confrontations in, 3, 123; cross-Atlantic ties with Caribbean, 134, 207 (n. 44); gender politics of, 134–35; as multiservice entities, 134–35. *See also specific stores*

Black Panther Movement (BPM): houses of, 2, 136, 143, 144, 209 (n. 84); formation of, 101, 138–39; police attack at Desmond's Hip City, 123; martial arts as self-defense tactics of, 139, 140; activism against police brutality, 139, 140, 142, 144, 145–46, 209 (n. 85); Black Panther Party compared to, 139, 142; Student Nonviolent Coordinating Committee compared to, 142; events of, 143; funding of, 144, 209 (n. 84); disbanding of, 151; sexism within, 151, 152, 154. *See also* Black Panther Youth League, Brixton, London

Black Panther Party for Self-Defense (BPP): and mainstream media, 96, 99, 107; uniform of, 98, 99, 107; cross-racial alliances in, 98–99; platform of, 99, 100, 120; and class composition, 99–100; membership of, 100, 101; and FBI, 101, 105; soul style of, 117; Black Panther Movement as first independent chapter of, 139; use of "pig" for police, 145; sexism within, 151, 152, 154

Black Panther Youth League, Brixton, London: soul style of, 11, 123–24, 138–44, 146; and police attack at Desmond's Hip City, 123; and style politics, 143; whites excluded from, 143–44

Black Parents movement, North London, 209 (n. 83)

Black Peoples Information Centre, 208 (n. 74)

Black People's News, 140, 147

Black Power movement: body politics in, 1; African-inspired clothing of, 3, 7, 163; and dress as political strategy, 3, 93; and language of soul, 9; and soul style, 68, 95, 139; and Student Nonviolent Coordinating Committee, 91, 92; and Afro hairstyle, 96, 176; philosophy of, 99; and Black Panther Party, 99, 101; and Black Power fist, 99, 117, 139, 143, 177, 213 (n. 74); and college students, 100; in Britain, 125, 132–33, 138, 139, 140, 143, 156; and black women activists, 151, 200 (n. 1), 210 (n. 109); sexism within, 152, 154

Black press: on Black Power movement, 6; and soul culture, 8; and language of soul, 10; and soul style as African-derived style, 20, 21–22, 65, 121; on African culture, 27; Wigs Parisian's advertisements in, 44; on natural hairstyles, 49–50, 51; and Grandassa models, 57–58, 63; and African Jazz-Art Society, 59; and civil rights movement, 67; and respectability, 70; on African diaspora, 121

Black pride: and Angela Davis posters, 2; and soul style, 5, 101–2; and James Brown, 6, 102, 105; and African Nationalist Pioneer Movement, 46; and Simone, 103; and Black Panther Youth League, 143; Afro hairstyle as symbol of, 152

Black resistance, Angela Davis's image as symbol of, 2

Blacks Against State Harassment (BASH), 142, 208–9 (n. 74)

Black Socialist Alliance, 208 (n. 74)

Black South African women: and miniskirts, 4, 159, 172, 174–75, 180; responses to black consciousness, 156–57; and style politics, 156–57, 159–60, 170, 179–80; and modernity, 159, 160, 165, 168, 180; and urban areas, 159, 161, 168–76; and respectability, 159, 171, 173–74, 175, 176, 179; and Afro look, 168–76

Black vernacular music traditions, 34

Black womanhood: redefined notions of, 4, 35, 91, 97, 121, 146, 156, 160, 168–69, 171–72, 175, 179; and histories of racial oppression, 170

Black women: redefining themselves against stereotypes, 1; soul style for, 2, 3, 4, 7, 8, 10; as activists, 3–4, 5, 10–11, 28, 30, 35–36, 37, 70, 72, 73, 74–75, 77, 87, 91, 97, 185, 186, 187, 191 (n. 12), 191–92 (n. 13), 200 (n. 1), 201 (n. 19); as targets of state-sanctioned policing, 4, 108; as soul sisters, 7, 10, 67, 91–92, 97, 98, 110–14, 117, 146, 186; enslaved women, 7, 54, 191 (n. 4), 200 (n. 6); and development of soul, 34–35; popularity of wigs and hairpieces, 44, 45–46, 48–49, 57; freed-women, 54, 70, 191 (n. 4); as fashion designers, 55; White Citizens Councils' attack on moral character of, 69; and Afro hairstyle, 108; movement through-out African diaspora, 156. *See also* Afri-can American college women; Africana women; Black British women; Black South African women

Black women's bodies: stereotypes of, 1, 14, 35, 58, 70, 72; body narratives of, 7; com-peting ideologies of, 14; as hypersexual-ized, 14, 72, 191 (n. 4); African women's bodies, 22, 26–27, 30; and Grandassa models, 53, 57; and African Jazz-Art Society's fashion shows, 56; redefining of, 87; in South Africa, 175

Black Women's Co-Op, 208 (n. 66)

Black working class: and album covers, 62; and intraracial tensions, 72, 80, 81; and Student Nonviolent Coordinating Com-mittee, 75, 76–77, 80–81, 84, 86, 90

Black youth: Angela Davis as role model for, 2; and soul culture, 6; and under-ground black fashion network, 9, 59, 199 (n. 60); African-based history and cul-tural aesthetic for, 53; and style politics, 55; blackness defined by, 97; and casual dress, 98; and Black Panther Party, 100; and soul style, 101–2; Afro-Caribbean

youth culture, 124, 133–38, 142–43; and cultural institutions, 133–34

Blake, Jackie, 140

Blue Note Records: and soul culture, 6; and language of soul, 33–34; and Donaldson, 41; album covers of, 60–62, 196 (n. 1)

Blues music, and language of soul, 6, 97

Bob Marley and the Wailers, 134

Bond, Julian, 86

Boot dance, 27

Boubous, 112

Bradford Asian Youth, 208 (n. 74)

Brathwaite, Cecil, 51–52, 57, 60, 63

Brathwaite, Ronnie, 51–52, 57, 60–61, 63

Breaker, E. Jeanne, 79

Briscoe, Rudel, 118

Britain: normative traditions of, 9; English-ness in, 125, 137; race relations in, 125, 149; immigrants in, 125–26, 137–38; citi-zenship laws in, 126–27; meaning of ghetto in, 133. *See also* London, England

British Empire, 125

Brixton Ad-hoc Committee against Police Repression, 209 (n. 74)

Brixton Black Women's Group (BBWG), 136, 151, 154, 155, 209 (n. 74)

Brixton neighborhood, London: record stores and black-operated cultural insti-tutions in, 123, 134, 142–43; meanings of blackness in, 124; de facto segregation in, 126; black youth culture in, 133–34, 136; soul geography of, 134–38, 147, 156; and blues parties, 136–38, 144; under-ground soul scene of, 136–38

Brooklyn, New York, 43–44, 102

Brown, Claude, 24

Brown, Ellen, 130

Brown, H. Rap, 102, 103

Brown, James, 6, 102, 105

Brown, Marion, 24

Brown, Oscar, Jr., 34

Brown, Palmer, 55

Brown v. Board of Education (1954), 69

Bryant, C. C., 82

Bubas, 21, 112

Buirski, Desré, 181

Bullock, Bette, 48
Burlesque shows, 27
Burrows, Stephen, 119
Buthelezi, Felecia, 179

Cabrera, Richard, 38
Caftans: and African fashion industry, 8;
    as African-inspired clothing, 89, 90, 112,
    205 (n. 59); and Afro look, 162, 166, 168
Camp, Stephanie, 200 (n. 6), 207 (n. 42)
Cannes Film Festival, 45
Cape Flats, Cape Town, 169, 177
Caribbean: national and cultural iden-
    tity in, 127; color-caste system of, 128;
    nationalist movements in, 138; black
    fashion models of, 197 (n. 13)
Carmen England hair salon, 132
Carmichael, Stokely: on Makeba, 27–28;
    government surveillance of, 36, 199
    (n. 59); and Student Nonviolent Co-
    ordinating Committee, 82, 90, 91; on
    Black Power, 91, 99; and Black Panther
    Party, 99; and African American college
    women, 102; marriage to Makeba, 103–4;
    on respectability, 200 (n. 4); on natural
    hairstyles, 202 (n. 37)
Carroll, Diahann, 13, 25, 84
Carter, Iris, 102
Casdulan, Frenchie, 118
Castro, Fidel, 99
Central Intelligence Agency (CIA), 36
Chaffe, Lois, 72
Chambers, Doris, 45, 46
Chang, Anne, 154
Charles, Ray, 38
Cherney, Mike, 43–44, 47–48, 65
Chicago Defender, 21
Chouinard Art Institute, Los Angeles, 60
Christianity, 173
Civil rights movement: and dress as politi-
    cal strategy, 3, 69, 175, 200 (n. 4); black
    women active in, 35, 67, 69, 71, 72, 73–74,
    200 (n. 1); Odetta's platform in, 36–37,
    38; and black middle class, 71, 98; orga-
    nizations of, 80–81; and Student Non-
    violent Coordinating Committee skin,

86; and fashion industry, 120; and local
    freedom efforts, 191 (n. 13). *See also* Stu-
    dent Nonviolent Coordinating Commit-
    tee (SNCC)
Clark College, 111, 112
Class issues: and social mobility, 7, 16; and
    fashion shows, 54–55; intraracial class
    tensions, 72, 80–83, 86, 99–100; and Stu-
    dent Nonviolent Coordinating Commit-
    tee, 80–83, 86, 87, 90; performance of
    class, 82–83; and cross-class alliances,
    87; and beauty politics in Britain, 128–
    29; and black identities in Britain, 156;
    in South Africa, 161, 165–66, 168, 169–70;
    elite as term in South Africa, 165–66,
    169, 171, 211–12 (n. 28); and performance
    of identity, 169. *See also* Black middle
    class; Black working class
Cleaver, Eldridge, 140
Cleaver, Kathleen, 92, 101, 107, 110
Cleopatra (1963), 45
Coif Camp Salon, 118
Coleman, Ornette, 24
Collins, Addie Mae, 36
Collins, Patricia Hill, 201 (n. 13)
Colonialism: white plantation owners' dic-
    tates on dress, 7; African women free
    of remnants of, 8; neocolonialism, 33,
    48; decolonization movement in South
    Africa, 35; African Nationalist Pioneer
    Movement's stance against, 46, 48; Pick-
    ens's protests against, 197–98 (n. 23);
    anticolonialism movement, 208 (n. 66)
Colorism: within black community, 45, 58,
    65, 114; and Grandassa models, 57–58
Coltrane, John, 24
Columbia Records, 33–34
Come Back, Africa (1959), 19–20, 23
Commonwealth Immigrants Act (1962),
    126–27
Communist Party USA, 2, 101, 105
Congo, 48, 197–98 (n. 23)
Congress of Racial Equality (CORE), 36, 37
Consumer market: African Americans as
    consumers, 44, 53–54, 55, 65, 199 (n. 60);
    and ethnic fashions, 65, 117

Cook, Ann, 118–19

Cooks, Carlos, 46, 47, 52–53, 59, 61, 197 (n. 19)

Coombe, Vivienne, 152

Cooper, Anna Julia, 70

Cooper, Carolyn, 7

Cornell University, 111

Cornrows: as element of soul style, 4; and Bantu education system, 17; and Student Nonviolent Coordinating Committee, 89; and African American college women, 95, 114; and Makeba, 103; and Black Panther Youth League, 143; and race pride, 152

Cosmopolitan (South African magazine), 180–81

Countercultural style, 55, 56, 90, 101

Courrèges, André, 164

Craig, Maxine Leeds, 2

Cranston, Beatrice, 53

Cultural Association for Women of African Heritage (CAWAH), 32–33

Cunningham, Beryl, 197 (n. 13)

DaCosta, Danny, 143

DaCosta, Geneva, 140

Dadzie, Stella, 128–29, 132–33, 140, 146, 154, 156, 210 (n. 109)

Dame Elizabeth hair salon, 132

Dance: dance halls, 7; highlife dance, 21; boot dance, 27; hard bop as dance music, 34; "whining," 135

Dar es Salaam, Tanzania, 3, 9, 53, 161, 174–75

Dashikis: in Angela Davis's FBI poster, 1; as element of soul style, 4, 60, 92–93, 112; and African American college women, 98; and black South African women, 159, 168

Davenport, Esther, 53

David and David, Inc., 118

Davidson's department store, 69, 201 (n. 12)

Davis, Angela: Afro hairstyle of, 1–2, 3, 105, 106, 107–8, 146, 177; and FBI, 1–2, 105–7, 108, 191 (n. 1); journalists shaping public image of, 2, 3; *If They Come in the Morning*, 2, 143; soul style image of, 2–3,

11, 184; British following of, 2–3, 133, 135, 140, 143; posters launching celebrity status of, 2–3, 135; and style politics, 4; and civil rights movement, 92; arrest of, 105–6, 108; acquittal of, 108; and African American college women, 115–16; influence on fashion trends, 118, 120

Davis, Eddie "Lockjaw," 34

Davis, James, 59–60

Davis, Janet, 127–28, 130, 132, 133, 138

Davis, Norma June, 75, 87, 201 (n. 19)

Day They Marched, The (Johnson Publishing Company), 83–84

Dean, Althea, 197 (n. 13)

Deaver, Brenda, 60, 63, 104

Denbigh Road Community Centre, Brixton, 143

Denim clothing: and repurposed fabrics of enslaved ancestors, 4, 76–77; and black women activists, 10, 77; and Student Nonviolent Coordinating Committee, 67, 68, 79–80, 82–83, 86, 87, 88, 89, 90, 92, 98, 99, 165; and African American college women, 86, 88–89, 95; as element of soul style, 92–93; and Students for a Democratic Society, 101; and fashion industry, 117

Denim overalls: as element of soul style, 4; and black women activists, 10; and Student Nonviolent Coordinating Committee, 67, 68, 77–78, 84, 87, 146; and sharecroppers, 77–78, 81–82, 91, 99; and March on Washington, 83, 84; androgynous self-presentation of, 84

Derrick's record store, London, 134

Desmond's Hip City record store, Brixton, London: Angela Davis poster in, 2–3, 135; and Black Panther Youth League, 123, 138–39; police attack of November 15, 1969, 123, 146–50; soul culture of, 135, 136; multiracial, mixed-gendered clientele of, 135–36

Desses, Jean, 45

Dhondy, Farrukh, 140, 209 (n. 84)

Diana Ross and the Supremes, 44

Diawara, Manthia, 192 (n. 30)

Feminine propriety. *See* Respectability

Feminist consciousness: of album covers, 61; of South African women, 169, 212 (n. 42)

Feminist movement: and style politics, 3; black feminism, 87, 144–45, 150, 152, 154–57, 160, 171, 210 (n. 109); women's rights organizations, 101; and Olive Morris, 144–45, 147, 150, 152, 154–55; and gender-nonconforming style, 146; and Black Panther Movement, 151; legacy of British black feminism, 156–57; and New Left, 200 (n. 2)

Ferguson, Renee, 114, 116

Flaaitaal (South African township slang), 19

Flamingo magazine, 63, 131

Fleming, Cynthia Griggs, 202 (n. 37)

Fleming, Juanita, 170–71

Folk music, 34, 200 (n. 2)

Fontaine, Walter, 118, 177–78

Ford, Herman, 105

Ford, Phyllis, 115–16

Forman, James, 86, 90

Franklin, Aretha, 112, 205 (n. 59)

Freedom, embodied notions of, 21

Freedom House, 80

Freedom Rides, 80

Freedom Summer, 90

Freedwomen, 54, 70, 191 (n. 4)

Free speech movement, 200 (n. 2)

Funk, 6, 34, 135

Garvey, Amy Jacques, 43

Garvey, Marcus, 46, 52, 197 (n. 19), 197 (n. 23)

Gaucho pants, 89

Gay rights movement, 101, 146, 200 (n. 2)

Gazebo, The (boutique), 112

Geles, 22, 112, 172

Gender politics: violation of gendered dress codes, 4; soul style as symbol of, 5; clothing as projection of, 7, 83–84, 86, 87, 144–45; and leadership, 84, 91; queering of gender line, 84, 145, 146, 149, 154, 175, 202 (n. 52); and androgynous self-presentation, 84, 175; and college rules

and dress codes, 87; and respectability, 105; and Afro hairstyle's gender neutralizing effects, 108; and black-owned record stores in London, 134–35; and British racism toward nonwhites, 149; and performance of gender, 149, 150; in South Africa, 159, 160, 168–70, 175; and *Drum* magazine, 169–71

Ghana, 21, 22, 53, 161, 175–76, 187, 196 (n. 6)

Giles, Harriet, 70

Gilroy, Paul, 208 (n. 52)

Givenchy, 60

Glover, Amye: dorm room decorations of, 2, 115–16; and style politics, 4; and soul style innovation, 7–8, 11, 113, 186; at Indiana University, 96, 105, 108–9, 115–17, 186; Afro hairstyle of, 104–5, 108–9, 115, 186; on Angela Davis, 108

Glover, Bennie Lou, 108

Glover, Seaburn, 108

Gomwalk, Clement, 146–48

Gospel, 34

Gosse, Van, 200 (n. 2)

Grandassa models: and language of soul, 10, 39; and Black Nationalism, 39, 41, 52–53, 55, 57, 90; on album covers, 41, 60–62, 63, 64, 196 (n. 1); and soul style, 42, 43, 57, 58, 64, 68, 90, 98; and natural hairstyles, 53, 56–57, 63, 104, 176, 199 (n. 50); and fashion shows, 55–58, 59, 102; exoticism of, 57, 58, 60; black press on, 57–58, 63

Grant, Jane, 144

Greek migrants, in Britain, 137–38

Greenwich Village, New York: Makeba in, 23–24, 28, 37; Simone in, 28–30, 37; Odetta in, 30, 36, 37; Lincoln in, 32; soul style scene in, 32, 41; bohemian culture of, 37, 89–90; and language of soul, 39

Grenada, 125–26, 137

Groove, 34

Gross, Michael, 211 (n. 22)

Guevara, Che, 99, 135, 184

Guinea, 22, 89, 104

Gwatkin, Nina W., 198–99 (n. 50)

163, 164, 165; British origins of, 163–64, 211 (n. 22); and Quant, 164, 211 (n. 22)

Miriam Makeba (1960), 25

Miscegenation, in Britain, 129, 136

Miss Black South Africa pageant, 183

Miss Natural Standard of Beauty contest, 46–47, 51

Miss Soweto pageant, 183

MIT, 114

Mixed-race people, 136, 162

Mixed-race women, beauty politics in Britain, 128–29

Mngweru, Betty, 173

Modernity: and urban areas, 6; and South African township residents, 16; and style politics, 16–17, 165; debates on, 20, 42–43; and African culture, 22, 163, 165, 175–76; role of beauty and style as markers of, 42, 165, 180; and natural hairstyles, 50; and black South African women, 159, 160, 165, 168, 180; and pan-Africanism, 175

Mokubung, Palesa, 183, 187

Monk, Thelonius, 24

Moody, Anne: and Student Nonviolent Coordinating Committee, 67, 69; and sit-in movement, 67, 72, 73, 74, 201 (n. 12); on clothing, 78; and March on Washington, 84; as soul sister, 91–92

Moon, Millie, 45, 46

Morehouse College, 88

Morel, Marion, 171

Morgan, Rose, 25–26

Morgan State University, 95, 111

Morris, Basil, 127, 150, 156

Morris, Errol, 127

Morris, Ferryn, 127

Morris, Jennifer, 127

Morris, Olive: soul style of, 11, 145, 156; and police attack on Desmond's Hip City, 123, 146, 147–50; effect of racism on, 126; migration to Britain, 127; and Black Panther Youth League, 139, 140, 142, 143, 144, 147; education of, 140, 208 (n. 66); and Kokkinos, 143–44; androgynous style of dress, 144–45, 146, 148–49; feminist politics of, 144–45, 147, 150, 152, 154–55; homophobic sexual threats against, 145, 149–50; anti–police brutality activism of, 145–46, 209 (n. 86); health of, 156; and antiapartheid movement, 208 (n. 66)

Morris, Yana, 127

Morris Brown College, 111, 114

Moses, Bob, 90

Moss Side neighborhood, Manchester, 133, 208 (n. 66)

Motown Records, 37, 44

Mowatt, Judy, 155

Mugler, Thierry, 163

Muhammad Speaks, 63–64

MUKHTI, 208 (n. 74)

Murray, Sunny, 24

Music industry, 33, 34, 36–37. *See also* Jazz music; Soul-jazz music

Nadelson, Regina, 107

Nairobi, Kenya, 53, 163, 176

Nash, Diane, 69, 92

Nassau, Bahamas, 59, 103

National Association for the Advancement of Colored People (NAACP), 80–81, 82, 100

National Geographic, 22

Nationalist Movement in Africa, 35

Nation of Islam, 65

Nat's Afro Wigs shop, Brixton, London, 134, 135

Natural hairstyles: and Black Power, 3, 91; and head scarves, 4, 172, 179; on album covers, 6, 41, 60, 61; and Makeba, 16–17, 18, 23, 25, 26, 28, 31–32, 199 (n. 50); differentiation in types of, 25, 56–57, 104, 108, 114, 162, 177, 186; and Odetta, 28, 31–32, 78, 104; and Simone, 29, 103, 186, 194–95 (n. 61); African-ness associated with, 32, 56–57, 58, 89, 162, 198–99 (n. 50); and respectability, 32, 202 (n. 37); and language of soul, 33; and Lincoln, 33, 55, 57, 78, 79; and Black Nationalism, 42, 55; and African Nationalist Pioneer Movement, 46, 47, 48, 49; and standards of beauty, 46–47,

48, 51, 55, 63, 132, 187, 196 (n. 1); debates on, 48–52, 65, 198–99 (n. 50); and Grandassa models, 53, 56–57, 63, 104, 176, 199 (n. 50); and African Jazz-Art Society, 55; and Tolliver, 58; and Student Nonviolent Coordinating Committee, 67, 68, 78–80, 91, 92, 146; and African American college women, 78–79, 87, 102, 114, 202 (n. 37); and March on Washington, 84; and Olive Morris, 146; and African diaspora, 156; and head wraps, 168. *See also* Afro hairstyle; Cornrows

Naturally fashion shows, 55–58, 59, 102

Negro, as term, 204 (n. 32)

Negro Digest, 50, 104

Nelms, Rose "Black Rose," 53, 61, 62–63

Nelson, Karlotta, 112

Nelson, Rema, 176

Nemiroff, Robert, 35

Neocolonialism, 33, 48

New Beacon Bookstore, Finsbury Park, London, 133

New Breed, 55, 112, 205 (n. 59)

New Left, 200 (n. 2)

New Negro movement, 43

Newsweek, 106–7, 205 (n. 39)

Newton, Huey P., 98, 140, 143, 152

New York Amsterdam News, 27, 44, 48, 49, 197 (n. 9)

New York City, 8, 9, 13–14, 15

Ngozi, Nonhlanhla, 17, 169, 183

Ngubeni, Thoko "Butterfly," 173

Nigeria, 22, 29, 50, 196 (n. 6)

Nile Queen hair and skin care, 196 (n. 6)

Nixon, Richard, 58

Nixon, Tricia, 58

Nkosi, Nkhensani, 181, 183–84, 187

Nkrumah, Kwame, 133, 196 (n. 6)

Nonjojo, Shirley, 168

Nonviolent Action Group, 200 (n. 4)

Norford, Thomasina, 49

Norman, Memphis, 72

Northwestern University, 111

Notting Hill Carnival, 138

Notting Hill neighborhood, London, 126

Ntu Stop, Harlem, 59–60

Obama, Michelle, 187

Obi, Liz, 140, 152, 156

Obote, Maria, 176

Obote, Milton, 176

Odetta: and language of soul, 10, 14, 33; influence on soul style, 14, 28, 32; natural hairstyle of, 28, 31–32, 78, 104; and Simone, 29, 30; and Black Freedom movement, 30, 31; caftan as signature garment of, 30–31, 90; as activist-entertainer, 35, 36–37; material success of, 38; name recognition of, 62

Ogunbiyi, Theresa, 50

Ohio Players, 119

Oh Yes!, 189

Olatunji, Amy, 43

Olatunji, Babatunde, 38, 43

Organization of Women of Asian and African Descent (OWAAD), 154–55, 155

Osakwe, Amaka, 187

Osei Duro, 187

Oxidine, Debra, 111–12

Packard, Sophia, 70

Padmore, George, 140

Palazzo pants, 168

Pan-Africanism: pan-African unity flag, 13; and Harlem, 43; and blackness, 60; in Britain, 138; and black feminism, 155; and repositioning of Africa in international community, 163; as rejection of Western modernity, 175; and Afro hairstyle, 176

Parks, Rosa, 84, 110

Patch, Penny, 80

Patton, Big John, 60, 63

Peoples News Service, 136

Peters, Brock, 38

Peterson, Maurice, 2

Phango, Peggy, 16

Pickens, William, 197–98 (n. 23)

Pilane, Meisie, 168

Pillay, Sonny, 23

Plantation system, 197–98 (n. 23)

Platform shoes, as element of soul style, 4, 112

Police officers in Britain: Afro-Caribbean youth's social spaces shut down by, 13; police brutality in London, 123, 124, 139–40, 142, 147, 155; geography of containment system of, 134; blackness associated with criminality, 136, 146; racial profiling used by, 136, 147; Black Panther Movement's antibrutality campaigns, 139, 140, 142, 144, 145–46; "Sus Law," 147

Police officers in South Africa, 159

Police officers in United States: black women beaten and sexually assaulted by, 4, 74–75, 201 (n. 19); Afro hairstyle as marker for harassment by, 108; British police compared to, 139, 142

Political alliances: and cross-ethnic alliances, 8–9; cross-racial alliances, 8–9, 90, 98–99; cross-diasporic alliances, 22

Political music culture: and Simone, 28, 30, 35–36, 37; and language of soul, 33–34, 35; and Odetta, 35, 36–37

Politics of hypervisibility, of black British women, 131, 151–52

Popular culture, 6

Powell, Enoch, 136

Pratt, John, 24–25

President Giant cigarettes, 26

Prestige Records, 33–34

Primus, Pearl, 25

Princess Tam Tam (1935), 196 (n. 6)

Princeton University, 111

Protest music, and Simone, 37–38

Quant, Mary, 164, 211 (n. 22)

Race and race relations: in Greenwich Village, 24; and African American college women, 97, 114; in Britain, 125, 126, 127–28, 129, 139–40

Radical chic, 97, 107, 146

Ramphele, Mamphela, 159, 176, 179

Randall, Dorothy, 117

Raymond, George, 67

RCA Records: and soul culture, 6; and Makeba's U.S. career, 13, 24, 34–35; and language of soul, 33–34; and Simone, 103

Reading's record store, London, 134

Reagan, Ronald, 2, 105

Record Corner, London, 134

Reed, Ishmael, 24

Reggae music, in Britain, 134–35

Religions, concept of soul in, 5

Respectability: black middle-class respectability, 1, 25, 27, 67, 68, 71–72, 75, 81, 88, 109, 194 (n. 46); and feminine propriety, 4, 10, 16, 23, 47, 58, 67–68, 72–73, 109, 110, 145, 146, 159, 170, 176; soul style subverting expectations of, 14, 16, 68; and apartheid-controlled short hair, 17; and Makeba, 25; and natural hairstyles, 32, 202 (n. 37); and fashion shows, 55; and Grandassa models, 58; politics of, 65, 69, 70–71, 72, 73–74, 170; and civil rights movement, 69; performance of, 69, 84; and Student Nonviolent Coordinating Committee, 69–75, 76, 79, 80–82, 146; and Victorian norms of womanhood, 70; and African American college women, 70–72, 105; and dignity of grooming regimen, 72–73; and March on Washington, 83; and Afro hairstyle, 105, 179; of black British women, 135; Olive Morris's challenging of, 145, 146; and black South African women, 159, 171, 173–74, 175, 176, 179; of freedwomen, 191 (n. 4)

Rhodesia, 63

Rhythm and blues, 34

Ribane, Nakedi, 168

Richardson, Gloria, 92

Richardson, Judy, 11, 78, 79–81, 86

Ricks, Willie, 91

Ringwood's Afro-American Journal of Fashion, 54, 198 (n. 41)

Rinoth, Haya, 164, 165, 174–75

Riverside Records, 33–34

Roach, Freddie, 34, 60, 64

Roach, Max, 6, 32, 33, 38, 56

Robertson, Carole, 36

Robeson, Paul, 36

Robinson, Gwen, 79, 86, 87, 202 (n. 37)

Robinson, Ruby Doris Smith: and Student Nonviolent Coordinating Committee,

experience, 97, 111; of Desmond's Hip City record store, 135, 136

Soul food dishes, 95

Soul-jazz music: pioneers of, 34; and Donaldson, 41; and Grandassa models, 42, 62; and reverence for U.S. South, 90; and language of soul, 97; in Britain, 135; in South Africa, 165. *See also* Album covers

Soul Power: and power of black community, 9, 102; and race-conscious fashions, 97; Makeba as icon of, 103–4; in London, 135, 136, 146, 156; black British women's use of, 144; gender nonconformity linked to, 145; and black women activists, 187. *See also* Black Power movement

Soul style: visual markers of, 1, 2; history of, 3, 15, 111, 184; and African-inspired clothing, 4, 42, 64, 121, 163, 186; popularity of, 5, 6, 55, 65, 97; circulation within African diaspora, 5, 8, 9, 59, 60, 121, 162, 163, 184, 192 (n. 30); global market for, 5, 18, 28, 98, 117–21; as response to social and physical violence, 6; and African American college women, 7–8, 95, 96, 97, 102, 104, 110–17, 120–21; and thrift stores, 8, 9, 112, 199 (n. 60); transnational geographical terrain of, 8–9, 41, 43, 59, 63, 145–46, 157, 187–88, 192 (n. 29); development of, 9, 28, 92, 192 (n. 29); fashion network for, 9, 59, 65, 199 (n. 58), 199 (n. 60); competing ideas about identity and activism, 10; commodification and marketing of, 10, 38, 64, 65, 90, 93, 97; of Black Panther Youth League, 11, 123–24, 138–44; as African-derived style, 20–21, 53, 65, 121; hybridity of, 21, 63; hypervisibility of, 64; of Student Nonviolent Coordinating Committee, 67–68, 79–82, 89, 90, 98; evolution of, 68, 97; and soul sister image, 91, 146; distinction between dressing down and dressing up, 98; in Brixton, 136, 138; and black South African women, 157, 159, 160–68. *See also* Style politics

South Africa: and Black Freedom movement, 4; gendered dress codes in, 4; Afrikaner culture, 4, 9; de jure segregation in, 10; antiapartheid activism in, 11, 13, 157, 159, 193 (n. 1); beauty and fashion culture of, 11, 16, 18, 159–60, 179–80, 181, 183, 211 (n. 24); Bantu education system, 16–17; drums banned in, 27; Makeba advocating boycott of, 35; uniform of domestic workers, 164; Afro look in, 165, 166; black hair care industry in, 179–80; democracy in, 180. *See also* Afro look; Black South African women; *and specific cities*

South African Students' Organization (SASO), 159

South Asians: and cross-ethnic political alliances, 9, 162; in Johannesburg, 15, 19; in London, 124; in Britain, 125, 126, 140; in Caribbean, 127; in Black Panther Movement, 140, 143

Southern Christian Leadership Conference (SCLC), 69, 91

Southhall Black Sisters, 154

Soweto, Johannesburg, 19, 20, 26, 165–66, 168, 169, 173, 180

Spellman, A. B., 24

Spelman College, 70, 73, 79, 87, 88, 95, 111, 114, 202 (n. 37)

Squatters' Union, 136

Stahr, Elvis, 101

Stefani, Gwen, 187

Stephens, Cooki, 114

Steve Allen Show (television show), 23

Stewart Models agency, 119

Stiletto heels, and black South African women, 159

Stoned Cherrie, 181, 183, 184, 187

Strauss, Levi, 77

Stroud, Andy, 38, 103

Student Nonviolent Coordinating Committee (SNCC): and feminine propriety, 10, 67–68; and Simone, 36, 37; and natural hairstyles, 67, 68, 78–80, 91, 92, 146; and sit-in movement, 67, 69, 72, 73, 74, 75,

United States; Student Nonviolent Co-ordinating Committee (SNCC)
Universal African Nationalist Movement, 197 (n. 19)
Universal Negro Improvement Association, 13, 46
University of Alabama, 200 (n. 4)
University of California, 105
University of Connecticut, 114
Urban areas: and development of soul style, 9; and modernity, 16; and African fashions, 53, 57; and street fashions, 55; and denim clothing, 86; and Black Freedom movement, 98, 116; and black South African women, 159, 161, 168–76
Urban League Guild, 45, 46

Vagrancy Act of 1824, 147
Vaseline Blue Seal, 26, 194 (n. 48)
Vietnam War, 101
Vlisco, 166

Wade-Gayles, Gloria, 73, 74, 79, 91
Walker, C. J., 130
Walker, Marilyn, 114
Warwick University, 154
Washington, Lynn, 102
Watts Riots, 98
Waymon, Eunice. *See* Simone, Nina
We Insist! Max Roach's Freedom Now Suite (1960), 33, 37
Wellesley College, 111
Wells, Ida B., 70
Wesley, Cynthia, 36
West Africa, 21, 22, 50, 89, 138
Western imperialism: Angela Davis's image used as emblem of, 3; natural African-ness in tension with, 26; in South Africa, 161; Afro look as marker of, 161, 175; Afro hairstyle as marker of, 176–77; and African fashion industry, 188–89; and foreign aid to Africa, 188–89
Western Kentucky University, 116
West Indies, 125, 127, 130, 137
"Whining" (dance moves), 135

White, Helene, 41, 53, 56, 60
White, William, 24
White Citizen Councils, 69
Whiteness: white ethnics, 9, 43; modern beauty culture associated with, 18, 31, 45, 47, 184; white liberals, 31; white male gaze, 58; white women as innately morally pure and passionless, 58; in Britain, 125, 137–38, 142–44, 152
White supremacy, 69, 149
White vigilante violence, 139
Wigs Parisian: African Nationalist Pioneer Movement's protest against, 3, 43, 47–50, 51, 197 (n. 23); in Brooklyn, 43–44; in Harlem, 44, 45, 46; advertisements of, 44, 197 (n. 9); and black hair care, 65
Williams, Clarence, 114, 116
Williams, Eric, 140
Williams, Gus, 55
Williams, Helen, 45
Windrush generation, 126–28, 140
Women's liberation. *See* Feminist consciousness; Feminist movement
Woolworth's, 69, 72, 199 (n. 60), 201 (n. 12)
World War I, 54

Xhosa culture: and African-inspired clothing, 4, 157, 162–63, 172; and Makeba, 13, 22, 24; jazz styles blended with tradition music of, 15

Yancy, Bobbi, 86
Young, Ena Au, 130–31

Zambia, 63
Zeta Phi Beta sorority, 108, 116
Zimbabwe, 63
Zinn, Howard, 88
Zoot suits, 7, 55
Zulu culture: and African-inspired clothing, 4, 157, 162–63, 172; jazz styles blended with traditional music of, 15; traditional clothing of, 22; and colonialism, 48; and natural hairstyles, 56
Zuvaa, 187